THE
HOPE
OF THE
GOSPEL

Books by J. D. Jones

The Apostles of Jesus

Commentary on Mark

The Greatest of These

The Hope of the Gospel

The J. D. Jones Classic Library

THE HOPE OF THE GOSPEL

Expository Sermons on
Christian Encouragement

J. D. JONES

kregel
PUBLICATIONS

Grand Rapids, MI 49501

The Hope of the Gospel by J. D. Jones

Published in 1995 by Kregel Publications, a division of Kregel, Inc., P. O. Box 2607, Grand Rapids, MI 49501. Kregel Publications provides trusted, biblical publications for Christian growth and service. Your comments and suggestions are valued.

Cover and book design: Alan G. Hartman

Library of Congress Cataloging-in-Publication Data
Jones, J. D. (John Daniel), 1865–1942.
    The hope of the Gospel / by J. D. Jones.
        p. cm.
    Originally published: London; New York: Hodder and Stoughton, 1919.
    1. Sermons, English. 2. Congregational churches— Sermons. 3. Christian Life. I. Title.
BX7233.J6H6   1995   252'.058—dc20   95-13298
                                                                                    CIP

ISBN 0-8254-2973-0 (paperback)

1 2 3 4 5 Printing / Year 99 98 97 96 95

Printed in the United States of America

Contents

CHAPTER ONE

A Root Out of a Dry Ground

*For he grew up before him . . . as a root out of a dry
ground.* —Isaiah 53:2

"A root out of a dry ground"! What idea does this figure suggest to
you? It suggests to me the idea of unexpectedness, unaccountableness,
miraculousness. A "dry ground"—that is not exactly the kind of place
we expect a root to shoot out from. A "dry ground"—that is not
exactly the kind of soil in which we expect plants to flourish. I notice
that when the bedding-out season comes round, gardeners, even when
they put their plants into prepared ground, take care to keep that
ground moistened and well watered. If they bedded their plants in dry
ground, they would not spring up at all. If a man took it into his head
to plant seeds on our highways, he need not look for flowers in the
spring. They are dry ground. And if by chance a root should spring up
out of dry ground, it is usually a very poor and stunted and shriveled
thing. Some time ago as I traveled through one of the Welsh mining
valleys my eye fell upon three or four trees that were growing out of
the very midst of a hill of coal waste. It was a most unlikely place in
which to see a tree growing at all, and I marveled at the vitality that
could exist amid such surroundings. But I also noticed that it was a
very precarious and poverty-stricken existence these trees on the coal
heap were leading. Compared with the trees that were growing in the
green and fertile fields near by, they were poor and sickly-looking
specimens. It is hopeless to expect a strong, vigorous, beautiful plant
to spring out of a dry ground.

But the prophet here asserts that, in the case of a certain historic Person, that hopeless and seemingly impossible thing actually happened. "He grew up before him," he writes, "as a root out of a dry ground." I need scarcely say to remind you that the Messiah is the subject of this great and overwhelming chapter. It may be, as scholars assert, that it was the afflicted nation of Israel that the prophet at first pictured under the figure of the suffering servant. But in this chapter 53, he has come to identify God's suffering Servant, not with the whole nation, but with one particular Person in it. In a word, in this moving chapter the prophet, by the Spirit, speaks of Christ. And this is one feature about the Christ which he notices— His unexpectedness, His unaccountableness, His miraculousness. He grew up before Him as a "root out of a dry ground." There was nothing in the soil out of which He grew to account for Jesus. The marvel of Christ's Person becomes all the more marvelous when we consider the conditions of His time and the circumstances out of which He sprang. The nature of the growth is always in accordance with the nature of the soil. You cannot expect a harvest from seed that falls on the rocky ground. If things grow at all out of dry and hard ground, they are bound to be feeble and sickly growths. But Jesus was no feeble and sickly growth. He was the "chiefest among ten thousand, and the altogether lovely." He was like the cedar of Lebanon for strength, like the lily of the valley for fragrance and purity, like the rose of Sharon for glory. By universal consent He was the best and noblest, and the highest and holiest of mankind, and yet He grew up as a root out of a dry ground. There was nothing in His circumstances or surroundings to account for Him or explain Him. He is as surprising, as inexplicable, as miraculous as would be, let us say, a crop of flowers springing up out of the asphalt paving of our public streets.

This, then, is the subject upon which I want to speak—the unexpectedness of Jesus. If you rule out all but humanitarian considerations, He remains as inexplicable as a "root springing up out of a dry ground."

Family

First of all, there is nothing in His family to account for Him. We make much in these days of the influence of heredity. Sometimes I begin to feel we make too much—that we press the doctrine of heredity so far that we endanger individuality and personal responsibility. But while I think that sometimes we are inclined to press the effects of heredity too far, that it does play a large part in human development is beyond cavil or dispute. Heredity is one of the factors that go to determine character and destiny. Parents reproduce themselves in their children. We inherit from our parents not only facial and physical characteristics, we inherit from them also mental gifts and moral qualities. Life supplies us with abundant illustrations of all this. We speak in England here sometimes of our "ruling families." Sometimes we do so angrily and resentfully. We are inclined to think and to say that certain families monopolize the government simply in virtue of their rank and birth. But really that is not so. Rank will not keep a man long in the ruler's place if the man himself is a fool. If we have ruling families it is because there is in such families a certain capacity for rule. Take the Cecils. Possibly we do not always agree with them. But no one can think of the Cecil family, from the great Elizabethan statesman downwards, without seeing that they possess a certain hereditary gift and aptitude for government. Government has become a tradition with them, and succeeding generations display an amazing instinct and aptitude for rule. And it is the recognition that gifts and qualities often descend from father to son, from parent to child, that makes biographers of great men begin their story with some account of the ancestry from whom their particular hero is descended. They do so because oftentimes acquaintance with a great man's parentage and remoter ancestry will help us to explain the great man himself.

But the study of Christ's ancestry does not help us in the least little bit to explain Christ. There is nothing in His family to account for Him. We know this on the testimony, not of any of Christ's friends, but on the testimony of His critics and foes. You remember Mark's account of our Lord's visit to Nazareth. The effect of His preaching was to create a feeling of wonderment and amazement among His hearers. "Many hearing him," says Mark, "were astonished, saying, From whence hath this man these things? and what is this which wisdom is given unto him, that even such mighty works are wrought by his hands?" The wonder would have been great had Jesus been the son of some great and learned rabbi. It was absolutely staggering when they thought of the house from which He had actually issued. "Is not this," they said in bewildered astonishment, "the son of Mary, the brother of James, and Joses, and Judas and Simon? and are not his sisters here with us?" They knew all about Christ's family. It was not His likeness to them that struck them, but His total unlikeness. When they remembered that Mary was His mother, and James and Joses and Judas and Simon His brothers, they wondered how Jesus could have come out of such a family circle. For Mary was just a plain peasant woman. And James and Joses and Judas and Simon were quite ordinary and humdrum men. You can see James for yourself in the epistle that bears his name. The man that reveals himself in that epistle—and from his position in the Jerusalem church we are justified in arguing that he was the ablest of the brothers—is a dry, bald, rather narrow man, with a good fund of common sense, but without any glint of the soaring vision that distinguished the Lord. There is all the difference between James and Jesus there is between a half penny dip and the noonday sun. Even the prejudiced Jews felt and acknowledged this difference; they looked at James—good, plain, commonplace man; then they listened to Jesus speaking His wonderful words of spirit and life, and, I repeat, they were left in a condition of bewildered amazement. "What is the wisdom that is given to this man?" they asked. There was nothing in our Lord's heredity to account for Him. As far as His family was concerned, He grew up as a root "out of a dry ground."

Surroundings

Then, in the second place, there was nothing in His surroundings to account for Him. Next to heredity, we moderns are inclined to lay chief stress upon environment. A man is largely made, we say, by the conditions under which he is constrained to spend his life— by the moral and intellectual atmosphere he breathes, by the company he keeps, by the education he receives, and so on. Now this truth, again, is often pressed to extremes. From the way in which some people state it, you might believe that every one bred in a pious home grows up pious, and every one reared in a slum grows up slummy both in body and mind. But life and experience prove that this is not so. Environment is not a determining factor; in the last resort a man can always rise superior to it. But while it does not exercise decisive and determining influence, it remains true that it does exert a large and important influence. A man's environment always colors his mode of speech, his manners, his whole mental and intellectual outlook. For instance, here we are living in the twentieth century. The twentieth century puts its unmistakable mark upon us: we speak its language; we use its measure of knowledge; we think its thoughts and beliefs. If any of us are guilty of making books, and so adding to that much study which the wise man declares is a weariness to the flesh, there is no need to put the date of publication on the front page. An examination of the contents will always be sufficient to locate the book within, at any rate, a few years of its right date. For involuntarily we reproduce in our books the ideas current in our day. They proclaim themselves as belonging to the beginning of the twentieth century. In the matter of thought and intellectual outlook we are the children of our time.

Or take, again, the matter of culture. The kind of culture we have received always leaves its mark. Let us suppose man has received no education worth speaking of. The lack will reveal itself in his speech, and not simply in his speech, but in his manners and tastes and whole intellectual outlook. On the other hand, if a man has enjoyed the advantage of a university training, that also will reveal itself, not simply in the correctness of his speech, but in something far more important, a certain unmistakable breadth of mind. The peasant lives in his narrow, contracted peasant world; the scholar lives in the vast and glorious universe which scholarship opens to him. Environment exercises enormous influence. I will not say a man is entirely made, but he is largely made by his surroundings.

But surroundings entirely fail to account for Jesus. He came from a humble peasant home. His reputed father was a carpenter in a Galilean village. The household—it is obvious from scattered hints in the Gospel—was a poor household. Joseph and Mary did not, as some poor Scottish parents do, scrape and sacrifice in order to send their son to a university. They were probably too poor to dream of sending their boy to Jerusalem, to sit with Saul at the feet of Gamaliel. All they could do in the way of education was to give him such as the village school at Nazareth provided. And even that education was not prolonged. The family expenses grew as one little child after another made its advent, and Jesus was taken from school and put to help His father in the workshop, and for fourteen or fifteen years He shared in Joseph's trade—He was one of the village joiners. And yet this Jesus, Himself a working man, bred in a working home and blessed with nothing beyond a peasant boy's education, "spake as never yet man spake." He surpassed in wisdom the greatest, wisest, holiest men of His own great, holy, and inspired race. There is nothing in His surroundings to account for it.

You cannot explain it on the ground of early advantages, for He had none. I do not wonder that the Jews were surprised. "Whence hath this Man these things?" they asked. "is not this the Carpenter?" "How knoweth this Man letters," they asked on another occasion, "having never learned?" They thought of our Lord's home, they thought of His education, they thought of Nazareth, they thought of those years in the workshop; and then they thought of His words of grace, His deeds of power, and His life of absolute holiness, and it left them utterly and hopelessly bewildered. There was nothing in His upbringing and surroundings to account for Him. As far as His environment was concerned, He grew up as a "root out of a dry ground."

Time

Then, in the third place, as there was nothing in His own immediate surroundings at Nazareth, so there was nothing in the mental and moral atmosphere of His time to account for Jesus. Now, there appear to occur in history certain seasons or cycles that seem to favor the emergence of genius. For instance, "the spacious days of Queen Elizabeth," in our own country, witnessed a wonderful efflorescence of gift and genius in almost every department of human endeavor. The new learning had but just reached England, and it created a new and vigorous life, with the result that England had great men in her councils, great sailors on her seas, and a great galaxy of poets to adorn her literature. But the days in which Jesus appeared were not such spacious days. Never did the national life of the Jews run so poor and thin. The chief glory of the Jew was his religion. But all the days from Malachi to Jesus were poor days for religion. You might say of them as the Bible says of those disastrous days of Eli—"There was no open vision." The oracles were dumb. There was no authentic divine voice. Religion had degenerated into legalism, and legalism issued in hypocrisy. The prophets had all died out, and the scribes, with their dry and thin pedantries, took their place. There was nothing in the condition of Israel favorable to the emergence of a great religious genius. There was no religious expectancy, no spiritual life. I think of Judea in these first years of the Christian era, and then I think of Jesus. The contemplation of the one does not help me to understand the other. As far as the religious condition of His day is concerned, Jesus is a "root out of a dry ground."

And not only is there nothing in the religious condition of our Lord's time to account for His appearance, but there is nothing in the state of religious thought to account for His teaching. I said a moment ago that we are all of us, in a very deep and unmistakable sense, the children of our time. In our ideas and beliefs we reproduce the ideas and beliefs current in our own day. But Jesus is in no sense a child of His day. That is not to say that, in historical and scientific matters, He did not share in the current beliefs of His time. But Jesus' sphere was neither history nor science, but religion. He did not come to anticipate Galileo and Newton and Darwin. He came to show men the Father. And in the matter of religion Jesus was in no sense a child of His own day. The comment of the people who heard Him preach was that He was "not as their scribes." The rabbi who came to Him by night was so staggered by His teaching about the kingdom that he cried, "How can these things be?" The charge brought against the first disciples was that by their teaching they were turning the world upside down. It was not the familiarity of our Lord's religious ideas, but their strangeness, their absolute newness, their revolutionizing character, that astonished His contemporaries. The fatherhood of God was not a religious idea of His time. The spirituality of worship was not a religious idea of His time. The new birth was not a religious idea of His time. The supremacy of love was not a religious idea of His time. The universality of the kingdom was not a religious idea of His time. I think of the Jews of our Lord's day identifying ritual with religion, dreaming of a material empire, and thinking that the kingdom was a Jewish preserve; and then I think of Jesus revealing the Father, declaring that God was a Spirit, and must be worshipped in spirit and in truth; preaching a spiritual kingdom, into which publicans and sinners, Greeks and Gentiles reborn, were free to enter, and into which no Jew could hope to enter until he was reborn; and I cannot find in the one any explanation of the other. On mere humanitarian grounds you cannot explain how Jesus so completely and absolutely transcended the thoughts and beliefs of His own time. You cannot understand how, such being the intellectual and spiritual atmosphere of His day, Jesus came to be able to speak these deep and eternal words of truth and life. A study of contemporary thought and faith will not enable you to account for the Sermon on the Mount or the fourteenth chapter of John. As far as the religious thought of His day is concerned, Jesus is a "root out of a dry ground."

Race

And, lastly, there was nothing in our Lord's race and nationality to account for Him. I am well aware that the Jew had, shall I say, a genius for religion. I am not forgetting that from the Jewish race came forth such great and inspired seers and psalmists and prophets as Moses, and David, and the writer of this immortal prophecy from which my text is taken. But His Jewish birth and lineage do not account for Jesus. The remarkable thing about our Lord is that there is nothing exclusively Jewish about Him. Moses and David and Isaiah never allow you for one moment to forget that they are Jews. It is for Israel that they write. It is the glory of Israel they predict. It is a kingdom of Israel of which they dream. But there is nothing parochial or sectional about Jesus. He is catholic and universal. I can detect no Jewish accent in His speech. He speaks with equal directness and force to all human hearts. There is nothing foreign about Him. Like His disciples at Pentecost, He speaks to every man in the language wherein he was born. As far as the Jewish nation is concerned, Jesus is a "root out of a dry ground." There is nothing in His nationality to account for Him.

And I will broaden my statement and say not only that there is nothing in the Jewish nation—there is nothing even in the human race to explain Jesus. You may remind me that the race has produced great teachers and leaders like Confucius and Buddha and Mahomet and Plato and Socrates. Yes, I know; but the fact that the race produced Confucius and Buddha and Mahomet and Socrates and Plato and Dante and Shakespeare does not make it a whit easier to understand how it could produce Jesus. For in the matter of wisdom and truth, a whole universe separates Jesus from the best and wisest of other teachers. There are falsities mixed up with their wisdom, but the wisdom of Jesus is all pure gold. We outgrow their teaching. The teaching of Jesus, after nineteen centuries, remains our wonder and our inspiration. Others guess at truth. Jesus talks about the eternities in the calm and assured accents of full and perfect knowledge.

But wisdom and truth are not the most wonderful characteristics of Jesus. Holiness is the most wonderful of all. I look abroad upon the human race, and I notice wherever I look that man has a sort of taint in the blood. "There is none that doeth good; no, not one." That terrible thing which the Bible calls sin—I see it everywhere. And the best and noblest of men are just the men who are most vividly and keenly conscious of it. The whole race, somehow, has become infected and corrupted. Original sin, and the corruption of men's hearts, are not theological doctrines, they are terrible facts of experience. But I look at Jesus and I see Him "holy, harmless, undefiled and separate from sinners." On the testimony of His foes, He was a man without fault. On the testimony of His own conscience—a far more wonderful testimony—He did no sin. I look at the race, stained, infected, corrupt, shut up, as the apostle put it, under sin; and then I look at the sinless and spotless Jesus. Can that stainless Person issue from that sin-stained race? Can such a stream, so fresh and sweet, issue from so bitter a fountain? If the race could produce one Jesus, why has it not produced some more? I look at the race and then at Jesus, and I can see nothing in the one to account for the other. The race could not produce Jesus. The race did not produce Jesus. Human nature is not equal to this great creation. The soil will not account for the flower. As far as the race is concerned, Jesus is a "root out of a dry ground."

What, then, shall we say of Jesus? There is only one thing that can be said of Him. He is not the product of the race. He is the gift of God. Start from purely human considerations, and Jesus remains as big a problem and as hopeless and insoluble a riddle as a root out of a dry ground. But my difficulties vanish and I can understand Jesus when, with the holy church, I say that Jesus does not represent so much the ascent of man, as the descent of God; not so much the climbing of the human into the Divine, as the condescension of the Divine to the human; that His birth was not a mere birth, but an Incarnation; that Jesus is not simply Son of Mary, but Immanuel, God with us. "I say," said Browning, and I say it with him—

> The acknowledgment of God in Christ,
> Accepted by the reason solves for thee
> All questions in the earth and out of it.

CHAPTER TWO

The Sound of the Trumpet

Praise him with the sound of the trumpet.
—Psalm 150:3

The loud, clangorous, exultant trumpet! "Praise Him," says the psalmist, "with the sound of the trumpet!" That crashing, triumphant note is to go sounding through our songs! But I am more than half inclined to believe that nowadays the psalmist's advice is more honored in the breach than in the observance. The trumpet is a neglected instrument. Or, at any rate, it is true to say that there are other instruments with which we are much more familiar, and in the playing of which we are much more expert. I hear much more of the wail and sob of the flute than I do of the piercing, shattering notes of the trumpet. We pitch our tunes in the minor key. We are subdued, hesitant, doubtful. We talk not as the New Testament does of victory and conquest; we talk of defeat, reaction, arrest. We lack that note of confidence and joy which was the characteristic mark of the invincible apostolic church. There is an old Jewish legend which tells how each morning in heaven the trumpets ring out; and when Lucifer, son of the morning, was asked, after he had fallen from heaven, what he missed most, he replied, "I miss most of all the trumpets that are sounded in the morning." And that is what I miss most in the individual Christian life and the corporate church life of today. I miss the trumpets that are sounded in the morning. I miss the note of courage, confidence, defiance. We are more familiar

with Misereres than we are with Te Deums. Our religion is marked
by sadness and melancholy rather than by the abandonment of joy
that sounds through this psalm with its summons to praise God
"with the sound of the trumpet," to "praise Him upon the loud
cymbals," to "praise Him upon the high sounding cymbals."

We have become self-conscious and morbid in our Christian
lives. We are much more given to examining our own conditions
than we are to letting our minds dwell upon the excellencies and
glories and conquering might of our risen and ascended Lord. Intro-
spection has its uses, but it may easily become morbid and perilous.
The man who is always taking his own temperature and examining
his own pulse may easily fret himself into a fever. And that is what
we have been doing as individual Christians and as churches. We
have been spending far too much of our time in diagnosing our own
conditions. We have pored over discouraging church statistics, and
tried to discern what is amiss. We have almost persuaded ourselves
that the church is sick, anemic, decayed, dying. And the result is we
are more in the mood for wailing than for shouting, for mourning
than for rejoicing.

The effect of this, again, is still further to cripple and paralyze the
church. Nothing is so enfeebling as despair. A depressed and discouraged church is almost bound to be a defeated church. Is it not a
fact that in the recent South African War some man who lived in
Ladysmith was imprisoned by Sir George White because by his
persistent prophecies of defeat he discouraged the hearts of the
garrison? The discourager is more to be dreaded than the avowed
and open foe. That was why the ten spies with their panic-stricken
report about the size of the inhabitants of Canaan, and the strength
of their cities, brought upon themselves the denunciations of Moses.
They "made the heart of the people to melt." They took all the spirit
and courage out of them, and doomed them to another long and
dreary sojourn in the wilderness. For Moses knew that to go up
against the fenced cities of Canaan with a people whose hearts were
melted within them was simply to court defeat and disaster. A
desponding and disheartened people is always a crippled and enfeebled people. And the discourager has been abroad among the
churches of Christ for long enough. He has been telling us that the
church is losing ground, and that the world is winning in the fight.
And the result has been enfeeblement and impotence, because the
hearts of our people are melted within them. It would be an

unspeakable blessing for the church if our discouragers, like the discourager in Ladysmith, could be put under lock and key. This sentence occurs in the latest Yale Lecture "As soon as the preacher finds himself pitching all his sermons in a minor key, he ought to resign or be granted a vacation." What we want is not discouragers, but encouragers—people who will say to the church today as the prophet did to exiled Israel long ago, "Comfort ye, comfort ye my people, saith your God. Speak ye comfortably to Jerusalem." Comfort ye! Be of good heart! Have a good courage! "For the Lord will come with vengeance, even the Lord with a recompense; He will come and save you."

One of the great religious needs of the present day is a healthy objectivity. We want to think less of ourselves and more of our Lord. We want to look in less, and out more. We have been far too introspective and subjective in our religion. We have thought far too much about our own moods and feelings. We have been far too absorbed in the contemplation of the obvious weaknesses of the church. I am not surprised that, such being the case, we have been depressed and discouraged and have harped on the topics of reaction and arrest. What Christian folk need to do is to think less about themselves and more about their Lord—their mighty and conquering Lord! I know there are many things to discourage us in the condition of the church; but, suppose we lift up our eyes, what do we see? We see Jesus "crowned with glory and honor," we see Him from "henceforth expecting until all his foes shall be made the footstool of His feet." Expecting! Calmly, confidently expecting it! The result is not a matter of doubt, it is only a matter of time. That is the vision we want to see—the vision of our enthroned Lord. That would bring the trumpet note back again. That would fill us with confidence and courage. And confidence and courage would spell conquest. "This is the conquest that conquers the world, even our faith." is there not a story told that during Napoleon's passage of the Alps the troops at a certain point were almost about to give up the effort in despair, beaten by the cold and the toilsomeness of the way? And then some genius suggested that the band should play the "Marseillaise." And as soon as the notes of that fierce and defiant song, into which the spirit of revolutionary France has instilled itself, fell on the ears of the tired soldiers, a new light came into their eyes, and a new strength seemed to come into their wearied limbs—they set themselves once again to breast the hill, with the result that soon the difficulties were all surmounted, and what looked like being a defeat was converted into a triumph. And that is what the soldiers of Christ—depressed, discouraged, disheartened, need to hear in these days—some Christian "Marseillaise," the piercing, defiant, exultant note of the trumpet. "If the trumpet gives an uncertain voice, who shall prepare himself for war?" But a church that hears the trumpet note shall go forth conquering, and to conquer.

When the church has praised God with the sound of the trumpet, she has been invincible and irresistible. It was so in New Testament times. That was the characteristic of the apostolic church. It was a very small church, and a very insignificant church, but it was a church blessed with magnificent courage and confidence. Its members flung themselves against an embattled world with a dash and an abandon that clean take the breath away. The trumpet never ceased to ring in their ears. *Marantha* was their watchword—"the Lord cometh"—and in the strength of that mighty hope they went everywhere preaching the word, and turned the world upside down. It was so in Puritan times. The church in those troublous days was afraid of nothing. "They praised God with the sound of the trumpet." You have noticed what a part the trumpet plays in John Bunyan's works? Mark Rutherford declares that the silver trumpet is the symbol of the spirit of the great Puritan dreamer. "Faith even when we are prostrate and the enemy stands over us, resistance to the uttermost, and then the voice of the silver trumpet and the trampling of the slain." That is the keynote of the *Pilgrim's Progress*—victory. From beginning to end John Bunyan sounds the trumpet—victory over the Slough of Despond, victory over Apollyon, victory over Vanity Fair, victory over Giant Despair, victory over death, and then—"all the trumpets sounded for him on the other side." And that is what I would fain recover for the church today— this note of exultation and confidence and triumph. We are saved by hope. A church that believes in itself and its Lord is on the way to victory. So let us cease our moanings and complainings, and let us triumph in the grace of God; let us exchange our miseries for plans and hallelujahs; instead of crying to God from the depths, let us "praise Him with the sound of the trumpet."

But someone may say, "What is the use of telling us to put the trumpet to the lips in face of the circumstances that confront us? We live in a world of gigantic wrongs and heartrending tragedies. The

fires of hell are burning at our very doors. Evil men wax worse and
worse, and good men faint and fail; what is the use of telling us to
put the trumpet to the lips? We do not feel any more like using the
trumpet than the exiled Jews felt like singing the songs of Zion in
pagan Babylon. They hung their harps on the willows, and for the
moment, at any rate, we, too, have put the trumpet by." But why put
the trumpet by? The time for the trumpet is every time. If we feel
this is no time for the trumpet, that is because we have allowed the
nearest facts to absorb our vision, and have not looked deep enough
or far enough. If we only looked up to God—then, in face of all
difficulties and discouragements, we would praise God with the
sound of the trumpet. That indeed is the test of faith—to believe in
victory in the day of seeming defeat, to believe that God is on the
field when He is most invisible, to ring out the trumpet blast in the
very face of exulting foes. "Many are the afflictions of the righteous"—we can all say that! But the psalmist put the trumpet to his
lips when he added, "but the Lord delivereth him out of them all."

What are the things that tempt us to lay the trumpet by? What are
the things that change the shout into a wail, and the Te Deum into a
sob? Well, perhaps principally these four things—the perplexities of
providence, the terrific and appalling power of sin, the blight of personal trouble, and the fear of death. And yet I am going to suggest to
you that, in face of these things, we can sing our song of exultation
and triumph, and praise our God with the sound of a trumpet.

The Trumpet in Face of Dark Providences

Firstly, then, even in face of the perplexities of providence we
may praise God with the sound of a trumpet. I know there are
certain tragic happenings in life that almost silence the song on the
lips of the cheeriest and the bravest. It takes all the faith a man is
capable of to put the trumpet to his lips in face of an appalling
calamity like that which took place at the Hulton pits the other day.
We torture ourselves trying to discover the reason for these staggering catastrophes. Why, we ask, if there be a good God, should so
many hundreds of people be involved in so sore and, as we think, so
undeserved a sorrow? Why should crimes, such as the atrocities of
the Congo, be permitted in a world in which goodness is supposed
to rule? Questions like these inevitably challenge us, and they are
hard; what is more, they are impossible to answer. And yet in face
of these heartbreaking providences I will put the trumpet to my lips.

"The Lord reigneth," cries the psalmist. What then? "Let the earth rejoice." "The Lord reigneth!" What then? Well, in face of Italian earthquakes and Lancashire explosions, praise God with the voice of a trumpet! For if God rules it means this: that, spite of everything that seems to suggest the contrary, love rules, and goodness rules. Lay hold of that fact—and the trumpet note will never be lacking. Do you remember how Browning sounds that note again and again throughout his poetry? That was Browning's fundamental faith: "Thou God art love; I build my faith on that." And, believing that, Browning had the trumpet continually on his lips! He was a triumphant, exultant, almost defiant soul! "This world," he cries, with all its tangled providences, with all its grief and tears, "this world means intensely and means good." "God's in His heaven," he cries in *Pippa Passes*, "all's right with the world." That is it—he praised God with the sound of the trumpet. And with the same vision we, too, shall gain the same triumphant faith. To see God in Christ is to say good-bye to doubt and fear. If God, who loved the world well enough to give His Son to die for it, rules the world, then, though dark mysteries are all about me, I will believe that love rules. Listen to the way in which Archbishop Trench praised God with the sound of the trumpet: "I say to thee," he wrote,

> Do thou repeat,
> To the first man thou mayest meet,
> In lane, highway, or open street,
> That he and we and all men move
> Under a canopy of love
> As broad as the blue sky above.
> That doubt and trouble, fear and pain
> And anguish, all are shadows vain,
> That death itself shall not remain.
> That weary deserts we may tread,
> A dreary labyrinth may thread,
> Through dark ways underground be led,
> Yet if we will our guide obey,
> The dreariest paths, the darkest way,
> Shall issue out in heavenly day,
> And we on divers shores now cast,
> Shall meet, our perilous voyage past,
> All in our Father's house at last.

"The Lord reigneth; let the earth rejoice. . . . Praise Him with the sound of the trumpet."

The Trumpet in Face of the Power of Sin

And, in the second place, in face of the terrific and appalling power of sin, we may praise God with the sound of a trumpet. I do not wish in the slightest way to minimize the power of sin. I would not have Christian people treat lightly the enemy they have to face. Men who treat their enemies lightly often pay in defeat the penalty of their rashness. The Scriptures do not hold cheaply the might of sin. Recall the apostle's words, "We wrestle not against flesh and blood, but against the principalities, against the powers, against the world-rulers of this darkness, against the spiritual hosts of wickedness in the heavenly places." The apostle would not have us underrate our foes. And yet, while we ought not to underrate the power of sin, neither ought we, as we confront it, to whimper and whine as if we were defeated men. The men of the Bible, when they confront sin, do it always with the trumpet to the lips. The victory is not to lie with sin. Sin is a broken and defeated power.

Our Lord, as He confronted sin, praised God with the sound of a trumpet; He triumphed over this monstrous and appalling world power. "Be of good cheer," He said to His timid and frightened disciples, "I have overcome the world." "I have overcome"—He blew His blast of victory over a broken and prostrate foe. It looked, in our Lord's own day, as if evil had overcome good; when the cross was set up in Jerusalem it seemed the very hour and power of darkness. But Jesus was in no whit dismayed. Facing it all, He sounded forth His note of conquest. "I beheld Satan," He cried, "fallen as lightning from heaven." "Satan fallen!" That is what our Lord saw. Sin broken! Evil destroyed! Wickedness overthrown! Never a note of doubt or fear fell from His lips. All through, He praised God with the sound of the trumpet. And His disciples caught His spirit. The evil world rose in its might against them. It used fire and stake to destroy them. But they never flinched or faltered! They never imagined for one moment the world could crush the church. They went forward to their battle with the assurance of victory in their hearts, and songs of victory upon their lips. You remember John's cry as he confronted imperial Rome, drunk with the blood of the saints, and bending all her strength to stamp out the tiny church: "Fallen, fallen," he cried, with a sort of fierce rapture, "is Babylon the Great!" And this is the vision with which his book ends—the Devil and the Beast and the False Prophet and death and hades are all cast into the lake of fire. It is on that triumphant note the Bible ends—sin destroyed, the new earth created! These New Testament saints sang to the Lord with the sound of a trumpet.

And we may sound the same triumphant note. There is no need for us to cower and quake in face of the embattled hosts of evil. The trumpet to the lips, my brethren! In spite of seeming reaction, sin is a broken and defeated power. When our Lord went down to death and the grave, He came to grip with sin. And when He rose again, He emerged victor from the conflict. The power of sin was shattered in the Cross. The decisive battle was fought and the issue settled then! It is true that there is often sporadic fighting after the fate of a campaign has been settled. After Paardeburg and the capture of Pretoria—which really settled the fate of the war—there was a good deal of fighting and not a few British reverses. But there could be only one end to the war, and every one knew it. It is so with the struggle against sin. The issue was settled on Calvary. The Serpent's head was bruised there. But though his power has been broken, the old Serpent is able to give considerable trouble before being finally destroyed. But there can be no shadow of doubt about the end. Sin is a broken power, on the way to become a power destroyed and rooted out! A look back over the long stretches of history will show that its defeat is no imagination. It has been losing power. It is on the way to destruction. Its empire is breaking down!

This is no time for melancholy fluting over failure. Sound the trumpet rather over the sure and certain triumph! You remember Isaac Watt's verse—

> Hell and thy sins resist thy course,
> But sin and hell are vanquished foes:
> Thy Jesus nailed them to His cross,
> And sang the triumph when He rose.

That is it exactly! Hell and sin are vanquished foes! That is the trumpet song you and I ought to raise. "Who art thou, O great mountain?" asked the prophet of some great mountain of difficulty that confronted Zerubbabel in his work of restoring the exiles. And then he added, with superb and splendid defiance, "Before Zerubbabel thou shalt become a plain." And so we may confront the mountain of sin and vice and evil and indifference that faces us today with a similar confidence and courage. Before the church of Christ it shall become a plain. Away, then, with all our fears and despairs! "Hell and sin are vanquished foes." Let us praise our God with the sound of the trumpet.

The Trumpet in Face of Death

I had meant in the third place to say that in face of personal trouble and affliction we may praise God with the voice of a trumpet. "Rejoicing," says the apostle, "in tribulation." He sounded the note of joy and triumph in the midst of trouble and loss because he knew all things worked together for good to them that loved God. But I pass that by to come to what is perhaps the greatest trouble of all, the fear of death. And in face of the last dread foe the Christian may still put the trumpet to his lips. Not every one can use the trumpet in the face of death. Before Christ came, men feared the end. They sobbed and wailed in their fear of death, "O spare me that I may recover strength ere I go hence!" cries one. "The grave can not praise Thee, death cannot celebrate Thee," cries another. But Christ has robbed death of all its terror! He has revealed it to us, not as an end but as a new beginning; not as the finish of life, but as the commencement of a life richer and nobler.

And in the faith begotten of Christ's resurrection men have been able to sound the trumpet in face of death. Listen to St. Paul, "O grave, where is thy victory? O death, where is thy sting? Thanks be to God who giveth us the victory through our Lord Jesus Christ"— that is the trumpet note. Listen to James Renwick, the young Covenanter on the scaffold at Edinburgh: "Yonder," he cried, as he heard the drums beat, "is the welcome warning to my marriage. The Bridegroom is coming. I am ready! By and by I shall be above these clouds, then I shall enjoy Thee and glorify Thee without intermission for ever"—that is the trumpet note. "I am going," said William Blake, the poet, "to that land which I have all my life longed to see"—that is the trumpet note. "How they ring out!" said Burne Jones; "I hope there will be trumpets in heaven." And that is what he wanted to hear at Browning's funeral—the trumpet with its defiant and triumphant note. The trumpet! the clangorous, exultant, triumphant trumpet!—that is the instrument wherewith to meet death and the grave! For—

> We bow our heads at going out, we think,
> And straightway find another palace of the King's,
> Larger than this we leave, and lovelier.

So, as strength fails and the eyes grow dim and life slips away, we shall be able to sing to God, not in any minor key—we shall be able to praise Him still with the sound of a trumpet.

The trumpet! That is the instrument I want to see upon our lips; that is the instrument whose note I wish to hear! We want courage, confidence, triumphant joy! And we shall get it by laying a fresh hold upon God in Christ. For the man who really believes that God was in Christ there can be no fear, no doubt, no gloom, no despair. For if God was in Christ—then love is on the throne, and sin is a broken power, and goodness works through sorrow, and death is but the entrance gate to life. Do you believe it? Then away with fear! Rejoice always! Sing your song of hope and victory in the day of seeming defeat. God will not fail nor be discouraged—so "praise Him with the sound of the trumpet."

CHAPTER THREE

The Place of Christian Experience in Christian Thinking

Now the natural man receiveth not the things of the Spirit of God. for they are foolishness unto him; and he cannot know them, because they are spiritually judged [or "tested"].   —1 Corinthians 2:14

No one can read the First Epistle of St. John without noticing how passionate and vehement he is in his denunciation of the heresy of those teachers who denied that Jesus was the Christ. That heresy, in the apostle's view of it, was the ultimate falsity, and meant the total subversion and destruction of Christianity. But apparently the apostle never imagined that this heresy would spread and submerge the faith. Over against the criticisms and negations of the Gnostics, he set the spiritual experience of the Christian man. "We have an anointing from the Holy One," he wrote, "and we all know." The Gnostic leaders might conjure up what difficulties they pleased, the Divine power of Christ was not a matter of theory or speculation to the plain Christian folk to whom John addressed his letter; it was an assured fact of their own experience—they had received the anointing from the Holy One and they all knew. These heretical teachers who plumed and prided themselves on their superior cleverness, who by their very name professed to be the "knowing people," were incompetent to judge upon a question like this.

26

They had not the necessary equipment for it. It lay clean outside their sphere of knowledge. The humblest believer in Ephesus who had had personal experience of Christ possessed an authority of judgment upon a question like this to which the subtlest Gnostic could lay no claim. For knowledge of Christian truth is not merely intellectual; it is experimental. It is they who have received the anointing from the Holy One who really know. It is upon this great contention of the apostle John that I want to speak briefly. My theme is: the place of Christian experience in the testing of Christian truth.

I have taken as my text, not that great word of the apostle John's which I have already quoted, but an equally great and striking word of the apostle Paul's in which precisely the same truth is enshrined. And this I have done to make it clear that this idea of the critical place of experience in the acquirement of Christian knowledge is no mere crank or obsession of the apostle John's. Paul is in full agreement with him. It is "the anointing from the Holy One" that enables a man to know, says John. "The natural man"—the unregenerate man—is unable, Paul says, to receive the things of God, for they are foolishness to him, and he cannot know them, because "they are spiritually discerned." It is not the merely clever man, but the man who has felt the power of spiritual forces who is competent to deal with spiritual issues. The judge of religious truth is not the critic, but the saint.

Let me call your attention first of all to the circumstances under which Paul penned this great statement of my text. He is recalling the manner of his early preaching at Corinth. He came direct to Corinth from Athens. In Athens he had tried to meet the Greeks on their own ground. "The Greeks," he declares in the previous chapter, "seek after wisdom." They prided themselves on their "culture." They were nothing if not intellectual. And when Paul went to Athens he did—what my friends tell me a good many of our preachers do still when they go for a Sunday either to Mansfield or to Cambridge—he tried to preach up to his audience. He gave these keen and clever Greeks the wisdom they desired. He preached a sermon—a wonderful and mighty sermon of its kind—upon natural religion. But apparently that Athenian sermon left Paul profoundly dissatisfied. It was the first and the last sermon of the sort he ever delivered. He made no more attempts to meet the Greeks on their own ground and give them the wisdom they reveled in. When he got to Corinth he entirely altered his tactics. He gave no more addresses on natural religion. "I, brethren," he writes in the opening verses of this chapter, "when I came unto you, came not with excellency of speech or of wisdom proclaiming to you the mystery of God. For I determined not to know anything among you, save Jesus Christ, and Him as crucified." Paul in Corinth was not the nimble intellectual disputant; he was the herald and the preacher telling the story of salvation through the Cross of Christ. He did not argue about his message; he simply proclaimed it. And what was the result of this preaching of the Cross? It was twofold. To those who accepted it and received it, Christ crucified proved Himself to be "the power of God, and the wisdom of God." The promise of salvation proved to be no deceptive illusion. By this crucified Christ men were delivered from their sins, and given the life which was life indeed. Satisfaction, peace, liberty, power—all came to them through Christ.

But to others the preaching of Christ crucified seemed sheer "foolishness." To the clever and rather conceited Greek, accustomed to apply the intellectual test to everything, the idea that the death of Jesus upon the cross in Jerusalem could result in blessing and benefit to a world, appeared simply silly and absurd. He laughed Paul and his preaching out of court. But Paul was not at all perturbed. That his preaching of the Cross should appear foolishness to the unsanctified reason of the merely clever man was only what might have been expected. But then, the merely clever man did not possess the necessary qualifications for judgment. For more is needed for the appreciation of spiritual truth than a clever intellect; there is needed also a regenerate heart. "The natural man receiveth not the things of the Spirit of God, for they are foolishness unto him, and he cannot know them because they are spiritually judged." Paul is in complete agreement with John; the only competent judge of Christian truth is not the scholar or the critic, but the saint.

The Insufficiency of Mere Reason

Now what are we to make of the principle the apostle here lays down? Does it amount to a repudiation of reason in the realm of religion? Is it a denial of the rights of the intellect? Is it a case of warning off the scholar and the critic, and reducing religion to a kind of Fleusinian mystery? By no means. There is no suggestion of hocus-pocus about the Christian faith. It appeals to men as reasonable and intelligent beings. This is the challenge it addresses to them: "Come and let us reason together, saith the Lord." It courts investigation; it welcomes inquiry. It calls upon men to serve and love God not only with the heart and the soul, but with the mind as well. There was not a touch of the obscurantist about Paul. He himself brought a mighty' brain to bear upon Christian truth. He is par excellence the thinker of the apostolic group. He would be the last in the world to challenge the function of the reason or to deny the rights of the intellect. On the contrary, he commends the Christian faith and the Christian service on the ground that it is essentially a reasonable service. No, this is not a denial of the rights of the intellect; it is not an assertion that the reason has no part to play in religion. But it is the assertion that reason by itself is not enough, that something more than a keen and clever intellect is necessary for the discernment of religious truth. And there is nothing unreasonable in the apostolic contention. He is really only laying down a principle the reasonableness and, indeed, necessity of which are freely acknowledged in other spheres of human learning.

As a matter of fact, there is very little of our knowledge that has come to us as the result of mere and pure reason. There is only one science that can with any semblance of truth be spoken of as a pure intellectual discipline, and that is the science of mathematics. And the science of mathematics is a purely intellectual discipline, and the reason alone is sufficient for it, simply because it is an abstract science and entirely remote from life. When once, however, you bring mathematics out of the purely abstract region and begin to apply it to life, you find pure reason will not carry you far. For instance, in the abstract you know that twice two makes four. But you cannot be at all sure that, if you put four men on to a job, you are going to get twice as much work out of them as you did out of two. To answer that question you need to know men—and to know human nature you need more than a clear brain; you need insight, sympathy, a heart. And that is typical of all our concrete and practical knowledge (and nearly all our knowledge is of this type): it has come to us, not by way of the intellect simply; all the complex forces of our personalities—feeling, imagination, conscience, will— have played their part. For it is a vast and complete mistake to suppose that the acquisition of knowledge consists in the reception of certain bare facts onto a blank mind. No mind is a blank mind, and no facts are bare facts. We come to the study of any facts with

minds already full of prepossessions, predilections, prejudices, as-
sumptions. If the process of knowing were simply the reception of
bare facts into blank minds, there would be among men absolute
uniformity of thought and belief. But, as a matter of experience, the
same facts mean one thing to one man and quite another thing to
another. And the reason for that is our minds are not blank minds.
We all look at the facts through our own special and peculiar spectacles. The nature of a man's perception depends upon his personality. What a man knows depends upon what he is. His conviction
depends upon his character. But I do not want in my sermon to drift
off into technicalities. I think I can—apart from technicalities—
illustrate and make real to you the truth for which I am contending,
that knowledge is not the result of intellect merely, but that emotional and moral factors are called into play as well.

Let me try to make it clear by a simple illustration or two.

To appreciate painting, you need much more than a clear eye and
the power to distinguish colors. You need more than a brain. You
need a certain moral and spiritual gift: you need sympathy with the
painter's mind and purpose. I remember when in Venice seeing an
American gentleman, sitting in a room which contained Titian's
glorious "Annunciation," listlessly turning over the leaves of his
catalogue, and looking the very picture of weariness and boredom.
And I overheard his wife say to him: "Come, along, John, to room
so-and-so; there's something besides saints there." John found absolutely no delight in the glowing canvases by which he was surrounded. The truth is, you need more than a clear eye to appreciate
a picture; you need a little of the artist's soul.

To appreciate music you need more than an accurate ear; you
need a little of the musical temperament. There are plenty of keen,
clever men to whom music of all kinds is an intolerable weariness.
Your Handel and your Mendelssohn, your Beethoven, your Wagner
—they are so much noise to them. To appreciate and understand
music you must have a bit of the musician's soul. To appreciate
poetry you need more than the power to read; you need that curious,
subtle feeling for the harmonies and cadences of words. Darwin, in
the later years of his life, confessed he had absolutely no taste for
poetry. He had a mighty intellect, but poetry, shall I say, is not a
matter of mind simply—poetry is poetically discerned.

Take one other illustration on a rather different plane. To understand men you need more than a clear head; you need also a

sympathetic heart. The power to read human nature, as we say, comes not so much through our intellectual faculties as through our emotional and moral qualities of insight, sympathy, sensibility. Before a man can understand another he must be in a certain spiritual correspondence with him. When it became known that Mr. John Morley (as he then was) had undertaken to write the life of Mr. Gladstone, men questioned whether he had all the qualifications necessary to make him a successful biographer. For the deepest and profoundest thing in Mr. Gladstone, the real secret of his life, was his religion, and Mr. Morley, it was understood, was not in sympathy with Mr. Gladstone in the matter of religion. And though we may think that in the actual result that difficulty was largely overcome, the feeling that prompted the criticism was perfectly sound and just. It is of no use asking a man to write a biography of another if he is not in sympathy with his subject. A picture of a great man drawn by some one out of sympathy with him—the Archbishop of Canterbury, let us say, drawn by some disappointed, embittered, persecuted Nonconformist, or Dr. Clifford drawn by a narrow and irritated Anglican—will not be a true picture, but a gross and lying caricature. To know a man thoroughly, intimately, truly, you need to be in affectionate sympathy with him.

Now it is this same principle, the validity of which you acknowledge in everyday matters, that Paul is applying here to the matter of Christian truth. It comes to men not through the mind only, but through the heart, the emotions, and the will as well. And to understand Christian truth you need more than intellectual cleverness; you need moral sympathy with the truth you seek to grasp; you need the Christian spirit; "these things are spiritually tested." The only difference is that, if this principle holds good in other spheres of human knowledge, it holds with tenfold validity in the apprehension of Christian truth. For Christianity is not a theory, it is not a set of maxims, it is not even a body of truth; it is a personal relation, it is an obedience, it is a life. Christianity, at bottom, is life in Christ.

Experience and Doctrine

Now I want to call your attention to this important fact, that in the Christian religion experience precedes doctrine. There is a certain body of doctrine which we recognize today as being the intellectual statement of the truth of Christianity. But, as a matter of history, Christianity did not begin as a set of doctrines; it began as a vital experience in the hearts of men. Experience came first, dogma came second. It was not the Christian doctrine that gave rise to the Christian experience; it was the Christian experience that gave rise to the Christian dogma. Men felt certain things, and then they felt constrained to try to give an intellectual account of them. Take the cardinal doctrine of the Incarnation. The apostles did not start with the doctrine. But Jesus Christ produced a certain impression upon them, and accomplished certain works in them, and coming to account for that impression, and those mighty and revolutionary works, they explained them by saying that Jesus was no mere man, but God manifest in the flesh. Take Paul's doctrine of atonement. That is not a mere dialectical exercise; it is not something evolved out of Paul's brain; it is not an intellectual tour de force. Paul's theory of atonement has been drawn out of the blood and fire of his own experience. The crushing burden of sin, the ineffectiveness of law, the redeeming and life-giving power of the crucified Christ—they were vital experiences with Paul before they were translated into doctrines. His doctrine of release through the atoning sacrifice of Christ is simply the attempt to give intellectual expression to what he had already experienced. Now if that be the true order (and I think that no one will dispute that it is), it follows that for the true appreciation of these great Christian doctrines an identity of experience, a sympathy of spirit is required.

Experience and Knowledge

So here we are back again at Paul's statement: "These things are spiritually tested." If Christian truth were purely intellectual, like the multiplication table or the problems of Euclid, the intellect would be sufficient for its apprehension. But Christian doctrine is simply Christian experience translated into speech. To understand and appreciate the speech into which it is translated you must first of all have some sympathy with and some share in the experience. Take the great and cardinal doctrines to which I have already referred.

Take first the matter of the Incarnation. The Gnostics in John's day challenged this doctrine. They denied that the infinite God could express Himself in a finite personality. They scouted the bare idea that God could become manifest in the flesh. It was not the least bit surprising that they should do so. From the merely intellectual point of view the doctrine seemed impossible and absurd. But to John and the Christians at Ephesus it was not impossible, and it was not absurd. They had felt and seen and handled the Word of Life. They had come into direct contact with Jesus; He had exercised God's power upon them and done God's work within them. The Incarnation to them was not an impossible thing; it was a sure and certain thing. Their conviction sprang from their experience. They had an anointing from the Holy One, and they knew.

Take next the great doctrine of the Cross with which Paul is dealing in this chapter. To the clever Greek the idea that forgiveness could come to the world through the death of Christ was simply silly. To the natural man it was mere foolishness. This is nothing to be surprised at. The natural man cannot know this great truth. The man who has never felt broken and crushed by his sin will never understand it. He does not realize the need of forgiveness, and so the whole idea of an atoning sacrifice becomes to him a ridiculous superfluity. But the man who has passed through Paul's experience finds no difficulty about Paul's doctrine. The man whose heart has been broken by his sin appreciates the Cross, understands the Cross. To the wise and prudent it seems a superfluity. To the penitent soul it is God's answer to his urgent and bitter need, and a great multitude of sin-burdened men and women have found in it their hope and comfort.

> Rock of ages, cleft for me,
> Let me hide myself in thee.

I might illustrate further in the matters of miracle and prayer. But I must draw to a close. There the broad truth stands—with nothing unreasonable or obscurantist about it—we must be Christians ourselves if we are to understand Christianity; a share in Christian experience is the condition of appreciating Christian truth. "These things are spiritually discerned."

Now all this has a very vital bearing upon our Christian apologetic. We are living in days when scholars and critics are dealing very freely with what we have been accustomed to believe are fundamental verities of the Christian faith. Now the scholar and the critic have their work to do. By all means let them examine into the structure of the Bible and scrutinize matters of date and authorship. By all means let them bring their knowledge to bear upon questions of text and interpretation. Scholarship is competent for that task. But when it comes to the substance of the Christian faith, when it comes to the great spiritual verities that constitute Christianity, I challenge and deny the competence of the mere critic to decide. I deny the sufficiency of mere scholarship. If a man is to judge rightly upon these high matters, he must be more than a critic, he must be a Christian; he must be more than a scholar, he must be a saint. And so, over against the negations and denials of a skeptical and unbelieving criticism, I set the experience of the spiritual man. Clever men are once again denying the Incarnation and scouting the Atonement. We need not be unduly alarmed. To the natural man, however keen and clever, these great Christian doctrines seem absurd, and they tell us so loudly and continually. But I say again, I challenge their competency to judge. How is a man to know who and what Christ is if he has never put himself in Christ's hands? How is a man to know whether the Cross is the power and wisdom of God or not if he has never felt the ache and burden of his own sin? These things are spiritually tested, and a man who has no experimental knowledge of Christ and who has never felt the sinfulness of sin is as incompetent to pronounce judgment upon the Incarnation or the Atonement as a blind man would be to pronounce judgment on color or a deaf man on sound.

For the appreciation of Christian truth Christian experience is necessary. And that is why it is that there are many things hidden from wise men which are revealed to babes, and an insight is given to the humble Christian to which gifted but skeptical scholars can lay no claim. So in these troublous days, over against the denials and negations of the critics I set the experience of the saints. And about the witness of the saints there is neither hesitation nor doubt. They know that Jesus is the Son of God, for they have felt His power in their lives. They know the Cross is a redeeming sacrifice, for it has brought redemption and life to them. And not only is this the experience of the saints of today; it has been the experience of the saints all down the centuries. The faith of John in Christ as the everlasting Son of the Father has been the faith of an unbroken succession of holy men and women all down the ages, because they have shared in John's experience. The faith of Paul in the atoning sacrifice of the Cross has been the faith of multitudes of other redeemed souls: through Augustine and Martin Luther and John Wesley and D. L. Moody the mighty evangelical succession has been continued, and the doctrine has been ratified and confirmed in the experience of that innumerable host of men and women who have been loosed from their sin by the blood. It does not trouble me very much that the mere critic sees nothing in these great doctrines. The faith is secure because multitudes by experience have found them true. And the saint—the man who has tried—the man who has made experiment—is the only competent judge of Christian truth. He is the true defender of the faith. The faith was once for all delivered, not to the critic or the scholar, but the saint.

Do you desire to know that Christ is Son of God? Do you desire to know that the Cross is the power of God? Then come and put yourselves in Christ's hands, and let Him work His will upon you. And come and kneel at His Cross, until both your sin and the Divine love shine out upon you. Then you will know. For knowledge of these things comes not by study and research, but by obedience and experience. "They are spiritually discerned." And when you have had that direct experience your faith is secure. "One thing I know," said the blind man to all objectors and critics, "whereas I was blind, now I see." "One thing I know," you will say, "Christ wrought God's work in me." "One thing I know," you will say, "I received redemption through His blood, even the remission of sins." Such a faith will stand foursquare, for it is based on the impregnable rock—the impregnable rock of knowledge and experience.

CHAPTER FOUR

The Immediacy of Religion

*Son of man, behold, they of the house of Israel say, The
vision that he seeth is for many days to come, and he
prophesieth of times that are far off.* —Ezekiel 12:27

I fancy that Ezekiel was a much-discouraged preacher. These
opening chapters of his prophecy are full of indications that he
prophesied to a skeptical and unbelieving people. They were, as he
puts it, a rebellious house. His words produced no effect upon them.
He had that most heartbreaking of all the preacher's experience—
he saw his most urgent appeals and his most solemn warnings alike
pass utterly unheeded.

And in my text I find one of the reasons why Ezekiel's ministry
produced such little effect. The people did not believe that his message in any way concerned them. The burden of Ezekiel's preaching was the sure destruction of Jerusalem and the dispersal of the
Jewish people. In a score of ways he tried to bring this solemn truth
home to the hearts and consciences of his hearers. They, however,
calmly pooh-poohed it. They said they had heard that kind of thing
before. Jeremiah had uttered similar bodeful prophecies. But day
after day had passed and nothing had happened. Jerusalem was still
standing. The people were still in possession of the land. So they
ignored and neglected the prophet's message. It left them absolutely
unmoved. They comforted themselves with the thought that if there
was any truth at all in the prophet's message, it related to some
faroff time. It had no immediate concern for them. Why should they

trouble about a distant future so long as they had peace and quietness in their own days? So they turned deaf ears to Ezekiel's appeals and dismissed his warnings with the remark, "The vision that he seeth is for many days to come, and he prophesieth of times that are far off."

The preacher is oftentimes still a much-discouraged man. Like Ezekiel, he finds that after his most urgent appeals the people are still unmoved, and that after his most solemn warning they remain quite unconcerned. Between him and them there seems to be a kind of wall of prejudice or unbelief, so that his most earnest words utterly fail to touch them. People have said to me sometimes after a service in which the gospel appeal has been given, perhaps, more plainly and directly than usual, "I wonder how the people can listen to that kind of preaching and go away apparently carelessly and unmoved." I wonder myself—with a sort of despairing wonder, too. But that has been the experience of well-nigh every preacher—even of the very greatest and mightiest. I find Isaiah, in the bitterness of his soul, saying, "Who hath believed our report, and to whom hath the arm of the Lord been revealed?" I find that after Paul had put all the powers of his heart and brain into that great sermon on Mars' Hill, "some laughed"—they found in it only matter for a jest. I find that John Wesley, the mightiest evangelist of modern times, had his depressing and heartbreaking times. In one town he would find a great door and effectual opened to him, and perhaps in the next would find the people like stocks and stones. In Newcastle, for instance, on the Tuesday and the Thursday a deep and gracious work of God was carried on in many souls. As he preached, men and women were pricked to the heart, many trembled exceedingly, six or seven dropped down as dead, some cried upon God out of the deep, and some found God gracious and merciful forgiving iniquity and transgression and sin. But on the Friday he went to a village called Whickham two or three miles away, and on the Sunday to another place called Tanfield-leigh, about seven miles away, and at these places he had a totally different experience. He spoke strong, rough words, he says, but he did not perceive that any regarded what was spoken. In Tanfield-leigh he expounded the first part of that great fifth chapter of Romans, in which Paul treats of the relation between the death of Christ and the forgiveness of sin—in other words, he made the subduing, overwhelming story of the sacrifice of Christ his theme; but, he writes, "so dead, senseless,

unaffected a congregation have I scarce seen. Whether the Gospel
or Law, or English or Greek seemed all one to them."

And that is the kind of experience the Christian preacher meets
with still. His words seem to fall absolutely impotent and dead.
Writers in the press discuss the "dearth of conversions." We do not
in these days hear people cry, "What must we do to be saved?"
Some people are inclined to lay the blame for this dearth of conversions at the preacher's door. They say that in modern preaching
there is not the same directness and urgency of appeal that was to
be found in the preaching of our fathers. I will not say that none of
the blame lies at the door of the preacher. There is an element of
truth in the charge that modern preaching lacks the note of urgency
and passion and personal pleading. And yet it is quite obvious that
the man who puts the entire blame down to the preacher's account
is ignoring some of the most glaring facts of our modern religious
life. For the same dearth of conversions is to be found in many a
church where the preaching lacks nothing in directness and evangelical fervor. Sunday by Sunday the warning is given and the
appeal is made, but how much response is there? Sunday by Sunday the way of life and the way of death are set before the people,
but they pass out apparently unconcerned. And that constitutes the
puzzle and the problem. Where the preaching is dull and cold and
lifeless, the lack of response is perhaps intelligible. But how are you
to explain the lack of response where the preaching is earnest,
urgent, and full of evangelical passion? The fault in such a case
cannot lie in the preacher; it must be in the people. It was so in
Ezekiel's case. It was not that Ezekiel himself lacked earnestness; it
was that the people themselves were encased in prejudices through
which his words completely failed to penetrate. And this prejudice
among other—that all Ezekiel's warnings referred to a time in the
remote future. They might have been sobered by the prophet's
warnings and have repented them of the evil if they could only have
brought themselves to believe that what he said was of present and
immediate importance. But, as it was, they listened to his warnings
and menaces with a smile and a shrug of the shoulders. There was
no need to hurry in the matter of repentance and reformation. The
ills the prophet foretold did not concern them. "The vision that he
seeth is for many days to come, and he prophesieth of times that are
far off."

And still the lack of conversion is not by any means due solely to

lack of earnestness in the preacher; it is due even more to certain
subtle prejudices and unbeliefs which make the hearers' hearts almost impervious to the gospel appeal. I sometimes think that there
never was a harder time for the Christian preacher than the present.
The movements of thought of the past fifty years seem to have
weakened the force of the sanctions with which the preacher was
wont to enforce his appeals. The doctrine of evolution, for instance,
has greatly weakened the sense of sin and responsibility; the decay
of the belief in hell has robbed the preacher of what George
MacDonald calls the "righteous use of fear"; a onesided doctrine of
the Fatherhood of God has created a weak and mushy kind of
optimism—we are all quite sure that everything and everybody is
going to come all right in the end; criticism has for many weakened
the authority of God's Word itself. And the result is the Christian
preacher is met by a subtle, unconfessed, but no less real unbelief
which minimizes and even nullifies the force of his warnings and
appeals.

But perhaps the thing that operates most powerfully in the way
of robbing the gospel appeal of its force is not any of the changes of
thought of the past fifty years, but the old feeling expressed in my
texts, feeling as prevalent today as it was in Ezekiel's day: the
feeling that religion is concerned with the distant and the remote
and the far-off. Most of the people who come into our churches
have some kind of a belief in God. In their hearts they acknowledge
that the gospel, with its witness about sin and the penalty of sin, and
the necessity of redemption through Christ, is true. Their very presence in the church indicates as much as that. But they persuade
themselves, also, that all these great issues are remote and distant.
They are not of immediate importance. There is no need to hurry.
And so they are able to put aside the most urgent appeal and the
most solemn warning by saying to their souls as these Jews did,
"The vision that he seeth is for many days to come, and he
prophesieth of times that are far off."

Now, what I propose to do in this sermon is to inquire into the
truth or otherwise of this widespread feeling that religion is only
concerned with the distant and the remote. Is it true that the preacher's
message is concerned mainly, if not entirely, with the days to come
and the times that are far off? If I were intent upon a kind of
debating-society argument, I should return an unhesitating "No" to
that question. But I am not arguing a case, I am simply wishful to

get at the truth and the whole truth, and so I answer both yes and no
to the question.

Religion and the Future

From one point of view it is true to say that the Gospel does lay
the emphasis upon the future. It witnesses to the unseen, the spiritual, the eternal. Over against this present world, with its sensuous
joys and material prizes, which is so apt to absorb and engross our
souls, it sets a world to come where judgment is moral and character is supreme. It is upon that world to come that the Gospel lays
supreme stress. It is to that world we really belong. It is by its
standards we are to judge ourselves. It is for its prizes we are to
labor. We live truly, only as we daily and hourly remember that we
are but pilgrims and sojourners here, while our real citizenship is in
heaven. From that point of view the Christian preacher is perforce
constrained to say much about the future. He is set in his place to
remind men that this world is not everything, that after earth comes
heaven, and after death the judgment. The Bible takes the long view
of life. To men so apt to take the short view, so apt to make their
portion in this life, the Bible speaks of the "days to come" and the
"times that are far off."

And I will be quite frank, and will say that, in my opinion it is
not less but more emphasis upon that eternal future we want. Heaven
and hell are rarely talked about even in the Christian pulpit in these
days. We are concerned almost entirely with the present and the
now. We live in materialistic days, when nothing is deemed of
value unless it can call itself practical. And the church has caught
the infection of the age, and nothing will suit us but what we call
practical religion and practical preaching. And so we banish the
future and the eternal out of our speech. We go in abject terror of
the charge of being otherworldly, and to purge ourselves of the
charge we pour cheap scorn upon those great hymns of the church
in which the saints have sung the glories of the land that is far off.
But what are we, I should like to know, if we are not otherworldly?
What are we here for, I should like to know, except to witness to
that otherworld? The preacher who ignores that other world and
concentrates his attention on this, as if this were all, is not serving
the present age, he is deceiving it, deluding it, betraying it. He is not
even the practical preacher he prides himself on being. There is no
great picture possible, says John Ruskin, unless there be in it what

he calls "heaven-light." And there is no great life in the present and the now possible, except as a man lives it in the light of the unseen and the eternal. Moses endured as seeing Him who is invisible. Paul declared his citizenship was in heaven. John Milton lived and labored as ever "'neath the Great Taskmaster's eye." There is no other possible way to greatness. Men must live their lives in the light of the eternal. They must keep the great judgment seat ever in view. And the church exists to witness to that eternal. The preacher's business is to remind men of the world to come. To its very core and heart the gospel is otherworldly. It takes the long view. Its emphasis is on the future. The vision it seeth is for many days to come, and it prophesieth of times that are far off.

Religion and the Present

And yet while from one point of view the Gospel lays stress upon the future, from another point of view it is the most immediate and pressing and urgent of all concerns—and that in a narrower and broader sense. Let me begin with the narrower sense, because it is the one which my text naturally suggests. It was about the threats and warnings of the prophet that these people said they referred to a distant future. When he threatened woe and destruction, they said, "We need not trouble. The vision he seeth is for many days to come, and he prophesieth of times that are far off." They lulled themselves into a fancied security, and all the time the destruction prophesied was at their very doors. "Say unto them," was God's command to His prophet, "Thus saith the Lord God, There shall none of My words be deferred any more, but the word which I shall speak shall be performed, saith the Lord God."

And the same kind of thing is said in their hearts by many of the men and women who assemble in our congregations. And especially by our young people. This is, indeed, the especial peril of young people. Life seems to stretch in almost endless length before them. To the young, twenty, thirty, forty years are like an eternity. And when they hear the gospel appeal and the gospel warning, they say in their hearts that the decision to which they are being urged need not be taken yet; and as to the perils of which the gospel speaks—ah, well they belong to the days to come and to the times that are far off, and long before those times arrive they will make the great decision and take their stand on the Lord's side. But is it a matter that can be delayed? Has it no concern with the present moment? Are the dangers of which, the gospel speaks—are they necessarily in the far-off future?

What is our life? A vapor, says the old Book, a shadow, the flower of a day. We know not what a day may bring forth. In the midst of life we are in death. And while we in our hearts may be saying, "Peace and safety," sudden destruction may be at our doors. In face of the tragic uncertainty of life, who can say that the Christian preacher, when he urges the necessity of the great decision is prophesying of the days to come and the times that are far off? The warnings and appeals of the gospel are of urgent, pressing and immediate importance. "Today, if ye will hear his voice." "Now is the accepted time, now is the day of salvation."

But for another and a broader reason, religion is a matter of present and immediate and urgent importance. The idea—prevalent though it is—that religion may be put off and put off, so long as it is not put off too long, proceeds on an entirely false conception of what religion is. People who say, "There's plenty of time; there's no need to hurry; I will decide by and by," regard religion as a kind of way of escape from peril. A fire escape, the irreverent might say. Their idea is that they may spend the best years of their lives in the service of self and sin, and then later on they will take themselves to religion, make it, as they say, "right with God," and so escape the punishment their sinful life would otherwise have brought upon them. Now, in all this there are all kinds of misconceptions involved. But I confine myself to this one—it proceeds upon an entirely false conception of religion. Religion is not something to die by, it is something to live by. The eternal life of which it speaks is not a future acquisition, it is a present possession. It is the present enjoyment of God; it is life lived now by the help and for the glory of God. Religion means nothing if it does not mean that. The religion which is a mere fire escape is no religion at all. Alike in its obligations and enjoyments, religion is for the immediate hour and the present day. The eternal life is not something which comes to us after death, when, as we say, we "get to heaven." It is something we may have and enjoy down here. Indeed, we must have and enjoy it down here if there is to be any heaven for us hereafter. For the eternal life is just the true life, the life for which man was made; it is life by faith in the Son of God; it is life in the Spirit; it is life lived in direct, personal fellowship with God. And that life we may and must live now, if we are ever to possess it at all. So long as men regard religion as a means of escape it is easy to understand why they should think there is no immediate reason for accepting it. But once a man realizes what religion really means—a life lived in God and a life lived for God—he will cease to charge the preacher with prophesying for many days to come, and for times that are far off.

For the duties of religion are present duties. Search the Scriptures, and you cannot fail to notice how much, for instance, of the apostolic teaching and of our Lord's teaching has to do with the common duties of every day. Our Lord and His apostles are not always talking about heaven—much of their speech is taken up with directions as to how to behave in the everyday relationships of husband and wife, master and servant, parent and child, neighbor and neighbor. The Bible, as I have already said, is full of the eternal, from cover to cover. It is a witness to the eternal. But that does not mean that it ignores the present. The eternal is brought to bear upon the present. The laws of heaven are to rule us here upon the earth. So the religion of Jesus is supremely practical. It is a religion for the home and for the shop, and for the office and for the council chamber. Unless our religion does go into our buying and selling, our daily labor, our social duties, our political activities, we are not truly religious at all. It is not about some vision for many days to come that the Christian preacher speaks. He speaks about something of present and immediate application. For whether we eat or drink, or whatsoever we do—that is the Christian rule—we must do all to the glory of God.

And the enjoyments of religion are as present as its obligations. When the Christian preacher talks of rewards and penalties, he is not talking of a time that is far off. He is talking of the present. For the penalties of sin and the rewards of religion are both experienced here and now. I will say nothing at the moment about the penalties of sin, except to say that when men postpone hell to some far-off future they do greatly err. I will confine myself to the rewards of religion. They are not something to be received when this life is done. They come to us then, perhaps, in fuller and richer measure. But, essentially, we may and can enjoy them now.

> The hill of Zion yields
>   A thousand sacred sweets,
> Before we tread its heavenly fields,
>   Or walk its golden streets.

Heaven is not a future but a present state. For the joy and the peace and the blessed fellowship with God (which constitute the bliss of heaven) may be enjoyed down here. What a tragic blunder those commit who postpone or delay the day of decision. They rob themselves of happiness and peace. "My peace give I unto you." Not, will give at some future day. But, I give now and at the moment as a present possession. No; it is not of the many days to come and the time that is far off that the preacher speaks when he speaks of the blessings and enjoyments of the Christian religion. He speaks to the present hour; for comfort, strength, hope, joy are ours here and now in Christ. It is not of a future happiness he speaks; even now we may lay hold on the life which is life indeed. I press this truth upon your own hearts and consciences. Perhaps some of you have been delaying and postponing the great decision, thinking that religion was more concerned with the future than the present. I preach a gospel for the present day and the life you now live—a gospel of vital and urgent importance if you are to discharge the duties of life aright, and if you are to know any of the deep joys of the soul. This practical, present-day gospel—have you received it? This life which is life indeed—do you possess it? Lay hold of it. Choose the better part now, that life may be strong, worthy and peaceful. And then when the days that are yet to come and the time which is far off (which nevertheless may be nearer than we think) arrive it will be well with us, for there will be offered to us an abundant entrance into the eternal kingdom of perfect peace and love and joy.

CHAPTER FIVE

The Law of Indirectness

And a certain man drew his bow at a venture, and smote the king of Israel between the joints of the harness.
—2 Chronicles 17:33

I have just one truth which I want to make vivid and real in this sermon, and that is this: that the best things in life are secured by not seeking them, that the noblest prizes are won by not striving for them. I know this sounds paradoxical—but all the facts of life bear me out when I say, there are certain things which we can never get by aiming at them; we only get them by aiming at something else. Pursue these things, and they elude and escape you; but think nothing about them, and go on your way doing your humble and faithful best, and they present themselves to you unsought. This is what the bishop of Ripon calls the Law of Indirectness. It is a great and immutable law of the spiritual life. The reason why so many people's lives are burdened with a sense of failure is that they have forgotten this law. They have devoted themselves to the direct pursuit of such things as pleasure, honor, life. And because they have pursued them, they have failed to lay hold upon them. For pleasure comes not to the man who seeks it, but to the man who, without thinking of pleasure, does his simple duty; and honor comes not to the man who aims at it, but to the man who, without thinking of fame or applause, cares only for the good that he can do; and life comes not to the man who conserves and saves it, but to the man who spends and loses it in the service of God and man. Happiness, honor, life,

and all the other supreme blessings, they are gained not by aiming
directly at them, but by aiming at something else.

I have taken as the text of my sermon a verse from the story
which the chronicler tells about the death of King Ahab. There was
war between Ahab and the King of Syria, and the contending armies
met at Ramoth Gilead. Now, for some reason or other, the King of
Syria regarded Ahab with deep and relentless hatred. It may have
been because Ahab was a cunning and insidious foe. It may have
been because he felt there never could be settled and permanent
peace so long as Ahab sat on the throne. It may have been because
every mischief and plot had Ahab for its instigator. At any rate,
when battle was about to be joined, he gave orders to his troops to
concentrate their attack upon Ahab. They were to fight neither with
small nor great, but only with the king of Israel. So what you have
is this: you have a whole army out for the specific purpose of killing
one bad man. Every arrow, so to speak, was directed at him. And
they all missed him. Spite of all their efforts, Ahab remained un-
hurt. And then some unknown soldier drew a bow at a venture. He
was not aiming at Ahab—he was aiming at no one in particular. But
that random shot smote the king of Israel between the joints of the
harness, so that about the time of the going down of the sun he died.
The great object which the Syrian army set out that day to accomplish was actually achieved not by the men who aimed for it, but by
some obscure soldier who did not aim at it at all. Now, I am going
to say no more about that unknown soldier and his casual arrow—I
simply remind you of the old story as an illustration of the truth I
want briefly to expound—that the prizes most highly to be desired
come not to the men who seek them, but to the men who never
think of them at all.

The Law in the Secular Realm

Let me, first of all, point out that the Law of Indirectness holds
good, at any rate in a measure, even in the secular realm. I do not,
of course, mean to suggest that the secular prizes of earth come to
us without effort. I do not mean to suggest that all we have to do is
to sit still and fortune will cause all her favors to fall into our laps.
There is but a poor lookout for the man who, like Mr. Micawber,
waits for something to turn up. The price men have to pay for
success in any walk of life is hard and continuous labor. Genius,
some one has defined as the faculty of taking pains. Accounting for

Sir Walter Raleigh's mass and weight of learning, a friend said, "He can toil terribly."

At the same time, it is true even in the secular sphere, that certain high distinctions only come to the men who do not directly seek them. Take poetry, for instance. A man does not become a great poet by studying the technicalities of verse-making. That is, as Dr. Boyd Carpenter says, "a schoolboy trade." If he wants to be a poet in the true sense at all, he must hold communion with nature, he must steep himself in the highest and loftiest thoughts of men, he must make his soul the temple of the holiest emotions and loftiest aspirations. A man needs more than a knowledge of metre and of rhyme to become a poet—he needs also a big soul.

Take the artist. The man who thinks of nothing but his artistry, whose whole attention is concentrated upon accurate drawing and the blending of colors, rarely becomes a great artist, except, perhaps, on the technical side. To paint a great picture a man needs to possess more than a knowledge of anatomy, the power to use his brush, and the ability to mix his paint—he needs large and elevated ideas. Take any one of the immortal pictures of the world. Take a Michelangelo, take a Titian; you are conscious as you gaze of much more than mere technical ability in drawing and painting; you are conscious that you are in touch with a mighty mind. The cultivation of the mind, the nurture of the soul—they do not seem at first sight to have much to do with the painting of a picture. But unless a man lays paints and brushes by, and attends to his soul, big painting will be forever beyond his grasp. The highest success in art only comes by not directly seeking it.

Take the orator. There are people in the world who profess to be able to teach others how to speak. They will tell you how to hold your hands, how to modulate your voice, how to give the appropriate emphasis. But elocution is not oratory. Indeed, a man must forget all about elocution if ever he wants to be an orator. Great speaking is forever beyond the reach of the man who is anxious about putting the right emphasis here and using the right gesture there. He becomes artificial, stilted, mechanical, ineffective. The first condition of power in a speaker is to forget himself. The mightiest effects are only secured by not seeking them. The man who speaks for effect fails to secure it. It is not the man who drills and disciplines himself in the technicalities of speech who becomes the great speaker, but the man who broods amid the great themes, who meditates among mighty thoughts, until these great themes possess him, until, as he muses, the fire burns, and he is constrained to speak with his tongue.

All these illustrations, I know, lie on the borderline between the material and the spiritual. And it is where spiritual considerations enter in that the law holds most completely true. But even such a secular matter as business illustrates the law up to a point. Who, for instance, is the man who secures promotion? Not the man who is always directly seeking it, asking for it, pulling wires in order to secure it. The man who gets promotion is the man who shows himself diligent, honest, trustworthy. Promotion comes not to the man who aims directly at it, but to the man who aims at something else—at doing the best in the place he has. We become masters not by directly seeking to be masters, but by resolving to be good servants. What is the best way of securing success? I know there are multitudes of people who make worldly success their aim; to make a fortune is their one object, and to the accomplishment of their ambition they bend their every energy. And it would be vain to deny that many who have thus made success their one aim have got the success they aimed at. We live in a very imperfect world, and unscrupulous men sometimes flourish in it like the green bay tree. But there is another and far better way of winning success, and that is by not seeking it, but rather by seeking to do honest work and to give value for money. Let a man make that his aim—always to do his best, to be honest and square in all his doings—and success, though perhaps slow in coming, will come at last unsought, and when it comes it will be sweet.

The Law in the Spiritual Realm

But now let me pass from the secular realm where this law only holds partially true, to the spiritual realm, where it holds entirely and absolutely true. The great prizes of the spiritual realm are only gained by not seeking them. When we seek them, we miss them. We get possession of them only by seeking something else. Now let me illustrate this in two or three directions.

(1) Happiness—Let me take first the great prize of happiness. Happiness is what all the world is really seeking—for deep down in our hearts there is the assurance that happiness is to be gained. But the tragic mistake the vast majority of men are making is just this: they make happiness their aim. Happiness or pleasure is the end of

all their striving. And because they make it their aim—they miss it. For the truth is, happiness is never to be gained by seeking it. If you want to be happy—I know it sounds like a paradox—you must not seek to be happy. You must seek something quite different. Seek to do your duty, seek to minister to others, and happiness will come unsought. "Those only are happy," wrote J. S. Mill, in a sentence it would be well we should all grave upon our hearts, "who have their minds fixed upon some other object than their own happiness; on the happiness of others, on the improvement of mankind, even on some art or pursuit, followed not as a means, but as itself an ideal end. Aiming thus at something else, they find happiness by the way." That is the law. You get happiness by not seeking it, by seeking something quite different. All experience teaches the lesson that men who make pleasure their aim never get it. You have seen that picture, perhaps, which represents Pleasure as a seductive female figure pursued by a host of devotees. And the notable point about the picture is this: not one of all that crowd of devotees is able really to lay hands on Pleasure and hold her fast. She is always just beyond their grasp. And that picture is a parable of life. Those who make pleasure their pursuit never know what pleasure really is. The professed pleasure-seeker is as a rule the most miserable of men. I could put one after another of them in the box and let them bear their own witness. It is unvarying, consentient, unanimous. You can sum it all up in Byron's words, "The canker and the grief are theirs alone." There is only one pessimistic book in the Bible. It is the book of Ecclesiastes. And the book of Ecclesiastes is the confessions of a pleasure-seeker. He had set out to get pleasure. He tried every resource. He drank at every spring. Whatsoever his eyes desired he withheld not from them. And the result of it all is— disgust, self-loathing and despair, and of his days he declares he has no pleasure in them. And you can parallel the preacher's experience from the experience of the pleasure-seekers of our own day. I heard a well-known novelist say that he has before today sat watching the people in Hyde Park. And the bored and weary and unhappy people were not the poor who had to work hard for daily bread: the bored and weary and abject people were the people whose lives were a feverish round of gaiety, and who lived for nothing but their own amusement. They had forgotten this immutable law that happiness never comes by seeking it. Seeking happiness always ends in disappointment and in misery. Happiness only comes to us as we seek

something else and something far different. Do you remember that
great passage in the Sartor into which Carlyle concentrates the pith
and marrow of his teaching. "Love not pleasure," he says, "love
God. This is the Everlasting Yea, wherein all contradiction is solved;
wherein whoso walks and works it is well with him." "Love not
pleasure—love God." That is what we are here for—not to please
ourselves, but to do God's will, to tread bravely the path of simple
duty and right. But what happens to the man who loves God, who,
without thought of self-pleasing, treads the hard and difficult way of
duty? why, this happens to him—happiness comes unsought. He
aims at duty—he hits pleasure. That is the truth Tennyson would
teach in the closing lines of that great ode of his on the death of the
Duke of Wellington—

> Not once or twice in our rough island-story
> The path of duty was the way to glory:
> He that walks it, only thirsting,
> For the right, and learns to deaden
> Love of self, before his journey closes,
> He shall find the stubborn thistle bursting
> Into glossy purples, which outredden,
> All voluptuous garden roses.
> Not once or twice in our fair island-story,
> The path of duty was the way to glory.
> He, that ever following her commands,
> On with toil of heart and knees and hands,
> Through the long gorge to the far light has won,
> His path upward, and prevailed,
> Shall find the toppling crags of Duty scaled
> Are close upon the shining tablelands
> To which our God Himself is moon and sun.

And that is not poetry. It is simple and blessed fact. It is the
people who never gave a thought to personal pleasure, but who
loved God and followed His leading, who have been the happy
people. Think of Jesus. He never gave a thought to His own personal happiness. That is how the apostle describes Him: "He pleased
not Himself." It was His meat to do the Father's will. He walked the
hard and rugged way of duty even though it led Him to the cross.
But as He marched along that hard and rugged way happiness came

to Him unsought. Jesus' heart was ever full of a deep and radiant joy. So much so, that joy—His joy—was that bequest He wished to leave to His disciples. When possessed of His joy, nothing would be lacking to their perfect happiness, their joy would be fulfilled. Think of Paul. He, too, never sought his own personal comfort or ease. All his thought was for others. He spent himself to the uttermost in the service of others. It entailed upon him a life of outward poverty and sacrifice and suffering. But Paul discovered this, that though he never gave a thought to his own happiness—happiness came. All his care was to fulfill the ministry God had appointed him; but as he went about his toilsome task joy blessed him. This is the man who could sing songs at midnight. This is the man who in the midst of his manifold sorrow was nevertheless "always rejoicing." And the experience of the Master and His great disciple is the experience of men and women still. They do their humble, faithful duty; they go their God-appointed way, and happiness comes. Now, we all want happiness. But we shall miss it if we make it the end of living. We get it only by not seeking it. "Love not pleasure, love God." Seek not your own enjoyment, but God's glory. And as you go faithfully and patiently about your Father's business, you will find deep and real happiness comes unsought. You shall "enter into the joy of your Lord."

(2) Honor—Let me illustrate the law, further, in the matter of honor. Honor, again, is a prize that multitudes desire to win. To be held in respect and affection by one's fellows is a great and splendid possession. But honor does not come to the man who seeks it; it comes rather to the man who, without any thought of personal profit or gain, lives for the good that he can do. The man who schemes for honor never wins it; he may win fame, he may win what we call "honors," but that deeper and nobler thing, honor—the respect and reverence and love of men—is never given to the man who aims at it. The world never honors the self-seeker. But let a man forget himself, and, without thought of reward and praise, spend himself out in the service of his fellows, and honor inevitably comes. Here, for instance, is David Livingstone doing his sacrificial work in Africa. No thought of personal fame moved him. His concern was simply and solely for the poor, downtrodden, enslaved African. But the honor he never sought for himself was given him freely, ungrudgingly, lavishly by a nation that learned to revere him for his self-forgetful labors. Here, again, is Lord Shaftesbury, spending

himself in the service of the factory children and the poor. He never sought honors for himself. He might have been a cabinet minister more than once had he chosen. He preferred to give his life to the help of the outcast and the downtrodden. Love. Serve. These were the motives of Lord Shaftesbury's life. But to this man intent simply upon sacrificial service, honor came unsought. His countrymen enshrined him in their hearts' affections. Here is General Booth— laboring like a giant for the salvation of the submerged tenth. He has never given a thought to his own reputation or position. He risked livelihood, he faced obloquy and contempt in his zeal for his redemptive work. At all costs he was intent upon saving men. And to this man, too, who never sought honor, whose one passion was the holy passion for souls, honor has come. There is no man England reveres more today. And if we see the law working itself out in the honor men pay to one another, we see it still more clearly in the honor which is paid in heaven. Heaven has no honor for the self-seeker. To aim at glory, so to speak, is to miss it. Heaven pays its honor to the men who forget themselves, and who live not to be ministered unto but to minister. The man who does his praying and almsgiving and worship to receive glory of men, who uses his religion to get a reputation, receives all his reward down here. But the man who, without thought of future glory or reward, does his simple and humble service because he loves men and loves Christ, will receive the honor he did not seek. For Christ Himself will declare his worth and proclaim his praise. "Inasmuch as thou didst it to one of these least, thou didst it unto Me."

(3) Life—Consider again the truth of this law in the matter of life. We get life—broad, full, abundant life—not by seeking it and saving it, but by giving it away. To save life is to lose it. To lose life is to save it. This is indeed the very heart of the gospel ethic. Self-culture was the motto of the Greek; self-sacrifice is the motto of the Christian. Life is what both the Greek and the Christian are after, but it is only the Christian with his self-sacrifice who really gains it. There are multitudes among us still who follow the Greek method. Self-culture is their ideal. They concentrate upon themselves. They give free play to the instincts and appetites of human nature. They take care of number one, as the saying goes. They do all this in the belief that they will enrich and broaden life for themselves. But it is a poor business. The man who goes in for seeing life, as they say, inevitably loses it. The younger son in the parable—and he is a type

of every young fellow today intent upon seeing life—instead of
finding abundant life in the far country, "began to be in want." He
lost life, for life is not mere bodily existence, mere breathing: real
life means a full, deep life of the soul. And the soul dies within the
man who gives himself up to the selfish and sensual life. And you
can see the same deadly process going on before your very eyes
today. The man who lives for himself—who thinks only of number
one—is daily losing life. All high and generous instincts perish
within him. Life becomes narrow, contracted, impoverished. His
soul shrivels within him. And "when faith is lost and honor dies, the
man is dead."

No! men never gain life by seeking it. They gain it only by
losing it and giving it away. Life expands and grows as a man
thinks not of himself but of others. Selfishness is the death of the
soul; sacrifice is its meat and its life. Look at our Lord. He gave His
life away. Virtue went out of Him. He did not shrink from the
uttermost sacrifice. He became obedient unto death—yea, the death
of the cross. He offered Himself a sacrifice on the altar of human
redemption. And by losing life He found life. Do you think we
would be remembering Christ today if He had thought only of
number one? He is enthroned in the affections of millions of men
today just because He lavished his life away. He gained His life by
losing it. And the same is true in their own degree of those who
follow in the Lord's steps. It needs no proof. We see it in actual life.
The men who live rich, deep, full lives are those who live the life of
sacrifice and service. If I wanted examples of human life at its best,
I would not look for them among those who take care of number
one; I would look for them among those whose motto is I Serve. I
was in Kidderminster not long ago. There is one statue in this town,
and, as far as I know, only one. It is not a statue of any of the great
manufacturers of Kidderminster who have established the town's
trade and made themselves fortunes in the process. It is the statue of
Richard Baxter, that faithful pastor who watched for souls as one
that would give account, who spent strength and life in ministering
to the people of Kidderminster; that is the man of men whom
Kidderminster delights to remember—the biggest, greatest man that
town has ever known. It is the man who gave his life away who
found it. "Shall save it unto life eternal." Richer life here and now!
and the assurance that that life is beyond the reach of death and
change. The body dies; the soul lives on. It is only the man whose

soul lives who has possession of the life eternal. And the soul lives by self-forgetting service and sacrifice. There is the law—the central law of the Christian faith. We gain life only by not seeking it. Seek life and you lose it. Give your life away and you shall find it unto life eternal. As Dr. Van Dyke puts it—

> Who seeks for heaven alone to save the soul,
> May keep the path, but will not reach the goal,
> While he who walks in love may wander far
> But God will bring him where the Blessed are.

(4) Goodness—I had meant to illustrate the working of the law in the matter of goodness. A word must suffice. It is the method of indirectness the Bible recommends even in the acquiring of a character. We acquire goodness best not by aiming directly at it, but by just loving Christ. You remember Christ's question to Peter. He did not ask him, "Do you promise to be good and brave and never to fall again?" He asked, "Lovest thou Me?" Jesus knew if Peter really loved Him that courage and goodness would follow. Be good—that is the appeal of the moralist. But the men who struggle and strain to be good often fail. "When I would do good, evil is present with me." "Love Me" is the appeal of Christ, and when men love Christ, goodness follows and becomes easy. That is the truth the conversion of every notorious sinner proclaims. To tell the drunkard to be sober and the profligate to be chaste is to waste breath. But the derelicts of the world learn to love Christ, and love emancipates them from their evil habits, and changes the sinner into a glorious saint. Love Christ—that is the preacher's message. That is the sum and substance of his appeal. That is all he asks for. It seems like the surrender of morals. It is, as a matter of fact, the surest way of making men good. The evangelist is mightier than the moralist. The indirect way is the quickest road to the goal. "Believe on the Lord Jesus Christ, and thou shalt be saved."

CHAPTER SIX

The Rainbow

*I do set my bow in the cloud, and it shall be for a token
of a covenant between Me and the earth.* —Genesis 9:13

This is not the story of the first creation of the rainbow. God had
been for ages setting His bow in the clouds. This is a case of the
investiture of a familiar sight with a new meaning. "It shall be for a
token of a covenant between Me and the earth." Noah and his sons
had seen the rainbow many a time before, for whenever the sun's
rays had fallen upon the glancing raindrops at a certain angle, this
glorious arch had sprung into being and spanned the earth. The
rainbow had been in existence, as Dr. Parker puts it, as long as the
sun and the rain had known each other. The scoffer who thinks he
has detected the Bible in another absurdity in that it says that the
rainbow was created for Noah's special benefit has simply entirely
misunderstood the narrative. For the Bible says nothing of the kind.
All that it says is that after a certain day the vision of the rainbow
became charged with new significance for Noah and his household.
You remember the old story. The great storm had practically sub-
sided. The sun at last had struggled through the dense clouds that
had for days and weeks covered the earth like a pall. Its emergence
from the cloud had, very likely, called the rainbow into existence.
And God, pointing to the bow in the clouds, says that from henceforth it shall be token of a new covenant of mercy between Him and
the earth. What was before a mere physical phenomenon receives
now a moral meaning. What had previously been natural becomes

henceforth sacramental. Every time that arch of many colors spans the heavens, it shall speak to men of God's forbearance and all-embracing love.

Nature—Sacramental

And I am tempted just here to pause in order to say that the rainbow in this respect is typical of nature as a whole. Nature is moral. Nature is charged with meaning. Nature is sacramental. There are plenty of humble men and women in the world today who know nothing about the scientific account of the rainbow. They cannot tell you how it is caused. They are unacquainted with the laws of light. But whenever they see the bow in the clouds, it whispers something to them about God's mercy and love. And the humblest and most ignorant of men to whose heart the rainbow whispers something about God, knows more of the inner meaning of the rainbow than the scientist who knows nothing about its spiritual meaning, but who can give you an accurate account of the natural laws which bring about the phenomenon of the rainbow on a rainy day. He knows most about nature, after all, who has penetrated to its inner, moral, spiritual significance. It is not the man who has all the natural laws at his fingers' ends, it is not the expert in geology or chemistry, who really knows the secret of nature; the man who has learned nature's inmost secret is he who sees in nature everywhere the print and impress of God. You do not understand man by simply becoming acquainted with the anatomical structure of his body and the chemical constituents of his brain. The anatomist will never with his scalpel discover the soul, and after all it is the soul that makes the man. And there is a soul in nature. The geologist with his hammer, the chemist with his crucible and test tubes and scales, the naturalist with his microscope will never discover it. Like the Sphinx of old, nature denies to them its secret. And those who have not discovered nature's soul can no more claim to know nature than the anatomist who is acquainted with all man's bones and muscles, but has never discovered that man is a living soul, can claim to know man. "Seeing they do not perceive, and hearing they do not understand." And just as the man, however ignorant of anatomy he may be, who has come to know that man is a living spirit has a far deeper, truer knowledge of man than the mere anatomist; so the man whose eyes have beheld nature's soul, who gazing, say, upon the bursting beauty of the spring has felt—as Wordsworth felt—

A presence that disturbed him with the joy
Of elevated thoughts; a sense sublime
Of something far more deeply interfused,
Whose dwelling is the light of setting suns
And the round ocean and the living air
And the blue sky and in the mind of man:
A motion and a spirit that impels
All thinking things, all objects of all thought
And rolls through all things.

That man has a far more real insight into nature than the mere scientist who can see nothing in nature save certain physical elements acted upon by certain physical forces.

We do not know nature so long as we only know the visible and the ponderable and the palpable. Nature is spiritual. Nature is sacramental. Nature has a soul, and the soul of nature is God. "In the beginning," we read, "God created the heaven and the earth." But God did not create nature and then cut it adrift. He is in nature. With His fullness He filleth all in all. It is God in nature that gives nature its unity and significance. And we do not know nature until, wherever we turn, in opening flower and bursting leaf and budding tree, in surging seas and the deep of heaven, we catch hints, gleams, suggestions, shadowings of the Infinite God.

"Without God was not anything made that has been made." And God's handiwork reveals His character. The artist when he paints puts his own soul into the picture. The author when he writes puts his own thought and belief and experience into his book. Well, nature is, if you like, a painting by the great Master Artist, and into the painting He has put His own soul. Nature is a book of God, a book of His own writing, just as surely as the Bible is.

The works of God. above, below,
Within us and around,
Are pages in the book, to show
How God Himself is found.

And all we need is the pure heart to read in it great messages from God. And the more clearly we see the spiritual through the material, the more easily our thoughts rise from nature to nature's God, the more fully and deeply do we understand nature itself.

The eye of the poet has always been quick to discern the spiritual meaning of nature—has always pierced through nature to the God who worketh all in all. "The heavens declare the glory of God," sang an ancient psalmist, "and the firmament showeth His handiwork."

> "'Tis thus at the roaring Loom of Time I ply,"
>   Goethe makes the Earth Spirit say,
> "And weave for God the garment thou seest Him by."

"To me," sang Wordsworth—than whom none saw the spiritual meaning of nature more clearly—

> The meanest flower that blows can give,
>   Thoughts that do often lie too deep for tears.

And Mrs. Browning had exactly the same vision when she sang—

> Earth's crammed with heaven,
>   And every common bush's afire with God.

To the seeing eye and the open heart the most familiar thing in nature carries the thought up to God, and they who see most of God know nature best. Have we this seeing eye? Is nature sacramental to us? Is it a clear shining mirror reflecting for us the image of God? Here is a daisy. A scientist begins to explain to me all about the structure of this simple common flower. He describes all its parts. He hurls technical terms at my head. He talks about the calix and the corolla, about the pistil and the stamens and all the rest. But when he has finished I can tell him something about the daisy that he has not mentioned. I can tell him that little flower speaks to me of the love and care of God. I can tell him how my Master, preaching to a vast crowd in Palestine of old, took this little flower in His hand, made it His text, and preached from it an immortal sermon upon the detailed and personal care of God. "If God so clothe the grass of the field which today is, and tomorrow is cast into the oven, shall He not much more clothe you, 0 ye of little faith?"

You have noticed how for the Scripture writers nature is charged with sacramental significance. The mountains remind them of the faithfulness and righteousness of God; the sea reminds them of His majesty and might; the stars remind them of the wisdom of Him who calleth them all by name; the winds are God's messengers; the lightning is God's sword; the thunder is God's voice. While Jesus finds the simplest things like the lilies of the field, the birds of the air, the springing corn, all charged with loftiest spiritual truth, just as to us common bread speaks of the broken body of Christ, and wine speaks to us of the blood of atonement. Yea, verily, nature is full of God, and in the dreariest and most barren spot of earth, the man of seeing eye and open soul will find something to carry his thought upwards and heavenwards, some ladder by which he can climb up to God, so that with Jacob he can say, "This is the house of God! This is the gate of heaven!" Do we catch the spiritual meaning of nature? Does it talk to us about God? Does it whisper to us of heaven and immortality? Let us not rest content with simply admiring the beauty of this glorious spring time—let us not rest, I say, until through the beauty of nature we see shining upon us the beauty of the Lord our God.

It was just this inner spiritual meaning of nature that God was teaching Noah here. Noah had seen the rainbow many a time before. He had admired it, very likely, for the beauty of its colors. But henceforth it is to be more to him than a natural phenomenon, he is to see more in it than the radiant beauty of its colors. Henceforward the rainbow is to have for him a spiritual meaning; it is to carry his thought up to God; it is to be the sign and symbol of a new covenant between God and the earth. But the rainbow in the cloud which Noah saw suggests to me much more than the sacramental nature of the world in which we live. It is suggestive to me of God's mercy and care even in the dark experiences of life. Many a cloud sails across our sky, but in the cloud there is always the rainbow. Let me speak briefly of God's rainbow in the cloud of sin, God's rainbow in the cloud of sorrow, and God's rainbow in the cloud of judgment.

God's Rainbow in Sin

I will begin with God's rainbow in the cloud of sin and guilt. I mention this first because it connects itself most closely with the narrative of which my text forms part. Without entering upon any critical questions in connection with the story of the deluge, it is enough for me that Scripture represents it as God's doom upon monstrous wickedness and sin. The story of the deluge, in a word, preaches those two stern and solemn truths that are woven into the very fabric of Scripture, that the human race is a sinful race, and that the wages of sin is death. Can you not imagine what Noah's feelings must have been like when he came out of the ark? Can you not imagine the dread fear that would possess his soul? For Noah, too, was a sinful man. How was he to know that a similar doom would not some day overwhelm him for his sins? The rainbow was given to reassure his soul. It was a pledge that in wrath God would remember mercy. It was the declaration to Noah that even though sin abounded, grace did much more abound.

Now that dark and gloomy and threatening cloud of sin is still in our sky—a cloud full of lightnings and thunders and bodeful of storm and tempest. We have all sinned and come short of the glory of God. There is none that doeth good, no not one. We are all of us shut up under the law of sin and death. But, thank God, *I can see His bow in the cloud!* The rainbow in the physical world results from the shining of the sun upon the dark rain cloud. And so today the sunshine of God's great love falling upon the black cloud of human sin creates the rainbow of mercy. When people tell us that there is no cloud big with storm and tempest above our heads, when they try to persuade us that sin is a mere bogey—it is at our peril we believe them. The cloud is there; sin exists. We have only to look into our own hearts to know it exists. And sin is no light thing—it is a terrible thing, an awful thing, a deadly thing. All the world is guilty before God. And God hates sin and is sworn to punish it. But if I had to leave it there, it would be a heartbreaking tale I had to tell. For it would be a message of doom and woe. But I have not to leave it there. God hates sin—but He loves the sinner. "He willeth not the death of any, but rather that all should turn unto Him and live." And His love falling on the big black cloud of our sins creates the beautiful rainbow of mercy. In a word, that is how God's love shows itself to guilty men—in the offer of pardon and forgiveness. "The wages of sin is death"—that is the cloud; "Come and let us reason together," saith the Lord; "though your sins be as scarlet they shall be as white as snow, though they be red like crimson they shall be as wool"—that is the rainbow. "The wrath of God cometh upon the children of disobedience"—that is the storm cloud; "Hereby shall we assure our heart before Him, whereinsoever our heart condemn us; because God is greater than our heart, and knoweth all things"—that is the rainbow. wretched man that I am, who shall deliver me from the body of this death?"—that is the cloud; "Thanks be to God, through Jesus Christ our Lord"—that is the rainbow. "I am carnal, sold under sin"—that is the cloud; "The blood of Jesus Christ His Son cleanseth us from all sin"—that is the rainbow. What God did in the wealth of His love in view of human sin was to give His only begotten Son, and as the result of what Jesus did on the Cross, mercy is made possible for every sinner. Christ crucified is the rainbow. He is God's pledge of mercy to a guilty world. "There is now no condemnation to them that are in Christ Jesus." The threatening and menacing cloud is in the sky of every one of us. Have we all seen the rainbow? We are all of us under the law of sin and death. Have we found mercy in the Cross of Christ?

There are two noticeable features of the rainbow: First of all it seems to unite heaven and earth together. Its ends are on the earth, its arch is in the sky. And so Jesus Christ, God's rainbow, has united God and man together. He has bridged the gulf that separated them. He has reconciled us to God by the blood of His Cross, having slain the enmity thereby. And, secondly, the rainbow seems to embrace the world. Between its arms it gathers all the earth that we can see. And in this it is but a type of the all-embracing love of Christ and mercy of God. "There's a wideness in God's mercy, like the wideness of the sea." It embraces all men within its sweep. It excludes none, denies none, rejects none. Jesus Christ is "the propitiation for our sins, and not for ours only, but also for the whole world." Yes, for everyone the rainbow is in the sky. To everyone God's mercy and grace are fully offered. Have we seen this rainbow? Have we received its message? Peace and joy enter our hearts when we have seen it.

> E're since by faith I saw the stream
> Those flowing wounds supply,
> Redeeming love has been my theme
> And shall be till I die.

But the cloud of sin is not the only one that has its rainbow; other clouds sail into our sky and make the days dull and gray for us. Sin is our sorest plague, but not our only one. "Man is born to trouble as the sparks fly upward," says the old Book. And it speaks true. Bereavement, sorrow, sickness, loss—these are some of the troubles that meet us as the days pass. And there is no one who has experienced them who does not know how dark and drear they make the day. But God's love shines on our manifold troubles and griefs, and in the dark cloud of our sorrows and distresses we may see His bow of promise and hope.

God's Rainbow in Sorrow

Here is a father, let us say, who has suffered the loss of a child. I have one such in my mind at this moment. I have had letters from him which tell me how black the cloud has been. But the cloud is not without its rainbow—and this heartbroken father has seen it. He got a glimpse of it here on Easter Sunday, and it wonderfully cheered him in his sorrow "He that believeth on Me shall never die"—that is the rainbow. "In My Father's house are many abiding places"—that is the rainbow. "We know that if the earthly house of this tabernacle be dissolved, we have a building of God, a house not made with hands, eternal, in the heavens"—that is the rainbow.

Here is another into whose sky the cloud of difficulty, and disappointment, and thwarted purposes, has come. It comes to all of us in turn. But if we only look, there is always a bow in it. Samuel Rutherford was transported from his beloved Anwoth into exile in Aberdeen. It was a heavy trial. But this is how he wrote to the parishioners from whom he had been snatched: "Why should I draw back when God driveth His furrow through my soul? He purposeth a crop." He had seen the rainbow. Here it is: "Whom the Lord loveth He chasteneth, and scourgeth every son whom He receiveth."

Here is another man into whose sky the dark and heavy clouds of sore temptation have sailed. He finds himself in some Pergamum or other where Satan's throne is. It is a ceaseless and grim fight with him from day to day, for honor and life. But even in that cloud I see God's bow. Here it is: "God will not suffer you to be tempted above that ye are able, but will with the temptation open up a way of escape"; and again this, "I also will keep thee from the hour of temptation which cometh upon all the earth to try them that dwell therein." Whatever the cloud, there is always the bow in the shape of this blessed and beautiful assurance, "All things work together for good to them that love God."

Have you seen the bow in the cloud? You men and women lying even now under the cloud of sorrow, disappointment, loss, temptation, is God's bow in the cloud? If we see nothing but the cloud, life is bound to be fretful, broken, anxious. But we shall be able to rejoice in tribulation and to sing songs at midnight, if only, arching our clouds of disappointment and trial and sorrow, we see the bow which tells us of God's unfailing love and care.

The Rainbow in Judgment

I have spoken of the rainbow in sin, and the rainbow in sorrow. Let me add just a word about the rainbow in judgment. "We shall all appear before the judgment seat of Christ," says Paul, "that each one may receive the thing done in the body, according to what he hath done, whether it be good or bad." "According to what he hath done, whether it be good or bad"—the words strike fear to my soul. For we have all done things we ought not to have done, and left undone things we ought to have done. All the sunshine fades out of my sky as I read this sentence, and I feel myself like the children of Israel at Sinai, in the midst of blackness and darkness and tempest. "According to what he hath done"—it seems to leave no ray of hope; "for if the Lord should be strict to mark iniquity which of us should stand?" But Paul's picture is not quite complete. I turn to John for the completion of the picture. Paul leaves me shuddering before the Great White Throne. John, by the touch he adds, gives me boldness in the day of judgment. Here it is: "And there was a rainbow round about the throne." The Great White Throne does not stand for truth merely; in it mercy and truth are met together: it does not stand for bare and sheer righteousness merely; in it righteousness and peace have kissed each other. There is a rainbow round about the throne. God's mercy will surround us. Our Judge will prove a pitiful and merciful Savior. He will "blot out, as a thick cloud, our transgressions and, as a cloud, our sins," and, remembering only our feeble love for Himself, our feeble efforts at goodness, our poor and unworthy attempts at service, He will say, "Come, ye blessed of My Father, inherit the kingdom prepared for you from the foundation of the world."

The rainbow in the cloud—have we seen it? There is only one way to see it, and that is to see God in Christ. He is God's bow to the world—God's pledge and promise of mercy and love to the world. To believe that God was in Christ is to see the rainbow of God's mercy telling us that where sin abounds, grace does much more abound; to believe that God was in Christ is to see the rainbow of God's love in every cloud of sorrow, assuring us that we are in our Father's hands; to believe that God was in Christ is to be able to face the Judgment Day with a brave and confident heart, for there will be a "rainbow round about the throne."

CHAPTER SEVEN

The Stars in Their Courses

The stars in their courses fought against Sisera.
—Judges 5:20

I have taken as my text a phrase from that fierce song of exultation and triumph which Deborah the prophetess sang over the defeat and death of Sisera. You remember the grim old story—typical of those primitive times from which it comes. The children of Israel had fallen under the domination of Jabin, king of Canaan, and Sisera was the instrument by whom their subjugation had been brought about. Sisera was Jabin's captain of the host, or, as we would say, he was Jabin's commander-in-chief. He was a mighty man of war and, as it seemed, an invincible general. He developed especially one arm of the service. Most great generals have had their favorite movements by which they have secured their victories. Sisera had his. He put his trust in the iron chariot plunging and tearing its way through the ranks of his enemies. He had nine hundred of these terrible chariots under his command, and the result was that no Israelite army could stand up against him. They feared the charge of these iron chariots. So for twenty years they bore the yoke and submitted to Jabin's oppressive rule. And then at length God kindled the passion for national freedom in the heart of a woman. Just as in later days France seemed to have almost resigned herself to British rule until Joan of Arc started her crusade and shamed the men into striking another blow for freedom, so in these far-off and primitive times it was from the lips of the prophetess

Deborah that the trumpet call came to Israel to cast fear aside and to break in pieces the oppressor. It was not easy to rouse the people from their torpor and despair. They thought of Sisera and his chariots, and a crusade for freedom seemed a desperate and hopeless enterprise. Reuben thought it best to sit among his sheepfolds, and Dan to remain in ships, and Asher to sit still at the haven of the sea. But Deborah's passion kindled a passion like her own. Issachar was with Deborah, and Zebulun and Naphtali "jeopardized their lives unto the death upon the high places of the field."

Ten thousand swords leaped out of their scabbards at Deborah's call; and ten thousand men—when summoned to risk life and limb for the liberty of their country—answered, as did Garibaldi's Italians in more modern times, "We are the men." Never did there go forth a nobler band to battle. Never did army face so terrible a task. But God was with that ten thousand! And when, led by Barak, they joined battle with Sisera and his nine hundred chariots at the brook Kishon, the Lord discomfited Sisera and all his chariots and all his host with the edge of the sword before Barak. Sisera himself fled ignominiously on foot from the stricken field; but he escaped death in battle only to meet with a meaner death at the hands of Jael, the wife of Heber the Kenite. And so Sisera, the man beneath whose oppressions the people had groaned for over twenty years, lay dead, and all his terrible chariots lay broken and shattered, and at last Israel lifted her head again and rejoiced in a recovered freedom.

This chapter from which my text is taken is entirely occupied with the song, the passionate and exultant song which Deborah sang over the defeat and destruction of Israel's foes. It is a fierce and almost vindictive song. I am not at all concerned to defend every sentiment in it. Deborah praises as a worthy and godly deed that act of Jael's which our more enlightened conscience stigmatizes and brands as a treacherous murder. Deborah had not learned of Christ. In the fierceness, vindictiveness, and savage scorn of her song, she reproduces the temper of her own pre-Christian day. But fierce and vindictive though it be, it is a mighty song. One cannot read it even at this distance of time without feeling the sweep and thrill of it. My text is a phrase from it. Deborah is recalling the fight, the wondrous triumph, and the destruction of the foe. Looking back upon it all, it seems to her that it was impossible for ten thousand untrained Israelites to have routed Sisera with his veteran army and his nine hundred iron chariots. There must have been some other power at work. There were other participants in the fight. "They fought from heaven; the stars in their courses fought against Sisera," she cries.

Now this is probably nothing more than poetic imagery! We are not told that the fight at the Kishon was attended by any unusual natural phenomena. It is probably just Deborah's way of saying that God was on Israel's side in the battle, that the whole universe was taking Israel's part. Though I would remind you that there have been mighty conflicts in the world's history, conflicts pregnant with vast and critical issues, where it has seemed as if nature itself were taking sides in the fight. There is more than one such instance recorded in Holy Writ. Let me remind you of one of them. The five kings of the Amorites made war against Gibeon, because Gibeon had made peace with Israel. The Gibeonites, unable of themselves to withstand the combined forces, sent an urgent appeal for help to Joshua. Joshua immediately responded, and by a forced night march hurried to their help, and fell upon the attacking kings at the break of day. Taken by surprise, the Amorites broke and fled. But people who were in that fight remembered it for the fact that it seemed as if heaven itself had intervened to complete the work Joshua had begun. For immediately after the battle an appalling hailstorm swept over the land. In that furious storm the fugitives were caught, and the rout was changed into ruin and destruction. The very forces of nature seemed fighting against the Amorites. It was the tempest that overwhelmed them—they were more who died with the hailstones than they whom the children of Israel slew with the sword.

We have a similar instance in the story of our own little island. When the Spanish Armada set sail for England, though it had received the blessing of the pope, it was intent upon an evil deed. For its object was the destruction of England's liberties and the uprooting of England's religion. It was the mightiest fleet the world had ever seen when it sailed proudly out of the harbors of Spain. There were a hundred and thirty mighty vessels in it, while to oppose it England could collect together only eighty vessels, scarce thirty of which were ships of the line. The disparity was ridiculous, absurd. Indeed, so conscious were the Spaniards of their superior strength that they called their fleet in advance the Invincible Armada. When it appeared off the Lizard yonder it stretched in the shape of a half-moon for seven miles across the sea. Now, about the skill and daring of Drake and Howard you already know right well. I do not want by a single word of mine to detract from the splendor of their exploits in the Channel and off the port of Calais. They showed that the great armada was not at any rate the invincible armada. And yet every one knows that it was not Howard and Drake who finally destroyed the armada. It was not Howard and Drake who put a final end to Spain's attempt upon English liberties. When Howard and Drake fell back for lack of ammunition, nature seemed to take up their work. As the fleeing ships tried to make their way round by the north of Scotland, wind and sea took up the work of destruction. On many a rocky island in Scotland, on many a cape on the west of Ireland those great galleons of Spain went crashing to their doom. Out of the one hundred and thirty ships that set sail, only fifty-four battered vessels made their way back, and it was not Drake's daring or Howard's fire-ships that had wrought the destruction. Wind and wave had done it. English folk verily believed that nature had helped them in the fight. "*Deus flavit*," so ran the inscription on the medal which Elizabeth struck to commemorate the mighty deliverance, "*et dissipati sunt*"—"God blew upon them and they were scattered."

Let me take one other story from still more modern times when the issue of a campaign was settled not so much by force of arms or military skill as by the elements of heaven. We have entered upon an era of a kind of Napoleonic worship. Books upon various aspects of Napoleon's career are continually issuing from the press. Now about the colossal ability of the Corsican there can be no doubt whatever. He was not only one of the great soldiers of the world, he was also a mighty ruler and statesman—the nearest approach to a superman that recent centuries have produced, and perhaps that is the reason why the age which has produced Nietszche's philosophy gives also its admiration to Napoleon. But colossal man though Napoleon was, I do not hesitate to say that he stood for all that was sinister and evil. He was animated by no great ideals; he was the foe of liberty and nationality, and to gratify an inordinate ambition he drenched well-nigh every country in Europe with blood. At the impulse of that frantic ambition of his, he resolved to invade Russia. At the head of the most imposing army he had ever commanded— six hundred thousand of the best troops in the world—he marched into that vast and inhospitable land. He penetrated as far as Moscow, but the Russians would neither own to defeat nor sue for peace. And then perforce he had to retreat. And what a retreat it was! All the way from Moscow to the frontier was littered with dying men and horses, and abandoned munitions of war. When at last the army straggled back into friendly territory it was found that out of the six hundred thousand who set out, less than one hundred and fifty thousand were left. And it was not the tireless Russians hanging upon the flanks and rear of the retreating army that had done the mischief. Winter had come on unusually early and upset all Napoleon's calculations. He was beaten and his army destroyed, not by Russia's soldiers, but by the blinding snow and the bitter cold. It looked as if the very heavens were fighting against him. It looked as if nature herself were resolved that his wicked schemes should not prosper. "God Almighty," Napoleon cried, "has been too much for me!"

Of course, the modern man will say that these interventions of nature's forces on the side of what we believe to have been justice and right were mere coincidences and nothing more. And yet I am not sure that our fathers, who with a simpler faith saw the hand of God in all these things, were not nearer the truth. "He maketh the winds His messengers," says one of the psalmists, "His ministers a flame of fire." "Fire and hail, snow and vapor, stormy wind," says another, "fulfill His word." And I find no difficulty myself in believing that God Almighty—who is in all and through all and over all, and without whom nothing happens—used these natural agencies (which are His ministers) to overthrow the oppressor and to defend the right.

I am content for the moment, however, to waive the literal interpretation and application of my text. And yet I want to claim for it that it sets forth in poetic form a sure and abiding truth. How shall I state the law, the principle, which I think it embodies? Let me state it in this way—the very constitution of the universe, the laws of nature are against the wrongdoer; the very constitution of the universe, the laws of nature are on the side of the man who does right. Sisera was to these early Israelites the personification of oppression and tyranny. Jabin the king scarcely counted; Sisera—this man with the nine hundred chariots—was the real oppressor. For twenty years he had planted his heel upon the neck of Israel; for twenty years he had enslaved them and tyrannized over them. Sisera to the Israelites was the personification and representative of the power of evil. And the "stars in their courses," stand for nature's powers, the laws of the universe, the constitution of things. And that is what Deborah says in my text, "The stars in their courses fought against Sisera."

Nature was against this evil man. The laws of the universe did battle against him. And what Deborah here says of Sisera is true of every evil man, of every evil interest, of every evil power, of all wickedness and wrong—the stars in their courses are fighting against them, the trend and constitution of things are working steadily and irresistibly for their defeat and overthrow. The universe is so made that it is against all wrong and on the side of right.

The Law in History

Now, when I come to try to demonstrate and illustrate the principle I have thus tried to lay down, I find myself in difficulties. It is a truth to be felt, perhaps, rather than to be proved. It appeals to our instinct rather than to our reason. And yet, by an illustration or two I can perhaps do a little to make the principle at once clear and believable.

I invite you, then, to consider, first, the truth of this principle on the broad field of human history and across great tracts of time. This is the principle—the universe is against wrong and on the side of right. The very constitution of things makes for the overthrow of all oppression and injustices and wickednesses. The Bible is never tired of insisting upon a certain sympathy between man and nature. Nature groans with man on account of his sin—suffers on account of his sin, and is infected by his sin. On the other hand nature rejoices with man in his righteousness and desire for holiness; sympathizes with him and helps him in his upward striving, and waits with eager desire for the revealing of the sons of God.

But all this to our practical and matter-of-fact age savors of mysticism, and we want something more definite and tangible than that if this principle is really to become to us a believable truth. Well, then, I invite your attention to this fact, that the principle I am trying to lay down represents an instinct bedded deep in the human soul. Let me remind you of that scene in the Jewish Sanhedrin when Peter and John were arraigned before it on the charge of preaching Christ in the streets of Jerusalem. The majority of the Council, irritated by the apostles' disobedience of their orders, were for killing them, and in that way effectually putting a stop to any further preaching on their part. But before they proceeded to that extremity, Gamaliel intervened. His suggestion was that they should let the apostles alone, and allow time to test the truth of the faith they preached. "Refrain from these men" he said, "and let them alone, for if this counsel or this work be of men it will be overthrown." If the faith was false, argued Gamaliel, there was no need to fret or fuss about it, for time would surely destroy it. Now what lay aback of that confidence of Gamaliel? This—the assurance that the laws of the world, the very constitution of the universe were against everything that was false and wrong; that the very "stars in their courses" would fight against a falsity and a lie. And that belief, I repeat, is bedded deep in the instincts of mankind. It is not Gamaliel alone who held it, all men hold it. It is an instinctive faith of the soul. We believe the world is on the side of right. We believe that the laws of the universe are such that wrong must come to naught. We have expressed that belief in our proverbs. "The mills of the gods grind slowly," we say, "but they grind exceeding small"—that is the truth on its negative side, that the constitution of the world is hostile to wrong. "Great is truth and must prevail"—that is the same truth on its positive side, that the whole universe is on the side of right and justice. And the faith which we have thus expressed in our proverbs, is a faith that is justified by the facts. The stars in their courses do fight against Sisera. There is a certain trend in things— undefinable, inexplicable—that slowly but surely brings every wrong to naught. The track of the centuries is strewn with the wreckage of giant oppressions and tyrannies which have thus been overthrown. Their overthrow has not been due to any particular person; all you can say is that time was against them, the course of the universe was against them, the stars in their courses warred against them and they fell. There is a power, as Matthew Arnold says, that quietly but surely "makes for righteousness."

Look at the one giant wrong of *slavery*. It was sanctioned by the usage of centuries. It struck its roots deep into the very fabric of society. When Sir Thomas Fowell Buxton first stood up in the House of Commons to propose the emancipation of the slave, the House laughed at him. The proposal struck them as a jest. But Sir Thomas was no whit dismayed. He knew the giant wrong would have to go. "The battle is not ours, but God's!" he said, as he faced the laughter. The battle is not ours—there were other forces making for the overthrow of slavery besides the labors of Buxton, and Clarkson and Wilberforce. Time was against slavery; nature was against slavery; the trend of things was against slavery; and despite all the slaveholders could do, that giant wrong came to an end—the very "stars in their courses" had fought against them. There is a law, a spirit, in the universe, and that law makes for righteousness and justice. In such a universe wrong lives a precarious life. In the long run, it cannot last. Many a gigantic iniquity has come to a full end already. And those that remain among us are under sentence of death. You have seen perhaps this notice on buildings that are doomed to destruction, This Building Is Coming Down. Well, I can see that same sentence written across many a vested iniquity that seems unshaken in its strength. I see it written across the face of the drink traffic, This Thing Is Coming Down; I see it written across barracks and forts and Dreadnoughts, These Things Are Coming Down; I see it written across all injustices of our social and business life, These Things Are Coming Down. Their doom is sealed, their end is sure, not because I see this and that good man doing his best to overthrow them, but because time, the course of the world, the makeup of this universe is against them—the stars in their courses are fighting against Sisera.

The Law in the Individual Life

And now for a moment further, let me illustrate the working of this principle on the plane of the individual life. If on the big plain of history there is sometimes a little difficulty in tracing out the working of this principle, there is none at all when we contract our vision and confine our study to the individual life. If there is one thing absolutely certain it is this: the universe ranges itself against the wrongdoer. The man who sins finds nature his enemy. The world is so made that it punishes and penalizes the man who does evil. Let Sisera stand for the wicked and evil man, and it becomes profoundly and eternally true that the stars in their courses fight against Sisera. You remember how strenuously Emerson insists upon this truth in his great essays on "Compensation" and "Spiritual Laws"; and let me say in passing it will do every one good to read, mark, and inwardly digest these mighty and masterly chapters. "All things," he says, "are arranged for truth and benefit." The universe is so made that it is helpful to the man who fulfills the law of his own being, and lives purely and soberly and righteously. But let a man violate that law, let him sin against his own health and purity, and at once nature becomes his enemy and chastiser. The stars in their courses begin to fight against him.

Take the physical laws of this human nature of ours. Let a man sin against his own body by sensual indulgence; let him give way to the drink habit; let him wallow in the mire of lust, and he finds the universe against him, he finds nature arising for his punishment. He reaps the sure and certain penalty of his wickedness and folly, in quivering limb, bleared eyes, raw-edged nerves, impaired health, premature death. When we postpone either punishment or reward to a future world, we do greatly err. Punishment is immediate and inescapable.

It is *immediate*. The Bible speaks of a coming judgment when the Lord Christ shall pronounce our doom. But, long before that day breaks, the wrongdoer begins to pay for his evil deeds. And long before he comes to reckon with the Judge of all, he has to reckon with outraged and insulted nature. Nature takes in hand the task of punishment. Nature makes war upon the sinner. "Crime and punishment," as Emerson says, "grow out of one stem. Punishment is a fruit that, unsuspected, ripens within the flower of the pleasure which conceals it." Remember that, you young people, when tempted to do that which is evil! You are setting yourselves against the universe! You are making nature your foe! And from her scourge there is no escape. The punishment is immediate, I say, and it is *unescapable*. Our courts have their lists of undiscovered criminals. For some of the perpetrators of those atrocities which so shocked our nation a few weeks ago, the police are searching still. But though undiscovered of Scotland Yard, no criminal, no sinner really goes unpunished. He may escape the police, but he cannot escape nature.

The worst punishment is not that which the law inflicts, but that which outraged nature inflicts on a man both in body and soul. And no man escapes that, because the penalty accompanies the sin. I know young folk often flatter themselves that they can get the so-called pleasures of sin without its penalties. You can no more halve things and get the sensual good by itself," says Emerson, "than you can get an inside that shall have no outside, or a light without a shadow." It is a hopeless enterprise! You may escape public censure! You may escape even the reproaches of your friends! But escape altogether? Never! The stars in their courses fight against Sisera! The world is so made that it antagonizes wrong. Sin is an offense against the law of the universe. No man can do wrong without making nature his foe. Let a man do wrong and the whole world seems to be one big eye, staring upon him and accusing him. I quote Emerson once again—

Commit a crime and the earth is made of glass. You cannot recall the spoken word, you cannot wipe out the foot-track and you cannot draw up the ladder, so as to leave no inlet or clue. Some damning circumstance always transpires. The laws and substances of Nature—water, snow, wind, gravitation—become penalties to the thief.

That is poetically spoken, but it is essentially true. Wickedness is not only wicked, it is foolish as well. The man who sins flings himself against the order of the universe. It can only have one issue—defeat, disaster, overthrow, ruin. "Whosoever falleth on this stone shall be broken, but on whomsoever it shall fall it shall grind him to dust." The world is so made—let every young man and woman lay the truth to heart—as to be against the sinner. The stars in their courses fight against Sisera.

The course of the world, the laws of nature, the constitution of the universe—they are against wrong and on the side of right. What does that mean? In other words it means this—this universe of ours is a moral universe. But you cannot attribute morality to a world that is purely material. Morality is an attribute of personality. It is only to a person, responsible and free, that right and wrong can have any meaning at all. If, therefore, this universe is a moral universe, if things are arranged for truth and benefit, if it ranges itself against all sin and wrong, there can be but one conclusion and that is this: behind this world making for righteousness, and making against sin, there must stand a Moral Governor; behind this moral universe there must stand God, loving righteousness and hating iniquity. If the stars in their courses fight against Sisera, it is because the God who calls the stars by name is Himself sworn to do battle against sin and destroy it. I look at this world by its very makeup helping the good man and making the way of transgressors hard, and I know this world did not come into being by chance; I know that the materialist's explanation leaves the most striking facts unexplained; I know that it is not accident that rules; through all, in all, over all I see the working of a righteous and holy God. The morality of the universe is simply the morality of God.

And the mighty truth about God the universe preaches to me is this—God is a God of righteousness! "I, the Lord, hate evil." That is why the stars in their courses fight against Sisera. The laws of the world are but expressions of the manner of God's working; and "I, the Lord, hate evil." Wrong is on its way to ruin. Sin spells disaster and defeat. "The wicked shall not stand in the judgment, but are like the chaff which the wind driveth away."

The righteous and holy God! There is a note of solemn warning in it! To the righteous and holy God only righteous and holy men are acceptable. Only those who are fighting in the cause of righteousness will be among them who rejoice at the finish. Are we on God's side? Are we living the brave and holy life? Without holiness no man shall see the Lord. Let us enlist on that side! Let us seek that holiness! And if we have no holiness of our own, let us remember for our comfort that the Lord who demands it is also the Lord who gives it. "The blood of Jesus Christ, God's Son, cleanseth us from all sin."

The righteous and holy God! There is in it a message of encouragement and cheer. The Infinite Power behind all is on the side of right and truth. Our hands hang down and our knees are feeble oftentimes as we note the slow progress of our work and the seeming impregnability of wrong and evil.

Sursum Corda! Lift up your hearts! The Lord reigneth! Righteousness is on the throne, and the final triumph is sure.

> For right is right since God is God,
>   And right the day must win;
> To doubt would be disloyalty,
>   To falter would be sin.

CHAPTER EIGHT

The Making of a Soul

In your patience ye shall win your souls.
—Luke 21:19 RV

I have quoted, as you will notice, from the Revised Version. The Revised Version, from the literary point of view, may have many defects, but it has at any rate one supreme and sovereign merit—it reproduces more exactly for us the sense of the original. In the Authorized Version my text reads, "In your patience possess ye your souls." That is to say, King James's translators treated this verse as if it were merely an exhortation to the disciples to be patient under the pressure of persecution and peril. But that is not what our Lord said at all. He did not bid these disciples possess their souls in patience. He said a far more striking and significant thing. He said that it was by patient endurance they were to win, to get possession of, their souls. "Ye shall win your souls!" It is a notable and suggestive saying. It is perfectly true that some of the commentators take all the suggestiveness out of it by explaining that it really means nothing more than this: that if the disciples remain steadfast in the midst of all their troubles, and do not turn apostate, then they shall win life in the resurrection of the just. This is, indeed, how the twentieth-century Testament translates the verse: "By your endurance you shall win yourselves life." But I cannot help feeling that such a translation is a case of conventionalizing and stereotyping what is a very unconventional and unusual expression. At any rate, in this sermon I am going to take the phrase at its

76

face value. Ye shall win—ye shall gain possession—of your souls. And the main and central suggestion of the phrase to me is this: our souls are not given to us ready-made, finished and complete. They have to be made. They are prizes to be won. We do not start with them—we gradually get possession of them. "Life," says Browning somewhere, "is a stuff to try the soul's strength on and educe the man." I know of no sentence that constitutes a more illuminating commentary on this word of Christ's. The soul is not an inheritance into which we are born; it is something we make and fashion and win for ourselves out of the varied discipline and experience of life.

The Origin of the Soul

Now there are questions about the soul which the wisest men have failed to answer. I will not refer just now to the question of the immortality of the soul, which was a fruitful and perennial subject of debate in the ancient world, because in Jesus Christ life and immortality have been brought to light; though I would remind you that even among Christian theologians the question of the inherent and native immortality of the soul is a moot point, a great theologian like Dr. Dale holding that the soul only gains immortality in Christ. Let me refer for a moment to the question of the origin of the soul. Where does the soul come from? How does it come to be at all? That question has divided Christendom into two camps, and divides it still. There are some Christian thinkers who take what is known as the creationist view, and there are others who take what is called the traducianist.

The creationist says that every soul is God's new and direct creation, that the miracle of Adam is repeated in the case of every man born into the world. God breathes into him the breath of life, and he becomes a living soul. Our bodies, the creationist says, we get from our parents, from the race of which we form a part; but the spiritual and immortal part of us we get from God Himself. And there is much to say for the creationist position. It conserves the truth of individualism. It agrees well with that conviction, deep-seated within us all, that at the core and center of his being every man is unique and stands alone.

The traducianist, on the other hand, maintains that every child is born—soul as well as body—of its parents. The soul, he says, is not newly created, it is inherited. It is only on the supposition that souls as well as bodies are inherited that you can account for the as well as bodies are inherited that you can account for the reproduction in the child not only of the parents' facial and physical characteristics, but also of their moral and spiritual qualities as well. It is only on this supposition, he says, that you can account for the universality of sin and the perpetuation of the bias to moral evil. The soul cannot be new created, for as soon as man wakes to moral consciousness he finds sin and evil already there. And, once again, the traducianist has a great deal to say for himself. The facts of experience lend color to his theory. Indeed, Dr. Clark, in his *Outlines of Christian Doctrine*, goes so far as to say that this is the only theory that fully accounts for the facts.

Now I am not going to attempt to decide between the two theories. It is like trying to decide between individualism and socialism. For the creationist theory that every soul is a new soul asserts the truth contained in individualism—that in the last resort man stands alone. And the traducianist theory that soul as well as body is inherited, asserts the truth there is in socialism—that every man is part and parcel of the race, and cannot be explained or accounted for apart from the race to which he belongs. And neither individualism nor socialism by itself is the whole truth. They are complementary to each other, and the whole truth is found in a synthesis of both. And so, very likely, both the creationist and the traducianist are right. Their theories seem to us to be mutually exclusive, but, if we knew all, we should see that in this case too there is a higher unity in which these seeming contraries blend and agree.

But I am not at all sure that both creationist and traducianist do not discuss the soul too much as if it were a ready-made and finished thing. "Where does this soul come from?" they ask. "Did God create it, or did the man inherit it?" But I venture with all reverence to say that neither God nor a man's parents are the factors chiefly responsible for the human soul. The man himself is. For the soul is not given—it has to be made. It is not inherited at birth—it has to be fought for and won. What man is born with is not, shall I say, with a soul finished and complete, but with the raw material of a soul, the possibility of a soul. Whether he has a soul—that noble and divine element which deserves the name soul—at the finish depends upon himself. The soul is the prize of living. It is the great reward that crowns the courage and loyalty of the man who fights the good fight. By your patient endurance ye shall win for yourselves souls.

Losing the Soul

Now possibly this idea of winning a soul may at first hearing seem a little bit strange and startling to us, but if we look at it from the reverse point of view the idea is common and familiar enough. No truth of the Bible is more certain than this, that a man may lose his soul. No fact of observation and experience is more sure than this—that the soul can decay, and shrivel up and perish. Lose the soul . . . win the soul; they are really but the obverse and the reverse sides of the same truth. Let us look for a moment at this matter of losing the soul. It will help us a little when we come to speak about winning the soul.

The soul can be lost—the Bible says so, and the experience of life confirms it. And when I speak about the soul being lost, I am not thinking for the moment about the fate of the soul after death. What may happen to the soul in the world to come I am content to leave in the hands of the wise and holy but loving God. But, short of that final loss, men lose their souls here and now, before our very eyes. We mistake when we postpone this loss to some future world. It is taking place now. We can see the deadly process going on. There are men and women among us who have less soul than they started with. Their stock of soul, shall I say, has been diminishing. There are some who seem to have no soul left. For, I repeat, the soul is not a finished article when we get it: it is a power, a capacity, a faculty. And like every other faculty it grows by exercise, it expands by being nourished and fed; but it atrophies and perishes through disuse and neglect.

How does the soul live? On what does the soul live? "My soul," cries the psalmist, "is athirst for God, the living God." "I," said Jesus, "am the bread of life." That is how the soul lives—by fellowship with God; by feeding upon Christ; by reproducing the life He lived; by kindness and love and sacrifice; by giving the utmost to the highest; by seeking what is lovely and true and pure and of good report. But when we forget God, when we neglect Christ, when we live for self and the world and sin, we impoverish and destroy the soul. And it is so easy to live this latter kind of life. The baser instincts of our own nature tempt us to it. That is a tremendous word of the apostle Paul's, and it stands for an experience of which every one of us knows something. "The flesh lusteth against the spirit, and the spirit lusteth against the flesh." We are torn by conflicting impulses. We are dragged in opposite directions, and on the issue of this internal conflict it will depend what becomes of our souls. For the soul expands and grows when we live for the spirit and crucify the flesh; but it shrivels up and perishes when we live for the flesh and crucify the spirit.

And we may see this latter tragedy taking place in case after case in actual life before our eyes. That is a notable word which our Lord spoke in His explanation of the parable of the sower. Explaining what He meant by the seed which fell among thorns, He said, "These are they that have heard, and as they go on their way, they are choked with cares and riches and pleasures of this life." "Choked with cares and riches and pleasures of this life." And what is it that is choked? Not the man himself. Apparently he is as much alive as ever. Very likely people thought him flourishing. It is the soul that is choked, stifled, strangled, destroyed. "Choked with cares and riches"—that is one way in which the soul is continually being lost. Saul gave once every promise of being a royal soul. He was intent upon the glory of God. But he was made king, and the cares of his position choked his soul. He became more anxious to establish a dynasty than to do the will of God. And so Saul, who started by being numbered among the prophets, finished up by losing his faith in God and turning instead to the witch of Endor. He had lost his soul. It had been choked with cares. Judas at one point in his life gave promise of being a great soul. When he enlisted among Christ's followers he was full of enthusiasm and vision and the spirit of sacrifice. But the love of money gradually got hold of his heart. And under the influence of that baleful love you can see the soul getting squeezed and stifled out of Judas, until at last he can carp and scoff at Mary's sacrificial love and sell his Lord for thirty pieces of silver. "Choked with . . . riches."

And we can parallel these cases by cases out of our own experience. Mammon is a deadly enemy to the soul. There is not one of us, perhaps, who cannot put his finger on men whose souls have been choked by riches. They began life with great enthusiasm and high ambitions. They delighted in God's house. They were foremost in God's work. They were even preachers and teachers of God's Word. But riches came, and prosperity came, and position came. And as their prosperity grew, their interest in spiritual things decreased. They are not to be found in the prayer meeting now; they are not to be found in the teacher's chair now; they are not to be found in the village pulpit now. They have lost interest in these things. They are of the earth, earthy. God has given them of the desires of their hearts, but the tragic sequence has followed—He has sent leanness into their souls.

And next to mammon there is nothing for destroying the soul like selfish and sensual pleasure. "Choked with . . . pleasures." When the younger son was spending his substance in riotous living in the far country, he was "lost," Jesus says. It was his soul that was lost. He had no soul left, so to speak. A course of selfishness and sin had eaten it up and destroyed it. And that is always the result of a life of selfish and sensual pleasure. It dries up and destroys the soul. It empties a man of high feeling, noble aspiration, and holy ambition. It dehumanizes him, it brutalizes him. It leaves him insensible to high appeal. It puts the mark of the beast on his very face. You remember that terrible sequence which Paul sets forth in the first chapter of his letter to the Romans—a "refusal to have God in their knowledge," "vile passions," a "reprobate mind": the repudiation of God; a life of sinful pleasure; a reprobate mind, a callous heart, a dead soul. And we see this tragic sequence in many a life. A course of selfish and sinful pleasure is the destruction of honor and truth and faith and fame. Is there not an old story which says that a painter once chose a child for a model of an angel because in its face there was such innocence and purity expressed? And many years later that same painter was searching the gaol for a man who should be a model of everything that was evil, and at length he discovered the man he wanted, a man out of whose face every gleam of soul seemed to have disappeared. And on inquiry it turned out that this degraded and soulless man was once the angel. That, then, is the tragic fact with which the experience of daily life makes us only too painfully familiar—a man may lose his soul. A life of selfishness and sin warps, impoverishes, corrodes the soul. A man may finish up with less soul than he began. He may end by having no soul at all.

Gaining the Soul

Now all this may help us to understand a little better what Christ meant by "winning" our souls. It is the obverse side of the truth I have been expounding up to now. The soul, I repeat once again, is not given to us ready-made and complete; it is given to us as raw material, the stuff which we may work up into souls if we will. Now if on the one hand that soul-stuff can be diminished and lost, it can on the other hand be multiplied and enlarged. If on the one hand, through neglect and abuse, a man may lose his soul, as that servant lost the talent he had buried in the earth, on the other hand the man who uses and exercises his soul may vastly increase his soul, just as the man who put his talent out to usury changed his single talent into five. A man in the process of life may become soulless, or he may become great-souled. He may finish up with less soul than he began, or he may finish up with vastly more. Soul may be lost; soul may be gained. That is the crown and reward of brave and faithful living—we shall gain soul, we shall make soul, we shall increase, enlarge, and multiply soul.

Now let me descend from that general statement to a more detailed and analytical consideration of the question, How may we gain soul?

I answer first by practicing the presence of God. It is for God the soul thirsts. It is by fellowship with God the soul lives and thrives. Let a man practice the presence of God, let him be much in prayer, and I care not what his outward circumstances may be, he will become a man of great soul. It is impossible to have a great soul without this. "If a man abide not in Me," said Jesus, "he is cast forth as a branch and is withered." Notice that word—he is *withered*. Apart from God the soul is like a branch divorced from the parent stem; there is no principle of life in it, it withers, it shrivels, it dies. Those of you who have read Stevenson's letters will perhaps remember one he wrote from Mentone after an attack of illness that had left him so prostrate that he was not allowed to speak or read. And this is what he says about those days when he was cut off from all mental stimulus and sustenance.

> As an intellectual being I have not yet begun to re-exist; my immortal soul is very nearly extinct. Being sent to the south is not much good unless you take your soul with you; and my soul is rarely with me here. I don't see much beauty, I have lost the key. I am a manacled and hidebound spirit, incapable of pleasure, the clay of a man.

Robbed of the stimulus of books, Stevenson's mind was dull and torpid and withered and dead. And as it was with Stevenson's mind when deprived of books, so is it with the soul when deprived of

God. Apart from Him the soul withers, like a dead branch. But in fellowship with Him it expands and enlarges and grows. If you want to gain soul, to grow in soul, practice the presence of God; live in the atmosphere of the eternal; be instant in prayer. The men of prayer—from the days of Jesus Himself down to ours—have gained to themselves souls

And in the second place, follow Christ and give your utmost to the highest. Men lose soul by surrendering the higher to the lower, the eternal to the temporal, God to the world. They gain soul by clinging to the high and eternal and Divine, whatever the cost. They gain soul by living as Christ did, not for the applause of men, but for the glory of God; not to be ministered unto but to minister. "Follow me," said Christ to Matthew in his tollbooth. It meant sacrifice. For it meant giving up a position and the prospect of wealth. But Matthew never hesitated. He rose up, left all, and followed Him. He lost in wealth, but he gained soul. "Thou shalt be my witness," said the voice to Paul on the way to Damascus. "My witness!" A witness to a crucified Christ! It meant a life of suffering and shame. But Paul never hesitated. He was not disobedient to the heavenly vision. He became a wandering preacher. He spent himself in the service of men. He lost everything the world counts dear, but he gained soul. And that is how we may win souls for ourselves, by following Christ; by living for love and the good that we can do; by giving our utmost to the highest. Every time we choose the hard right way, rather than the easy wrong way, we gain soul. Every time we sacrifice ease and comfort to do service to our fellows we gain soul. Every time we say a kindly word and do a loving deed we gain soul. When F. N. Charrington gave up a fortune to fight the drink, he gained soul. When Frank Crossley gave up comfort in Bowdon and went and lived in Ancoats to minister to the poor, he gained soul. When Dr. Peter Fraser gave up position and fame at home to go and be a missionary in the far-off Khassia hills, he gained soul. For the soul lives and grows and expands on love and kindness and sacrifice. Our hearts are always enlarged when we run in the way of God's commandments.

But to gain soul is a costly business. It is an easy matter to lose soul; it costs effort, sacrifice, agony to gain it.

> Our flesh and sense must be denied,
> Passion and envy, lust and pride.

That is the way to gain soul, and that is not easy. To "crucify the flesh with the affections and lusts thereof "—that is the way to gain soul, and that is not easy. To do the right in scorn of consequence is the way to gain soul, and that is not easy. To subordinate self and be willing to spend and be spent for others is the way to gain soul, and that is not easy. To hold cheap what the world most values and to live for the unseen and eternal is the way to gain soul, and that is not easy. That is why Christ says in my text, "In your patient endurance ye shall win your souls." We have to set our teeth; to go through with it; to stick to it; to hold fast. It is not a spasm of unselfishness we want, but a life of it. We shall be often tempted to ask, is it worthwhile? We shall be often tempted to fall in with the world's ways. But on that side lies loss of soul. It is by patient endurance, by steadfast loyalty to the highest and the best, by faithful following of that Christ in whom that best is embodied, that we gain soul. You have heard or read of James Smetham? He was an artist, and a great artist, an artist appreciated by men like Ruskin and Rosetti. Now the temptation came to Smetham to paint for money, to sacrifice his artistic ideals in order to make a fortune. If only he had condescended to become a fashionable portrait painter, he might have ended his days a rich man. But he put the temptation far from him. Nothing but the highest and the best should come from his brush. He never won popularity; he died a poor man. But by his patient allegiance to his ideals he gained his artistic soul. And side by side with that story of Smetham I will put this story of a man of business. He was being pressed to do what he believed to be a dishonorable thing. "Every one does it," said the other to him. "Are those the only conditions on which I can get the order?" he asked. "Yes, they are," replied the other. "Then I must do without it; I have a conscience to live with," was the uncompromising reply. He lost the order, but by his steadfast loyalty to truth and right he gained soul. And to gain soul is the vital and all-important thing. The soul is the great prize of living. To be great-fortuned is as nothing compared to being great-souled. Life is a failure or a triumph as we lose or gain soul.

Now, what about ourselves? Which are we doing? Let us turn the searchlight upon our own lives for a moment. Is the kind of life we live making or destroying soul? Which is it with us—are we living the selfish or the sacrificial life? Are we loving the world or are we following Christ? Is it mammon and pleasure with us, or is it

God? To gain a soul—that is the supreme end and aim of life. Live for that! Contend earnestly for that! Sacrifice everything for that! Count all things to be loss for that! Nothing else matters but that! Life is a triumph if by your steadfast loyalty to the highest and the best you have gained soul. But if you fail to gain soul, it matters not what else you have acquired, life is a disastrous and lamentable failure. You may have acquired fame and fortune, you may have amassed all the wealth of Araby and India, but if you have failed to gain soul, life ends in sheer and irretrievable loss. For the soul is the eternal part of us; the soul is the divine and heavenly part of us; the soul it is that prepares us and makes us meet for the inheritance of the saints in light. "And what shall it profit a man to gain the whole world and lose his soul?"

CHAPTER NINE

The Work of Grace

By the grace of God I am what I am.
—1 Corinthians 15:10

In one sense that is true of every man—believer and unbeliever, Christian and non-Christian. Whatever a man is—he is it by the grace and favor of God. We sometimes draw a distinction between the kingdom of nature and the kingdom of grace. The distinction is one that we find convenient and practically useful, but it may very easily become a false distinction if we understand by it that grace is the realm of God's working, while nature is a realm from which God's operations are excluded. As a matter of fact, God is in nature as well as in grace. He is in the common events of the common day just as certainly as He is in the great spiritual experiences of life. He is all in all. He girds men, though they do not know Him. He orders their paths and their lying down. They are what they are by the Divine permission and grace. Here is an illustration of what I mean right to my hand. I take up a coin of the realm and I find graven on it the words, "George V, by the grace of God King of the Britains." King, how? By succession, by hereditary right? Yes, no doubt. But in the deepest sense of all, "King . . . by the grace of God." George V is monarch of these realms only by permission and favor of God, and he will continue our monarch just so long as God permits him. By the grace of God he is what he is.

And what is true of the king is true of everyone. In God's hand our breath is, and His are all our ways. In Him we live and move and have our being, and apart from Him we would not be at all. Have you noticed that sometimes when an artist is billed to appear at some concert or other entertainment, the information is added that he appears "by permission of so and so"? What it means, I suppose, is something like this. Sometimes impressarios bargain with artists for their entire and exclusive services. If any such artist appears under any other auspices during the term covered by his engagement, he does so "by permission" of the man who has bargained for the right to his exclusive services. Now that illustrates in some measure the relation between man and God. We are His people and the sheep of His pasture. He and He alone keepeth our soul in life. Should God take away our breath, we die and return to our dust. Whatever we are, we are by permission of God. So it is not only true that George V is king by the grace of God—but it is equally true that you are a doctor by the grace of God, and you are a lawyer by the grace of God, and you are a merchant by the grace of God, and you are a businessman by the grace of God, and you are a mechanic by the grace of God. Believer and unbeliever, Christian and non-Christian, good and bad, they are on absolutely the same level here. Inasmuch as they would not exist at all without God, and inasmuch as their continuance from day to day depends upon God, it is true of every man that by the grace of God he is what he is.

But the word "grace" has a special meaning in my text. It means here—as indeed it means throughout the New Testament—not simply the goodwill of permission, of which I have just been speaking and which God shows to all men, even to the unthankful and evil; it means here the active and positive favor and goodwill which God shows to all those who are in Christ Jesus. The essential meaning of grace is love. But it is love with a certain connotation, love that takes a certain direction. So that it is true to say that, while all grace is love, all love is not grace. I mean this: love can be shown by an equal for an equal, by a higher for a lower, by a lower for a higher; but grace can only be shown by a higher for a lower. We can love God, but it would be a blasphemous impertinence to talk about our being gracious to Him. But God is gracious to us. Grace, then, is, as Dr. Whyte says, love that flows down; it is love that stoops; it is the love of the Highest for the lowest. And so it stands in Scripture for the love of God for man. And it was that love that made Paul. "By the grace of God I am what I am."

The Energy of Grace

Now will you notice, to begin with, how Paul's words in my text imply that grace is active, operative, energizing. Grace had made Paul. We need to have enlarged ideas of the power that resides in those forces which are immaterial and spiritual. As a result of the prevailing materialism, we are inclined, as Dr. Jowett says, to think far too meanly of spiritual ministries, and to think far too highly of the more palpable ministries of the physical universe. As a matter of fact, the mere mechanical forces are insignificant from the standpoint of power and influence, compared with the intellectual and spiritual. Take the one illustration of thought. What do you say of thought? Do you reduce it to a mere movement of the physical substance of the brain? Do you say it is like the flitting of a shadow—here and then gone, leaving no trace of itself behind? Why, a thought is a living creature, as Luther would say, having eyes and teeth. Let it out, it will pass from mind to mind and life to life, molding, shaping, guiding each, and you can set no bounds to its influence.

But the greatest energy of all is *grace*—God's loving thought for men. That is a truth about grace we need more clearly to realize. Grace is not a mere sentiment, it is not an amiability—it is a force, a power, an energy. "Grace, 'tis a charming sound," says one of our hymns. Yes, there is something beautiful and winsome about the very word *grace*. But I never think of that line without feeling its absurd inadequacy! Grace—a charming sound! Why, it would be just as appropriate to say that Niagara was a charming sound! What is the dominant impression Niagara makes as it hurries along seething, swirling, roaring to its final leap over the rocks? That of power—resistless, boundless, incalculable power! There is power in Niagara to do the work of a continent well-nigh. Ask the people of Buffalo, that great town twenty miles or so away, what Niagara is to them? And they will answer you—power. It is Niagara that runs their cars; it is Niagara that drives their machinery; it is Niagara that lights their streets. Niagara chained, harnessed, put to use, is doing the work of Buffalo. And grace is a perfect Niagara of power! Charming sound, indeed! It is a resistless tide of energy, it is a sweeping flood of force! That is the representation of grace given to us in the New Testament! It is not a mere sentiment, a charming sound, but an active, energizing force!

Take a reference or two in illustration of my point. "Be strengthened," writes Paul to Timothy, "in the grace that is in Christ Jesus.

Strengthened in the grace—grace is the fountain of power and might; the secret of triumph over cowardice and fear. "God our Father loved us and gave us eternal comfort and good hope through grace," writes Paul to the Thessalonians. Eternal comfort and good hope through grace—grace begets courage and confidence. It is like the coming of reinforcements to a sore-pressed army. It fires the heart and nerves the arm. It changes doubt and despair into the assurance of victory. We have comfort and good hope through grace. "Be not carried away by diverse and strange teachings, for it is good that the heart be established by grace," writes the author of the epistle to the Hebrews. "Be not carried away," he says; these Hebrew Christians were being driven backwards and forwards by changing tides of opinion, they were like the surge of the sea—there was neither steadiness nor stability about their lives. And how was this instability of theirs to be counteracted and remedied? By grace. It was grace that would establish the heart, and enable them to stand foursquare to all the winds that blew—established by grace. And yet one other illustration let me give you. It is the most sweeping of them all: "God is able to make all grace abound unto you," writes Paul to the Corinthians, "that ye having always all sufficiency in everything may abound unto every good work." Notice the sequence! "God is able to make all grace abound unto you." Abundant grace! What next?

"That ye having always all sufficiency in everything may abound unto every good work." Abounding grace—abounding work! Abounding grace—abounding power! Power for anything and everything! Abounding grace—always all sufficiency for everything. The apostle strains language to describe the force resident in grace—always, all sufficiency for everything! There are no impossibilities to a man reinforced and strengthened by the power of grace. God is able to make all grace abound unto you that you may abound unto every good work.

Now this potent energy of grace had been at work in the life of St. Paul. Ever since that memorable day when he met with Christ outside Damascus the love of God had been the dynamic of Paul's life. "The love of Christ constraineth me." That love had saved him, cleansed him, comforted him, strengthened him; that love had enabled him to bear and to do and to suffer; that love had given him his knowledge, his peace, his joy. Indeed, looking back upon his life, Paul realizes that all that he has known and all that he has done, all that he is in character and power is due entirely to the fructifying and energizing love of God. Without grace he would have been nothing; to grace he owes everything. "By the grace of God I am what I am."

I want now to examine a little more closely and in detail into the work of grace as illustrated in the life of Paul. "By the grace of God I am what I am," says the great apostle. What, then, had grace done for Paul? Well, I answer first—

Saved—by Grace

Grace saved him. Paul rejoices, in his epistles, that he is a sinner saved. And saved how? By grace! In speaking first of Paul's salvation, I am speaking of the very greatest thing grace did for him. If Paul had been asked, as Sir James Simpson, the great Edinburgh physician, was asked, what was the greatest and most welcome discovery of his whole life, he would have answered, as that great doctor answered, "The discovery that I have a Savior." Yes, the best and brightest and happiest day in all Paul's life was the day when, through Jesus Christ, he was delivered from his load of shame and sin—when he was saved by grace. If you have made any study at all of the literature of the saints, you will have noticed this—it is marked by a keen and vivid and overwhelming sense of sin. It is the very holiest of men who so realize the sinfulness of sin that they abhor themselves. Take these as illustrations:

> "When I look at my sinfulness," said Samuel Rutherford, "my salvation is to me my Savior's greatest miracle. He has done nothing in heaven or on earth like my salvation."

> "When a man like me," says Luther, "comes to know the plague of his own heart, he is not miserable only— he is misery itself—he is not sinful only, he is absolute sin itself."

"I am made of sin," says Bishop Andrewes, in his tear-stained *Book of Prayers*. While John Bunyan has described his condition in the very title page of his book, *Grace Abounding to the Chief of Sinners, A Brief Relation of the Exceeding Mercy of God in Christ to His Poor Servant, John Bunyan*. But none ever felt the shame and ache and torture of sin like Paul did. He was the bondslave of sin. Sin reigned over him and dwelt in him. His sin gave him continual sorrow of heart. He was a persecutor, blasphemous and injurious, and he would dispute with John Bunyan his claim to being the chief of sinners. And this sin of his made Paul's life a burden to him. His day was filled with pain, and by night he made his couch wet with tears, and day and night he cried, "My sins, my sins, who shall take away my sins?" And from this haunting, torturing, crushing burden of sin grace delivered him. It was nothing he had done or could do that brought him deliverance. From first to last it was the Lord's doing. Grace had done it all. "The Son of God loved me, and gave Himself for me!"

"It was Paul's accustomed manner," says the immortal dreamer in his touching introduction to *Grace Abounding*, "ever to open before his judges the manner of his conversion; he would think of that day and that hour in which he first did meet with grace; for it supported him." Yes, Paul was constantly going back to the day and the hour when Christ met with him and took his sins away. And why was he always reverting to that day and that hour? Not simply, as John Bunyan says, "because it supported him"; and not simply in order to give glory to God. But chiefly for this reason: in order to bring hope to the sin-burdened men and women to whom he spoke. The story of Damascus was in itself the mightiest argument. Paul himself was the evidence and proof of his gospel. There was none beyond the reach of that saving and redeeming grace which on that day and that hour saved Paul, the "chief of sinners." "Where sin doth abound," was the gospel Paul preached to a groaning world, "grace doth much more abound." There is no one so sunk in sin, so enslaved by sin, so defiled by sin as to be beyond the uplifting, emancipating and cleansing power of grace. "In whom we have our redemption," writes the great evangelical apostle to his Ephesian converts, "through His blood, even the forgiveness of our sins, according to the riches of His grace." It matters not how deep our sinfulness may be—though, like Bishop Andrewes, we feel ourselves to be made of sin, though like Bunyan we fall at the sight of our own vileness deeply into despair, though like Paul we feel ourselves the chief of sinners—Christ's grace is so rich and full that it can bring redemption and forgiveness of sins to us. We are helpless to rid ourselves of the burden or to deliver ourselves from its pain—but God's free love is able to deliver and redeem. We are saved by grace.

Thy grace, alone, O God,
  To me can pardon speak,
Thy power alone, O Son of God,
  Can this sore bondage break.

An Apostle—by Grace

But salvation was not the only thing grace bestowed upon Paul. "By the grace of God, I am what I am."—Well, what was he? Not only a sinner saved—but a Christian apostle. And how came he to be an apostle? By the grace of God. That indeed is the precise reference of my text. Paul never ceased to wonder at the marvel of his salvation. But next only to the marvel of his salvation was the marvel of his apostleship. Paul was "lost in wonder, love and praise" when he thought of his apostleship. For of all men he seemed the least worthy of this high honor and dignity. "For I am the least of all the apostles," he writes in the verse before my text, "that am not meet to be called an apostle, because I persecuted the church of God—but by the grace of God I am what I am." It was God's grace that had lifted him up to that height and conferred upon him that honor. Indeed in one place he calls his apostleship a "grace." "To me who am less than the least of all saints was this grace given, to preach unto the Gentiles the unsearchable riches of Christ." How was it that he who was less than the least of all saints became an apostle? By grace. Grace did more than save Paul, it brought him to honor and dignity.

And this again is one of the works of grace. This is one of the perpetually recurring effects of grace. This is a result of grace that is illustrated in the life of every Christian. It is perfectly true we do not become apostles. But it is still true, is it not, that grace does not stop its work at forgiveness, but goes on to promote a man to honor and renown? Grace finds the sinner in the gutter and makes a saint of him. Paul in one of his letters speaks of men being "adopted as sons through Jesus Christ unto God." What an honor is this that men should become sons of God, and should have mansions in the Father's house! How came such an honor to the lot of sinful men? Through grace. We have received the adoption that we might be "unto the praise of the glory of His grace." You see the grace of the father in the parable in forgiving the prodigal who had wasted his substance and broken his heart. But the father did not stop at mere forgiveness, did he? He went on to show the glory of his grace by giving him the best robe, and a ring for his hand and shoes for his feet, and restoring him to the son's place. And so you see the grace of God, in the remission and forgiveness of sin; but you see the glory of His grace in this, that He sets these sin-stained men and women on thrones and gives them crowns, and clothes them in white, and makes them kings and priests unto God. We sing sometimes about the glories of the saints, about their bliss and unspeakable joy. Once these saints in glory were like ourselves—

> They wrestled hard as we do now,
> With sins and doubts and fears. . . .

But if we ask them,

> —whence their victory came?
> They with united breath,
> Ascribe their conquest to the Lamb,
> Their triumph to His death.

Yes, they sit on their thrones, but not, shall I say, as a result of their own merit. They cry, "Not unto us, not unto us, O Lord, but unto Thy name be the glory." They cast their crowns before the throne of the Lamb, and every victor confesses, "By the grace of God I am what I am."

A Successful Worker—by Grace

"By the grace of God I am what I am," says Paul. And what was Paul more than a saved sinner, and a called apostle? He was also a successful worker. And how came he to be a successful worker? By the grace of God. I scarcely know where to begin when I speak of Paul as a worker. Never surely did any man toil as he did. He traveled innumerable miles; he preached innumerable sermons; he suffered unspeakable hardships. He took the whole world for his parish—and as the result of his unwearied labor he dotted all the lands between Antioch and Rome with Christian churches. He was called into the service last of all the apostles, one indeed born out of due time. But so earnestly, so unsparingly, with such consuming zeal did he fling himself into the service, that Paul, modest man though he was, can speak in the verse of my text as having labored "more abundantly than they all." And then he at once corrects himself. He knows that his vast toil, and the success he met with were not to be put to his own credit, but to the divine love aiding him and strengthening him. "Yet not I," he adds, "but the grace of God which was with me." The excellency of the power, Paul knew, was of God and not of himself. Grace made Paul a successful worker. He knew there would never have been a church established or a soul saved but for the grace of God that was with him.

Grace it is that makes men successful workers still. "Apart from me," said Jesus Christ, "ye can do nothing." Notice that! Apart from the Divine help we are utterly and entirely impotent. But assisted by the Divine grace there is nothing we cannot do! "If God be for us," said Paul exultingly, "who can be against us?" And again, "I can do all things through Christ, who strengtheneth me." Men have attempted what looked like impossible tasks with very scanty material resources, but the grace which was bestowed upon them was not found vain. Carey went to India, with a church at home indifferent to missions, and a government in India opposed to his coming. He, the Northampton shoemaker, flung himself upon the ancient and hoary paganisms of that country. It seemed a mad enterprise, but the grace was not found vain. Robert Morrison did the same in China, and the grace was not found vain. Lawes and Chalmers went to the savages of New Guinea. It seemed a hopeless undertaking to Christianize New Guinea. But listen to this: "I have seen myself," said Dr. Lawes, "six murderers and cannibals live peaceful lives. I have seen shameless thieves and robbers become honest. I have seen the lascivious and filthy become pure. I have seen the quarrelsome and selfish become unselfish and kind"—the grace was not found vain. And that grace avails for us. In face of the paganism of England; in face of those multitudes of people whom the churches do not touch; in face of the work at our own doors, in the church, in the Sabbath school, in our homes, that grace will not be in vain. Let us fling ourselves upon God, and we too shall accomplish great things, and yet not we, but the grace of God which is with us.

A Steadfast Christian—by Grace

"By the grace of God I am what I am." And I had meant to have added that in addition to being a sinner saved, and a called apostle, and a successful worker, Paul was a persevering Christian—through grace. This same grace which redeems, and calls, and strengthens also keeps. Paul had his share of temptation and difficulty and trial in the Christian life. Many of those associated with him found the life too hard and turned back. But Paul never faltered. He bore up against deprivation and suffering and loss—through grace. He tells of one of his trials—a thorn in the flesh, he called it. He besought the Lord thrice to take it away. But God's reply was, "My grace is sufficient for thee." And what grace did in the case of that particular trial, it did in the case of all the trials and temptations that beset him. Grace proved sufficient, so that at the end he could say, "I have fought the good fight; I have finished the course, I have kept the faith."

And grace is still sufficient. The forces of the world all tend to drive a man into sin and shame. But here is another force that is stronger than the pressure of the world, and which will keep a man pressing towards the highest and the best. A boat left to itself will naturally float with the current. If you want to drive it up the river you must have within the boat some force stronger than the force of the current—such as, for instance, the force of steam. The natural tendency for men is to go with the stream, and the stream carries us to shame and death; to breast the stream we need some force within us stronger than the world without us, and that stronger force we have in the grace of God. We have but to receive God's grace and we, too, shall be able to keep ourselves unspotted from the world and to endure to the end. God's grace is a keeping grace. To every struggling soul, to every one who feels the fierce force of the world's temptations, God says, "My grace is sufficient for thee."

Here, then, we are surrounded by infinite redeeming, uplifting, strengthening, keeping energy. It is ours for the taking. This Divine energy can be ours. When we are in Christ, all this wealth of saving force flows into us. Of His fullness we can all partake, grace upon grace. "Now unto Him that is able to guard you from stumbling and to set you before the presence of His glory without blemish in exceeding joy, to the only God our Savior through Jesus Christ our Lord, be glory, majesty, dominion and power, before all time, and now and for evermore. Amen."

CHAPTER TEN

Nicodemus

Now there was a man of the Pharisees, named
Nicodemus, a ruler of the Jews: the same came unto
Him by night.   —John 3:1–2

And the chapter which tells of that meeting between Jesus and
Nicodemus, and of the conversation that took place between them, is
one of the classic chapters in this great and classic gospel. How came
Nicodemus to seek out Jesus at all? How came a "teacher of Israel" to
seek out the Galilean prophet? How came the Jerusalem rabbi to sit at
the feet of a young teacher from Nazareth? Dr. Alexander Whyte, in
his lecture on Nicodemus, assumes that there is behind the story of
their meeting a whole chapter of unrecorded history. His own surmise
is that Nicodemus was one of that Pharisaic deputation—and possibly
the chief of it—which was sent from Jerusalem to Bethany beyond
Jordan to inspect John the Baptist's work and to report upon it. He
was one of those who heard John testify to the near approach of that
Messiah whose shoelatchet the Baptist declared himself unworthy to
unloose. He was one of those who heard the Baptist's call to repent
and be baptized, and who declined to yield obedience to it. And ever
since that day, says Dr. Whyte, conscience had been troubling
Nicodemus. He knew he ought to have gone down into the waters of
Jordan with the outcasts and publicans of Palestine—for sin lay heavy
on his soul. And it was this uneasy, accusing conscience of his, says
Dr. Whyte, that drove him, Pharisee, rabbi, ruler as he was, to Jesus,
in hope of relief.

That is an ingenious and by no means an impossible surmise, and the great Edinburgh preacher makes happy and effective use of it in his discussion of the conversation between the rabbi and the Lord. But it must be said that for Dr. Whyte's assumption there is absolutely no warrant in Scripture. It is a mere guess—a happy guess perhaps but a guess and nothing more. And there is really no need to assume as much as that to account for Nicodemus's visit to Christ. Even if Nicodemus had never been to John's baptism and had never heard John's testimony, there is enough in what the Evangelist tells us in the latter half of the previous chapter to account for his visit. It was Christ's first visit to Jerusalem after the beginning of His public ministry. Attention has been called to the fact that Jesus never appeared in Jerusalem without, by some action of His, practically proclaiming Himself the Messiah. In Galilee He kept His messiahship hidden; in Jerusalem He asserted it and insisted upon it. At this, the first Passover of His public career, He had announced His messiahship in bold and striking fashion by exercising authority within the temple, and sweeping it clean of that mob of traffickers who defiled its precincts. "My Father's house," He had called it. He set aside priests and Levites. Theirs, at best, was but a delegated authority, and they had abused it. But He was the real Lord of the temple. This action—and certain other signs which He did (probably miracles of healing mercy)—stirred Jerusalem to its depths. Jesus was the subject of universal discussion. Who is He? was the question that passed from lip to lip. They discussed that question in the homes of the poor; they discussed it in the seats of the mighty. "Many," says John, "believed on Him, beholding His signs which He did." That is to say, there was born in the hearts of many the hope that at last their long-expected Deliverer had come. And these, I will hazard the guess, belonged for the most part to the ranks of the humble and the poor. And what of the rulers? Well, I will hazard this other guess, that Christ's action had moved the rulers not to faith, but to wrath. When He said that someone had turned His Father's house into a house of merchandise, it was upon them His accusation fell. They knew they and none other were the guilty parties. When with His scourge of small cords he drove traders and money changers pell-mell out of the temple, it was upon priests, scribes, and elders His lash fell. And that day there was born in their souls a hate that at length glutted itself in the Cross. They had not repented at the preaching of John;

they did not repent at the preaching of Jesus. Hardened by sin and encased by prejudice, all they cared about was to get this uncomfortable Preacher put out of the way. None of the rulers or of the Pharisees believed on Him.

To this rule there was but one exception, and that one was Nicodemus. Nicodemus had witnessed the Lord's walk and work during that memorable Passover week, and he was puzzled, perplexed, perturbed. He did not allow prejudice and hate to make his judgment blind. He knew Jesus was no impostor or devil, as his associates were already beginning to say. Of one thing he was quite sure: that no one could do the mighty works which Jesus did except God were with Him. But was He anything more than a great and good man? Was He anything more than a prophet? Could it be that He was the long-promised Savior? These were the questions that puzzled Nicodemus, and gave him no rest. And at last, in his honest and determined desire to know, he went and sought out Jesus for himself. "Now there was a man of the Pharisees, named Nicodemus, a ruler of the Jews; the same came unto Him by night."

Nicodemus's Caution

By night! Under cover of darkness! When all the world was indoors or asleep! That was the time Nicodemus chose for his visit. And, fastening upon that fact, the commentators have emphasized Nicodemus's timidity, until he has come to stand for most of us as a type of the hesitating, dubious, fearful disciple. And by so thinking of him I am persuaded we have done a great injustice to Nicodemus. For the characteristic, the outstanding characteristic, of Nicodemus is not his caution, but his candor. I do not deny that he was cautious. I do not deny that his manner of approach to Christ suggests a fear of discovery. It is perfectly true that Nicodemus did not want to be seen. To be seen was to be committed, and Nicodemus was not prepared to commit himself as yet. Caution was certainly an element in his character. But let us not be too severe on his caution. There were at least two things that combined to make Nicodemus cautious.

(1) There was the fact that he himself was not sure. He did not know what to make of Christ. He was perturbed, but not persuaded. He was considering, but not convinced. Some of the people, seeing Jesus' signs, had jumped to the conclusion that He was the Messiah. But Nicodemus dared not jump to conclusions. He was a teacher in

Israel. He was a ruler of the Jews. He was a man of weight and authority, and therefore of responsibility. Now we all know that caution grows with responsibility. A cabinet minister, for instance, dare not allow himself the freedom of speech which a private member of Parliament not only claims, but often exercises. Newspapers report the cabinet minister's words; the people of the land look to him for information and guidance; so he feels constrained to be exact and accurate and measured in his speech. And that but illustrates a law. If a man occupies a position, in virtue of which people look up to him and are guided by him, the responsibilities of such a position teach him circumspection and caution. Public men need to be careful what they say and where they go. Now Nicodemus was such a public man. He was one of the leaders of Jewish thought. He counted in Jerusalem. What he said and did mattered. They say of our great preacher, Dr. Enoch Mellor of Halifax, that whenever a public meeting was held at which he was present, where some question—social, municipal, political—was being discussed, the Halifax people would never be satisfied until they knew what "their Enoch" (for so they called him in their homely Yorkshire fashion) thought. Well, it was something like that with Nicodemus. He counted in Jerusalem. The people looked up to him and depended upon him. Such a man had to be circumspect in his attitude towards Christ. While he was undecided in his own mind, he dared not visit Christ openly. Such action might lead the populace astray. It was, from one point of view, an honorable caution that led him to come to Jesus by night.

(2) Then there was the additional fact that all his own associates—priests, scribes, rulers, Pharisees—had taken up an attitude of hostility. I am quite prepared to hear some one say that if Nicodemus felt that Jesus had come from God, he ought not to have given a second thought to the priests and rulers and Pharisees. He ought to have done the right thing, in scorn of consequences. I admit that is so. But at the same time let us do Nicodemus the bare justice of remembering that he had everything to lose by an open confession of his attachment to Jesus. The rulers were so embittered against Jesus they would have stuck at no half measures if Nicodemus had attached himself to Him. You remember what they agreed upon later—that if anyone dared to confess Jesus they would excommunicate him and cast him out of the synagogue. That is the kind of measure they would have meted out to Nicodemus. They would

have stripped him of his offices and honors, and the ruler of the Jews would have found himself a pariah.

Let us always remember this: the higher a man's social position is the harder it becomes to risk all for Christ. That is why Jesus said on the one hand: "How hardly shall they that have riches enter into the kingdom of God"; and on the other: "Blessed are ye poor, for yours is the kingdom of God." That is why, as a matter of fact and history, not many wise, not many mighty, not many noble were called; but God called the poor and the despised and the weak to be the first citizens of the kingdom. That is why to this day there are more of the poor than the rich in the membership of Christ's church. I confess I have it not in my heart to criticize Nicodemus's timidity. My feeling is rather of thankfulness that in my own discipleship I was not exposed to so fierce and searching a test. I do not know how I should have stood the test. I do not know whether I would have come to Christ at all. For this was what coming to Christ meant for Nicodemus—counting all things but loss. Peter, James, and John, we are told, at the call of Christ rose up, left all, and followed Him. Yes, but all they had to leave was their boats and their nets! Nicodemus had position and wealth and fame and power—all to leave! Let others denounce Nicodemus's timidity if they like. I see this white-haired old Jewish leader stealing out to Christ's humble lodging on that dark and windy night, and I am amazed at the devotion that made him go at all! But admitting that the stealthiness of his approach argues caution and timidity, I repeat once again that to lay the emphasis there is to misread Nicodemus's character entirely.

Nicodemus's Candor

Nicodemus's distinguishing and dominant characteristic is not his caution, but his candor. In all his class he was the one glorious exception. The rest of the rulers and Pharisees condemned Christ straight off. "Have any of the rulers or Pharisees believed on him?" they asked later, as if that fact triumphantly disposed of the claims of Christ. No, not one! They had never even taken the trouble to inquire into His claims. They knew He came from Nazareth, and that was enough for them. They dismissed Him and His mighty works with the comment that He had a devil. But Nicodemus was a glorious exception. He was a man of honest and candid mind. Before he formed a judgment, he insisted on examining the facts. That was the plea, you remember, that he advanced in the Sanhedrin when they wanted to seize Christ. "Doth our law judge a man," he asked, "except it first hear from himself, and know what he doeth?" That question exactly hits off Nicodemus's temper and mental attitude. He would neither approve nor condemn until he had first heard from the man himself. And that is exactly how he dealt with Jesus. He had been stirred, moved, arrested by what he had seen and heard of Jesus. Questions had been started by Him which he could not answer. And so, honest man that he was, he went straight to the fountainhead. He went and saw Jesus for himself, and listened to what He had to say.

To what in our own society shall we compare Nicodemus? Well, perhaps a university don, the master of one of our old colleges, is the modern representative of Nicodemus. Well, picture the old don going to sit at the feet of a new Teacher. He had the spirit of the true scholar—the open, guileless, receptive spirit. He had the passion for truth. No pride of place deterred him. He was resolved to know the truth, even though it hailed from Nazareth! So to the lodging of Jesus the old man went by night—You remember how Bunyan says that when they came to the Delectable Mountains, Christian and Hopeful met with four shepherds feeding their flocks. And the names of the shepherds were Knowledge, Experience, Watchful, and Sincere. Now Nicodemus was a shepherd of the people. He was a ruler of the Jews; he was a teacher of Israel. And he answers to the shepherd Sincere whom the pilgrims saw. There was no guile in Nicodemus, no hypocrisy, no prejudice. He was honest, transparent, true. What he wanted was the truth. He was freer from prejudice even than Nathanael was—although Jesus pronounced that disciple to be an Israelite indeed—for he never asked: "Can any good thing come out of Nazareth?" He went and saw Christ with his own eyes, and listened to Him with his own ears. He was like those noble Bereans of whom Luke writes: he examined for himself. He brought himself face-to-face with that Jesus whose deeds had so startled and staggered him. That is the Nicodemus I find in this narrative: the student eager to know, the honest seeker after truth, the man of honest and candid mind. The rest of the Pharisees went away and plotted how they might take Him by subtilty and kill Him; but Nicodemus, under shelter of the night, came and spoke with Jesus face-to-face.

And Nicodemus's candor won its great reward. That word

candor is a beautiful word. It means literally "brightness, burning whiteness." A candid mind means literally a white mind, a clean mind, a pure mind. Now candor is a condition of knowledge in every branch of learning. Prejudice is fatal to perception. If you want to understand history, for instance, you must come to it with an open mind and let it speak to you. If you come to it with a prejudiced mind, it will never reveal its truth to you. If you want to understand science and the laws of this great universe, you must come to its study with an honest mind. Nature never reveals her secrets to the man with a prejudice. And all this is tenfold more true when the knowledge you speak of is the knowledge of God! "Blessed are the pure in heart," said Jesus, "for they shall see God." The pure in heart—the people of the white, the candid mind—they are the people who see. Nicodemus had the candid mind—and he saw. This chapter does not say so, but from what I know of Nicodemus's subsequent history I am quite sure of this, that before the close of the great and moving conversation recorded in this chapter, he knew in his heart he had found in Jesus the Son of God, the King of Israel. To the candid mind the truth was revealed. The pure in heart saw God. And that is the reward that always comes to the candid mind, the clean and honest soul. It sees! It finds! It is satisfied! Do you remember the title of one of G. J. Romanes's early work— perhaps the work that made him most widely known? It was called *A Candid Examination of Theism.* In that book he pronounced against theism—he denied that there was a God at all. But it was a "candid" examination. And so G. J. Romanes did not end in the dreary regions of negation. To the upright there ariseth light in the darkness. The honest soul sooner or later arrives at the truth. The pure in heart shall see. And it was no wonder that Romanes, who wandered so far from faith in his early days, should, with his candid mind, end his career by reposing trustfully in the love and compassion of Christ.

And that, I believe, is the great reward that candor always earns. God never denies Himself to the honest seeker. There may be dreary tracts to traverse, steep paths to tread, dark ways to pass, but, if the honest heart is there, the day of discovery shall surely dawn. Every one that asketh receiveth, and he that seeketh findeth, and to him that knocketh it shall be opened—every one, that is, who has the pure heart, the candid mind! That is the indispensable condition. To no other search is discovery promised. Indeed, if you have not the pure heart and the honest mind, the search is a sham, a pretense, a make-believe. But, given the candid mind, there can be no failure. Soon we shall be crying exultingly, like the first disciples: "We have found Him of whom Moses in the law and the prophets did write." We have found Him for whom our souls hungered and thirsted, and in whom every aspiration finds satisfaction and content. "Ye shall seek Me and find Me, when ye shall search for Me with all your heart."

Nicodemus's Courage

Candor—that is Nicodemus's chief characteristic. That is the reason of this secret visit. Dr. Edersheim says that Nicodemus must have been tremendously in earnest to have paid the visit at all. He was like some of our modern martyrs of science: he was determined to have the truth at all costs. Or if you still think there was a touch of cowardice in the secrecy of the visit, if you will not allow Dr. Edersheim's contention that even in this secret visit he showed courage, Scripture makes it abundantly plain that Nicodemus gained in courage as the days passed by, and the man who began his Christian career by coming secretly to Jesus by night, before very long was owning his faith in and love for Jesus on that dark and dreadful day when the cross was erected and the Twelve forsook Him and fled. When the sun shines with the broad light of noon the stars are all invisible. They are clean dazzled out of sight. But when the night falls they emerge out of their hiding, and pierce the black sky with their points of light. And so exactly in the night of Christ's trial and death, quiet, unobtrusive, secret friends of Christ stole out into the open, and among these were Joseph of Arimathea, who provided Him a grave, and Nicodemus, who brought hundred pounds' weight of spices for the anointing of His body. I do not believe myself that Nicodemus ever was a coward; but if he was, he became a hero before the finish. In the day when all Jerusalem wreaked its wrath and hate and spite upon Jesus, this man stood forth and said: "I loved Him and I believed in Him."

And if you ask me how he got this magnificent courage, I reply, he got it from his Master. "When they perceived the boldness of Peter and John, they took knowledge of them that they had been with Jesus." The boldness! No one could be a coward in the company of Christ. He breathed boldness! He inspired bravery! No one dreamed of shrinking, "by this Captain led." And if Nicodemus

ever was a coward, he put on courage when he put on the name of
Christ. "How can a man be born when he is old?" he asked despair-
ingly of Christ. How can a man go back upon himself? Remake
himself? Make a fresh start? Nicodemus did not see how such a
miracle could ever be! But if he ever was a coward, then he himself
was an example of that miraculous transformation. He was an old
man when he came to Christ. But he was born again, though he was
old. He was delivered from all his cautions and timidities, and
enabled bravely to confess Christ in the day of Christ's rejection
and shame. And so it came to pass that Nicodemus, who at his first
visit came to Jesus by night, one glad day heard his name confessed
by Christ as a friend, a brave and loyal friend, before His Father and
before His angels.

I had meant to have noticed one other point; it must be mentioned in just a sentence. Nicodemus was a scholar. He was the
teacher of Israel. And so, when I see him seeking Jesus, I seem to
behold scholarship at the feet of Christ. I mentioned a moment ago
that it was the poor and the despised and the weak and the things
that are not who responded most readily to the call of Christ. And
yet I would not forget that the man of commanding intellect was
also to be found among Christ's disciples. It would be a real difficulty in the way of accepting Christianity, says Dr. Gwatkin, if it
did not attract the best men of every time. But it does! It had a Paul
and an Origen and an Athanasius and an Augustine, in the early
days; it has had a Newton and a Kepler and a Faraday and a Clerk-
Maxwell and a Tait and a Kelvin in these days of ours. The mightiest minds find in Christ their Master. And at the head of the
procession of the gifted and the learned who own Christ as Lord is
this great teacher of Israel who came to Jesus by night.

Our Lord satisfies the highest as well as the humblest. We are
sundered from one another by great chasms of difference. We are
rich and poor; we are gifted and commonplace; we are learned and
ignorant. But, whatever our condition, Christ is our sufficiency. He
meets every need. He satisfies every want. He answers every aspiration. He stoops to the lowest. He is mightier than the mightiest. If
only we come to Him, as Nicodemus came to Him, we shall be
constrained exultingly to say—

> Thou, O Christ, art all I want,
> More than all in Thee I find.

CHAPTER ELEVEN

Prejudice and Its Cure

And Nathanael said unto him, "Can any good thing come out of Nazareth?" Philip saith unto him, "Come and see."
—John 1:46

You remember the story. Philip had found the Messiah, or rather the Messiah had found Philip. And then Philip, with this new joy in his heart, had set off to find his friend Nathanael that he might communicate the good news to him. He burst upon him as he meditated beneath the fig tree, and without a word of introduction blurted out the glad tidings. "We have found Him, of whom Moses in the law, and the prophets, did write, Jesus of Nazareth, the son of Joseph." But instead of receiving the news with joy, Nathanael shrugged his shoulders and smiled incredulously at his friend. That word "Nazareth" staggered him. Nazareth! Who had ever heard of Nazareth, that poor despised village, being associated with the Messiah? Moses, in the law, and the prophets had written of the Messiah, but never once had the name of Nazareth been mentioned! Philip had evidently been deceived, and so Nathanael answered Philip's ecstatic outburst with the sad and incredulous question of my text: "Can any good thing come out of Nazareth?" And when I read that incredulous question of Nathanael's, I feel that had it not been for his open and candid mind, instead of being one of Christ's chosen twelve, he might very easily have become one of that blind and unbelieving crowd who hounded Christ to His doom and nailed Him to the tree.

Nathanael's Prejudice

For what lies aback of Nathanael's incredulous question? Nathanael's prejudices. Nathanael had his own preconceived notions of what the Messiah was to be like and where He was to hail from. He was a great student of Scripture, but He had studied it, shall I say, through the spectacles of the rabbis. Nathanael was looking for the Messiah; he was one of those who were "waiting and watching for the consolation of Israel"; but the Messiah he looked for was not the Suffering Servant of the fifty-third of Isaiah. He was not the Man of Sorrows and acquainted with grief, the root out of a dry ground who had no form nor comeliness: the Messiah Nathanael looked for was the Messiah the rabbis had taught him to expect—a great prince clothed in purple, surrounded with all the pomp and splendor of royalty. And so it came to pass that when Philip burst upon him with the announcement, "We have found Him, of whom Moses in the law, and the prophets, did write; Jesus of Nazareth, the son of Joseph," Nathanael's preconceived notions all rose up in arms, and prevented him from receiving and believing the message. "Can any good thing come out of Nazareth?" he exclaimed incredulously. And Nathanael all but missed his Savior that day through his obstinate and inveterate prejudice.

I could say a great deal, if there were need for it, about the mischievous and disastrous consequences of prejudice. If you will cast your eye back upon the history of the centuries you will find that the greatest obstacles in the way of human progress have arisen from the blind and ignorant prejudices of men. Look where you will, you can see prejudice busy at its unreasoning and wicked work. Take the realm of the mechanical arts. When Arkwright invented the spinning frame he had to flee for his life from the infuriated mob at Preston, who thought his invention would ruin their industry. He fled to Nottingham to experience the same stupid and unreasoning opposition, and to have his mills burned down to the ground. When George Stephenson talked about an engine which would run by steam more quickly than the lumbering old stage coaches, what storms of ridicule and scorn he had to face! It was in spite of a prejudiced and hostile people he invented his locomotive and began to build his railways.

Take the realm of pure science. When Galileo discovered that instead of the sun going round the earth, the earth went round the sun, a prejudiced church flung him into prison and tried to make him recant his own discovery. When Roger Bacon, our first great English philosopher, was busy making his discoveries in chemistry and physics, he was accused by the ignorant prejudice of the time of having dealings with the Devil and he languished for ten years in prison. When Darwin propounded his great theory of evolution, there are some of us who can remember how the whole ecclesiastical world was up in arms, and how every weapon of insult and of ridicule that ignorant prejudice could lay hands on was used against the great scientist and the theory he propounded.

Take the realm of theology. Prejudice has done its ignorant and mischievous work in the church. Think of the treatment meted out to the early Methodists in the eighteenth century. Think of the treatment accorded to the Salvationists in the nineteenth. And I do not know that I might not say the same thing of the heresy hunts that have taken place in well-nigh every communion, including the hunting of the critics which is the favorite occupation of some prejudiced folk to this very day. Yes, prejudice has much to answer for. Blinded by prejudice men have rejected the most splendid gifts; they have persecuted the prophets; they have slain their benefactors. But the most deadly work of prejudice is this: that through it men have rejected and repudiated the Christ. They have denied the Lord who bought them. They have said, "We will not have this Man to reign over us."

Prejudice and Christ

Recall your Gospel history! "He came unto His own," says John of Jesus, "and His own people received Him not." "How often," said Jesus Himself of the Jews, "would I have gathered your children together, as a hen doth gather her brood under her wing—and ye would not." Would not? Why not? Through prejudice. The Jews rejected their Savior because He differed so utterly from their conceptions of Him. They had never dreamed of a man whose dress was to be the seamless robe. They had never dreamed of a man who should issue from a carpenter's shop in Nazareth. They had never dreamed of a Messiah whose court should consist of twelve Galilean peasants. They had never dreamed of a Messiah who was to be the friend of publicans and sinners. They had never dreamed of a Messiah whose state and origin should be such! "Search and see," said the Pharisees, almost literally repeating this incredulous objection of Nathanael's, and evidently regarding it as a clinching and conclusive argument, "that out of Galilee ariseth no prophet." It was not because they had discovered any moral defect in Christ that they rejected Him. They had to confess they could find no fault in Him. They were offended in Him because He traversed and disappointed all their expectations. If you want to know to what lengths of wickedness prejudice can go, read the story of Jesus Christ. It was prejudice that rejected Him; it was prejudice that mocked Him; it was prejudice that spat upon Him; it was prejudice that cried, "Not this man, but Barabbas"; it was prejudice that nailed Him to the tree.

And does not prejudice lead men still to reject and repudiate the Christ? John Bunyan, with that rare and wonderful insight of his, has noted the terrible part prejudice plays in the spiritual history of men. In his great allegory, *The Holy War*—that allegory which, as Macaulay says, would be counted the finest allegory in the world if, out of his teeming brain and inspired imagination, he had not also written *The Pilgrim's Progress*—he pictures the soul as a walled city having five gates, Ear-gate, Eye-gate, Mouth-gate, Nose-gate and Feel-gate, representing, I need scarcely say, the five senses. When Prince Emmanuel's forces come to capture Mansoul they direct their attack first upon Ear-gate. But Diabolus, says Bunyan, had taken his precautions to meet it, for he had stationed "one old Mr. Prejudice, an angry and ill-conditioned fellow, and put under his power sixty men, called deaf men—men advantageous for that service, forasmuch as they mattered no words of the captains nor of the soldiers." Which, being translated into plain prose, means this— that men's ears are closed against Christ's appeals.

It was so eighteen hundred years ago in the case of the Jewish nation. "Ye would not come unto Me that ye might have life." Old Mr. Prejudice—that angry, ill-conditioned fellow—defended Ear-gate so well in those far-off days, that instead of receiving Christ and accepting His gifts, the Jews would have none of Him and brought Him to the Cross. And still old angry and ill-conditioned Mr. Prejudice is doing his terrible and deadly work. With his sixty deaf men he still guards Ear-gate against all the appeals and calls of Emmanuel. Why, I will venture to say that prejudice is at this very day keeping thousands and tens of thousands of people away from Christ. Trace their indifference to Christ, their repudiation of Christ back to its cause, and you will find old Mr. Prejudice at the bottom of it. The fault is not in Christ; it is in the preconceived notions and prejudices of the men and women themselves. For it is so easy to become prejudiced against Christ. False conceptions and presentations of the Christ are as current today as they were eighteen centuries ago.

(a) Some are prejudiced against Christ by what skeptics have written about Him. There are some, like John Stuart Mill, who have been brought up in unbelieving homes, who have been taught false ideas of Christ from their very infancy, and to whom Christ has never been shown except in caricature. There are many in our own day who gather their notions of Jesus from the articles in the *Clarion* and from other representations equally perverted and unfair.

(b) And there are some who are prejudiced against Christ by the dogmas under which theologians have often buried Him. Study the history of religious revolt, and you will find it is not against Jesus that men revolt; they revolt against the religious theories which men have made, and the doctrines which they have formulated. Men reject Christ only because they have been taught that Christianity is identical with this or the other ism.

(c) And once again, men are prejudiced against Christ because of the inconsistencies of Christian people. This is the most frequent and the most appalling cause of prejudice against Christ. Men judge Him by His followers. We have no right to complain of this. Every Christian is Christ's representative. He is supposed to reproduce Christ's spirit and temper and life. He is Christ's photograph to the world. Paul speaks about "commending ourselves to every man's conscience in the sight of God." We are so to live as that men will respect us and honor us, and from what they see in us learn to honor and revere our Master. But we can only do that, as the apostle says, "by the manifestation of the truth"; that is, by giving a true picture of the Christ. But how many of us are giving this true picture? Selfishness has no place in the true picture; pride has no place in the true picture; malice and envy have no place in the true picture; guile and greed have no place in the true picture. How many of us are giving to the world the true picture of Jesus? It is a terrible thing to say, but alas, it is a true thing—Christ suffers for your sins and mine. Men will have none of Him because of what they see in us. They see our selfishness, our pride, our envy, our malice, our greed, our guile, and they say, "That's your Christianity? we will have none of it." 1 am not exaggerating. If all who name the name of Christ only lived the life, I believe the indifference of men would soon be a thing of the past. I believe those who are now careless or even hostile would come crowding to us saying, "Verily God is in you, and there is none else, there is no God." But as it is they are not won; they are estranged, repelled. They are prejudiced against Christ because of our inconsistencies. They watch our lives, and then see no beauty in Christ that they should desire Him. Yes, it is that angry, ill-conditioned Mr. Prejudice who keeps the gates of the heart against Jesus. A caricature Christ keeps men from coming to the real Christ. It has been the case with men and women all down the centuries; it is the case with men and women still. And of all those who are prejudiced against Christ, who are hindered from accepting the gospel by false notions and preconceived ideas, this man Nathanael, with his question, "Can any good thing come out of Nazareth?" is a pattern and type.

The Cure for Prejudice

"Can any good thing come out of Nazareth?" said Nathanael incredulously. And what answer did Philip make to the question? This: "Come and see." Mr. Prejudice had spoken in Nathanael's question. Philip did not attempt to argue the matter out with him. He did not set himself to prove that Nazareth was not so insignificant and not so contemptible a place as it was made out to be. He did not begin to quote Scripture and prophecy to prove that it was right and fitting that the Messiah should hail from Galilee. To argue the matter out would have taken a long time, and at the end of it Nathanael might be of the same opinion still; for Mr. Prejudice, remember, is an angry and ill-conditioned person. Philip knew a quicker and better way than that of argument and proof. He appealed to experience: "Come and see," he said. The only effectual way of dispelling Nathanael's prejudice and convincing him that Jesus really was the Messiah was to bring him and Jesus face-to-face. "Come and see," said Philip. And to his everlasting credit Nathanael came and saw, and his prejudices all died when he came face-to-face with Christ, and soon he was at the Lord's feet saying, "Thou art the Son of God, thou art the King of Israel."

"Come and see," that is the best cure for prejudice. It is so in every department of life. It was actual experience of the spinning jenny that at last convinced the Lancashire folk of its utility. It was actual experience of the locomotive that dispelled silly prejudices and made men realize the superiority of the railway to the stage coach. It is actual face-to-face intercourse with men that dispels dislikes and suspicions and ignorant aversions. And in the same way it is the actual vision of Christ Himself that will scatter all prejudices against Him. Come and see—that is, as Godet says, "the simplest and profoundest apologetic."

When we meet with men who are prejudiced against Christ, what shall we do with them? Try and argue the matter out? Try to prove that they are mistaken? I show you a more excellent way. Say to them, Come and see. Men's prejudices against Christ all arise from their ignorance of Him. When men and Christ come face-to-face prejudices disappear. What are we to do with the people who reject Christ because they stumble at this dogma or the other? Are we to set about demonstrating that these dogmas must be true? Are we to send them to books that prove the doctrine of the Trinity, or establish some theory of the Atonement, or settle the question of the miraculous? No. I would say: "Leave the Trinity and the Atonement and Miracles alone for the present. Come and see!" What are we to do with men who have taken their notions of Christ from skeptical literature? Send them to other books written to refute such skepticism and prove the truth of the Christian religion? No! Tell them just to come face-to-face with Christ as He is presented to us in the gospel story. Come and see! Jesus Christ Himself is the final apologetic for Christianity. He is His own best defense. Many books have been written in defense of the Christian faith; learned scholars have elaborately demonstrated its reasonableness. I am grateful for their labors. But for my own part, if I had to deal with a person prejudiced against Christ, I would never put a volume of apologetics in his hands. I would bid him study the Christ at first hand; I would not send him to the Bridgewater Treatises or to the Present Day Tracts. I would say to him, Come and see.

Come and see—that is the appeal the preacher has to make. Do not look at Christ through the spectacles of Renan or of Blatchford or anybody else. And do not even take your views of Him from what you see in the men and women who bear His name. No! come and see Him directly, immediately, face-to-face. Come and see Him sitting on the hill with the crowds standing round, while He pours out words of wisdom such as the world had never heard before. Come and see Him passing from place to place in Galilee, casting out devils and healing their sick. Come and see Him, in his compassion, touch the leper. Come and see Him in the house of Jairus, and

in the home at Bethany. Come and see Him going to lodge with
Zacchaeus, sitting at meat with publicans and sinners, speaking His
words of redeeming hope to a fallen woman. Come and see Him
without leisure so much as to eat, in His desire to minister to others.
Come and see Him with the little children in His arms. Come and
see Him girded with the towel, washing His disciples' feet. Come
and see Him in the Garden, bearing other people's sins and sorrows; come and see Him mocked and buffeted in the judgment hall;
come and see Him meekly and yet triumphantly dying upon the
cross! Yes—come and see! Christ does not need that any one should
speak for Him. If men will only let Him, He will speak for Himself.
It is always some false Christ, some unreal Christ, men repudiate
and reject. When they come face-to-face with the real Christ all
prejudices disappear; aversion and indifference change to passionate love, and they are at His feet like Thomas, crying, "My Lord
and my God."

The Result of Vision

Look at what happened to Nathanael. He came and saw. And
what was the result? All his prejudices against a prophet hailing
from Nazareth vanished, and the noblest confession of all came
from his lips: "Rabbi," he cried, "Thou art the Son of God, Thou art
King of Israel." That is what always happens. I remember, when
attending the International Council meetings at Boston, hearing Dr.
Cave tell the following incident. He had been preaching one Sunday in one of our best-known churches, and, after the service was
over, a young fellow came in, thanked him for his sermon, and then
blurted out to him, "Christ is not to me what He is to you. I am
especially set against your miraculous view of Jesus." Dr. Cave did
not attempt to argue the matter with him, but answered, "Will you
oblige me by reading carefully, in private if you can, the Gospel
According to St. John?" "Certainly," the young fellow replied, "but
what about the miracle question?" "We will discuss that later on,"
said the doctor. A few weeks passed, and the young fellow called.
"I have done what you asked," he said, "and I have very much
enjoyed reading the gospel. Jesus was a remarkable man, but to my
mind the miraculous element spoils everything." Dr. Cave was disappointed, and all the response he could make was, "Now oblige
me, my friend, by reading that gospel once more." A few weeks
later the young man returned again, but there was a change this

time. His very step, said the doctor, was alert and his face brighter. "Well," said he, "things are different?" "Yes," answered the young fellow, "and I can scarcely say how; but as I read, a miracle happened to me, for I knew I was speaking to Christ and Christ was speaking to me. All my doubts and questionings fell away because of my new experience." You see what had happened. Prejudices, doubts, difficulties, they had all vanished when he came face-to-face with Christ.

And you have perhaps heard of this incident that happened in Hyde Park. An infidel lecturer, addressing a crowd of men, was drawing a coarse and hideous caricature for them of the character of Jesus, and the men, as they listened to him, began to laugh and jeer at the Christ of whom he spoke. And it happened that Frank Smith, then of the Salvation Army, was passing by, and his heart was hot at the dishonor done to his Lord; and when the lecturer had done, he appealed to the sense of fair play always to be found in an Englishman's breast, and asked the men to listen while he told them the other side. And then he began to show them the real Jesus—the Jesus who worked for years in a carpenter's shop; the Jesus who was the friend of the poor and the outcast and the downtrodden; the Jesus who loved little children; the Jesus who went about doing good; the Jesus who preached the infinite value of the one lost soul; the Jesus who in love for men died upon the cross; the Jesus who did no sin Himself, but for whom no one had sinned so deeply as to be beyond the reach of His hope and His love; the Jesus who had been the spring of all philanthropic, ameliorative, and redemptive movements all down the centuries; and as the men listened a great awe stole over them, heads were bared, and when Mr. Smith had finished, these men, who but a few minutes before had mocked and jeered, gave three cheers for Jesus Christ. It was a rough way of expressing admiration, perhaps. But think of it—a crowd of English workmen in Hyde Park giving three cheers for Jesus Christ. What did it all mean? Just this: they had come and seen, and prejudice had given place to admiration.

And that is always the result of the face-to-face vision of Christ. When men see Him through the medium of books or creeds, or the representation His followers give of Him, it is quite possible they may see no beauty in Him that they should desire Him; but when they come and see, they find Him to be the "fairest among ten thousand, and the altogether lovely." Only they must be willing to come and see. They must have Nathanael's open and candid mind and be willing to come face-to-face with Christ. There are some people who never give Christ a chance. They love their prejudices more than the truth. They read everything, they snatch at everything that confirms them in their preconceived notions. They will read Strauss and Renan and Blatchford, they will seize upon the inconsistencies of Christian people, but they will not come face-to-face with Christ in the Gospels. Such conduct is without excuse. Men who act so love darkness rather than light. Come and see! Have the honesty and candor at any rate to look Christ in the face. If you do so, I have no fear for the result. When a man comes and sees, Christ conquers. He may be prejudiced against Him today, but every prejudice will vanish in His presence, and the experience described in our hymn will be repeated—

> Lord, I was blind, I could not see
>   In Thy marred visage any grace,
> But now the beauty of Thy face
>   In radiant vision dawns on me.

CHAPTER TWELVE

Immanuel

And they shall call His name Immanuel; which is, being interpreted, God with us. —Matthew 1:23

Matthew, in my text, is quoting, as you are all aware, a great and famous passage from the prophet Isaiah. The commentators are by no means of one mind as to the interpretation of that passage, nor are they agreed as to the person to whom it refers. In less critical days than ours the passage was accepted as messianic. Our fathers found the Incarnation and the Virgin Birth both foretold in the passage. And that is the idea that simple, believing folk for the most part hold to this day. They believe that the prophet, by the Spirit, spoke directly and specifically of Mary and of Jesus. But modern scholarship now steps in and says that we have no right to interpret this passage as prophesying the Virgin Birth, for the simple reason that the word translated *Virgin* means nothing more than a "young woman," whether married or unmarried. And they go on further to say that the child Isaiah had in mind was no far-off child, but a child immediately to be born. Some obliterate every messianic reference by explaining that all Isaiah says is this, that a certain young wife would give her child about to be born this glorious name "Immanuel," in token of her faith that God was still with Israel. The majority, however, still hold that the word carries with it messianic expectations. What they say is that Isaiah expected the Messiah to appear in the person of the little son of one of the royal wives, whose birth was expected quite soon.

115

From the critical and historical point of view, I am quite willing to believe that this interpretation is the right one. It proves nothing, however, beyond this: that Isaiah spoke larger and better than he knew. The Old Testament writers are continually doing that. They are constantly indulging in glowing hopes about persons in their own day which those persons do not realize. The psalmist, for instance, sang a song about the marriage of Solomon in which he spoke of Solomon's world-wide and abiding dominion. Solomon did not fulfill the anticipations of that song. Without knowing it, the old singer had been indulging in hopes which only the greater than Solomon could fulfill. And in much the same way Isaiah indulged in soaring hopes about the young prince soon to be born—possibly Hezekiah—which, good king though he was, Hezekiah entirely failed to satisfy. "And they shall call his name Immanuel, God with us." The name was too big for Hezekiah. He did not answer to it. He did not fulfill it. As far as Hezekiah was concerned, the name was an unfulfilled prophecy.

But here comes in the remarkable fact, that though in its primary application the prophecy was falsified by the event, and Isaiah lived to see it falsified, he left the prophecy standing in the book of his prophecies. The meaning of which I take it is this, that though mistaken in his choice of person in whom the hope was to be fulfilled, the hope itself was no treacherous or delusive one. Some day, Isaiah knew, the great and glorious Person would appear in whom men would feel that God had in very truth come to dwell in the midst of them, and who would fittingly answer to this majestic name—Immanuel, God with us. So he left the prophecy standing, and it became the great and inspiring hope of Israel. Centuries passed, and one and another great man appeared, but none of them answered to the name. Josiah, Nehemiah, Judas Maccabaeus—the name was too big for them all. And then Jesus was born of the Virgin Mary, in Bethlehem of Judah, and Matthew, thinking of the life that had that humble and insignificant beginning, finds the great and glowing anticipation of the prophet at last fulfilled. There had appeared in the world at length one who answered to this majestic name—"Immanuel, which is, being interpreted, God with us."

Those of you who remember your Sir Thomas Malory's *King Arthur* will recollect the story he tells as to the way in which Arthur was discovered and declared king of Britain. When Utherpendragon died he left apparently no heir, for Arthur, his only son by Igraine, had been smuggled away by Merlin as soon as ever he was born, and had lived in obscurity ever since. The realm therefore fell into great confusion, many of the great barons coveting the crown for themselves. Then the archbishop of Canterbury, according to the old story, summoned all the barons and knights to London on Christmas Eve, and on Christmas Day held service for them in London's greatest church. When they emerged from church, they saw in the churchyard a great square stone—like to a marble stone, Malory says—and in the midst of this stone a steel anvil, and stuck into the steel anvil by its point a naked and gleaming sword. And written on the sword in letters of gold were these words: "Whoso pulleth out this sword out of this stone and anvil, the same is rightwise king born of England." So one after another of the great lords who coveted the kingdom addressed themselves to the task. They tugged and pulled and strained, but not one of them was able even to move the sword. And then came Arthur, the unknown son of a simple knight (as people thought him), and without effort or trouble pulled the sword out of its resting place. At Candlemas, at Easter, and at Pentecost the process was repeated. Barons and knights came from far and near to try their strength upon that sword; but none prevailed save Arthur, and he always pulled it out easily. And then the people recognized that in the man whose hand was mighty enough to draw Excalibur from its sheath and wield it with consummate ease the king of England had been found.

Well, if I may use that old story to illustrate my present theme, this great and majestic name became the test which was applied to every one among the Jews who excited any hopes that he might be the promised deliverer. Did he answer to this name? What Excalibur was to those old British barons, this name was to all the great men who appeared in Israel. Whoso answereth to this name, the same is the Son of God and King of Israel. And none answered to it until Jesus came. He was not at all the kind of Person men expected. They objected to Him, as those old British barons did to Arthur, that He was of humble birth and lowly parentage; they said that no good thing could come out of Nazareth. But, for all that, He and He alone answered to the name; He and He alone fulfilled the name. Hezekiah, Josiah, Nehemiah, Judas the Maccabean all fell short; but Jesus answered and fulfilled every expectation. The name fitted Him like a glove. So candid and open souls—like Nathanael and the writer of this gospel—greeted Him as the promised Savior, the King of Israel, because in Him was fulfilled that which was spoken by the prophet, saying: "Behold, the virgin shall be with child and shall bring forth a son, and they shall call His name Immanuel, which is, being interpreted, God with us." This great faith about Christ was born of their experience of Him. Just exactly as Arthur proved his prowess by easily drawing and wielding Excalibur, so Jesus made the men and women about Him feel He was Immanuel by the words He spoke and the deeds He did. He produced the sense of God within them; He did the works of God upon them. It was because they had found God in Him that they were sure and certain that Isaiah's great word found its fulfillment and satisfaction in Jesus.

Having said so much about the prophecy, I want now to concentrate your attention upon this glorious and majestic name which the evangelist here applies to Christ. He says that, if you would think of Him rightly, you must think of Him as "Immanuel, which is, being interpreted, God with us." The tendency in these days is to whittle away the uniqueness of Christ, and almost to deny the solitariness of His splendor. Men talk about Him as "the prophet from Nazareth, "the comrade Christ," "the Galilean enthusiast," the "friend and brother" of men. From one point of view, I have no quarrel with these terms. They are all true so far as they go. But they do not go far enough. He was a prophet—but He was also much more than a prophet. He was the comrade of men—but He was also much more than their comrade; He was their Master and Lord. He was an enthusiast; the zeal of God's house consumed Him—but He was much more than an enthusiast; He was the mighty quickener of earnestness and zeal. He was men's friend and brother—but He was also infinitely more; He was their King and their God. I hate even to come near the heated sphere of controversy, but this much I feel constrained to say: when we attempt to whittle away the uniqueness of Christ and to empty Him of His dignities, we are not getting "back to Christ"; we are getting away from Him. To those who stood nearest to Him He was no mere man. Spite of His humble home and His seamless dress, His glory flashed and blazed before their eyes. They heap up dignities and honors upon Him; they add title to title. And at the finish all the dignities and honors and titles they give Him leave His essential glory undescried. For this Jesus to them was more than man: He was God manifest in the flesh, Immanuel, God with us.

God in Human Life

Now let me ask what this name thus applied to Christ really means, what it involves and implies. If Jesus be really Immanuel,

God with us, what mighty truths does the fact proclaim? Well, first of all, this: that God has appeared in human life, that in Christ God became a man. Now I know that this at first sight seems a stupendous and incredible thing—that the infinite God should take flesh and subject Himself to the limitations of our human life. But, staggering and stupendous though the suggestion that God should become a man is, I am prepared to assert that second thoughts will show that an incarnation is not an incredible thing, but a supremely rational and natural thing. I cannot fully develop the argument. I can only suggest certain considerations to be pondered over at leisure.

I should argue for the naturalness and almost inevitability of the Incarnation on two grounds. I should argue it, first, from the *nature of God Himself*. If God is a Personal Being, it is natural that He should reveal Himself. As Dr. Illingworth says, "We cannot conceive a Person freely creating persons, except with a view to hold intercourse with them when created." I do not and cannot believe in a deaf and dumb God. I believe in a God who can and who will hold intercourse with the creatures He has made.

And I should argue it, in the second place, from the *nature of man*. The characteristic of man is this: he is *capax Dei*. He has a capacity for God. He is a moral and spiritual being. This at once makes incarnation possible and likely.

It makes it possible. The chief objection to the idea of incarnation proceeds on the assumption of the vast and infinite distance that separates God and man from one another. But while there is between God and man all the difference there is between the finite and the infinite, the whole history of mankind, as well as the unvarying testimony of the Bible itself, emphasizes the fact that God and man are essentially akin. How shall I express it? The kinship between God and man is deeper and more vital than the difference. God breathed into man the breath of life, and he became a living soul. In the image of God created He him. God is Spirit, and man is spirit too. It follows from all this that if God must reveal Himself, it is in and through man He must do it, for only in man can He do it adequately or fully. He can show His power in the material universe, His wisdom on the field of history; but to show His love, His self-sacrificing and redeeming love which is His essential nature, He had to reveal Himself in the person of man. Man's nature makes it possible for Him to do so.

And it makes incarnation not only possible, *it also makes it likely*. For human nature is not only capable of God, it is also eager and athirst for God. "Thou hast made us for Thyself," said Augustine, and the history of mankind bears testimony to the truth of his word. The soul of man cries out for God, the living God. It thirsts for God; it pants for God; it longs for God. By a kind of universal instinct, men everywhere seem to realize that in the knowledge of God standeth their eternal life. And so, wherever you see man, you see him groping after God, if haply he may feel after Him and find Him. Now I believe these instincts are prophetic of their own fulfillment. Yes, if you will have it so, I believe an instinct is an argument, and a desire is equal to a demonstration. God does not invest a man with useless powers. He does not mock him by planting within him instincts impossible of fulfillment. If He gives man an ear, it is because there is a world of sound to be heard; if He gives him an eye, it is because there is a universe to be seen; if He gives men this instinct for God, it is because there is a God to be seen and known. As a matter of fact, all through the world we find glimmerings and expectations of the Incarnation. The Christian faith is not the only one that speaks of God manifest in the flesh. Isaiah was not the only one who dreamed of Immanuel, God with us. The Greeks, for instance, have many a story to tell of the descent of the gods in the likeness of men, to dwell for a brief space with mortals. Like the instinct for God Himself, the instinct, shall I say, for a human God is well-nigh universal. All these pagan myths, all these pathetic stories of visitors from heaven, speak of the instinctive cravings of the human heart. I consider mankind, with its universal and pathetic desire for a human God, and, unless I am to sacrifice the character of God and conclude with Heine that He is a kind of Aristophanes making cruel sport of the creatures He has made, I must believe that an incarnation is not only possible, but likely and even inevitable. The whole world yearned for Bethlehem. It was not Isaiah's great prophecy only that was fulfilled, but the anticipation and passion and desire of a world were satisfied when, in Jesus, God became Immanuel, God with us. That is the first mighty truth this title proclaims—in Christ God Himself entered human life.

And the second truth this title proclaims, is indeed, a consequence and corollary of the first.

God Knowable
Because God in Christ has become Immanuel, God with us, He is now a God to be known. I need only say just a word about this,

because the truth is so perfectly obvious. This is not to say, of course, that men had no knowledge of God before Christ came. Men could not gaze at the works of God without being reminded of His power and Godhead. The world inevitably suggested the thought of a Creator. But you can never learn a person's character from the works of his hands. A watch may tell you that there must be a watchmaker, and that the watchmaker is possessed of great cleverness and skill, but the watch can give you no inkling of the nature of its master's temper and spirit. The fact is the real secrets of personality can never be disclosed by means of things.

Personality can only express itself through personality. God could never disclose His nature by means of the stars. He could never reveal His heart in storm and tempest. It was only in and through a person that God could reveal to men His real name and nature. You have only to read the Bible to discover how inadequate and how mistaken men's notions of God were before Christ came. You have only to think of foreign lands to know how inadequate and mistaken men's notions of God are to this day where Christ is not known. Apart from Christ, Huxley's word is quite true: the highest altar man can raise is to the unknown and the unknowable God. But, in Christ, God has made Himself known. The veil which lay over the face of all the peoples is taken away. "He that hath seen Me hath seen the Father." This is the true God and eternal life.

> For Mercy has a human heart,
>   Pity a human face,
> And Love the human form Divine,
>   And Peace the human dress.

"Immanuel, which is, being interpreted, God with us"—that means a God in human life, and therefore a God to be known. But God with us means more than God in our midst; it also means God on our side. As good old Matthew Henry puts it: "By the light of nature we see God as a God above us; by the light of the law we see Him as a God against us; but by the light of the gospel we see Him as Immanuel, God with us, in our own nature, and (which is more) in our interest." That is the great gospel which is proclaimed by this title, and which was exemplified in the Christ who bore it—God is not against us; He is for us, and with us, and on our side.

God as Redeemer

He is with us to redeem and save us. Let me call your attention to a suggestive little sequence of which my text forms part. A verse or two before my text Matthew tells the story of the angel's announcement of Christ's forthcoming birth. He told Joseph what the child's name was to be. "Thou shalt call His name Jesus," he said, "for it is He that shall save His people from their sins." And then the Evangelist goes on straightway to say that all this was the fulfillment of Isaiah's prophecy that a virgin should bear a son, whose name should be called Immanuel. That is to say, according to the Evangelist, the birth of a Savior was the coming of Immanuel. God became Immanuel, God with us, when He stooped to redeem and save. And that is what we see in Christ—the loving God, the seeking God, the redeeming God, the saving God. In the law, as Matthew Henry says, He is God against us; He is a God making demands, threatening us with penalties, filling us with fear. But in Christ He is a God proffering help, keeping mercy, rich in forgiving grace, filling our hearts with hope and peace. He is Immanuel, God with us. Have you ever thought of this, that God, in order to become a saving God, had to become God with us? He had to identify Himself with us. He had to share our lot. For sin cannot be blotted out with a stroke of the pen. Sin can be taken away only by being borne. Its pain and curse can be removed only by being endured. And that is why God in Christ took flesh. That is why He lived our life, and faced our temptations, and bore our sins, and carried our sorrows, and died our death.

He did it all that He might become a Redeemer. He qualified Himself to be a Savior by taking all the shame and pain of our sin upon His own head and heart. That was the supreme object of the Incarnation. The Incarnation was in the interests of Redemption. God in Christ has become God with us to rescue and redeem us.

God as Present Helper

He is with us, again, not simply to rescue us from our sins: He is with us as our Friend and Helper every day. You have noticed how men and women in the Gospel story grew strong and brave in the presence of Christ. The unstable Peter grew steadfast, the miserly Zaccheus grew generous, the defiled and polluted Mary grew holy when Christ was nigh. Somehow or other, He helped them to be their best. He came between them and their temptations. He was a shelter to them from the tempest. And Christ is still the same. In

Him, God is our Friend and Helper. We have our temptations and fierce trials still, but in Christ we overcome.

"God's in His heaven," says Browning; "all's right with the world." I have quoted that with approval many a time, and in the sense in which Browning meant it, it is a message of infinite cheer. But if you interpret it literally there is not much comfort in it. If God were only in His heaven, it would be a poor lookout for us. But God is not simply in some distant heaven. He is Immanuel, God with us. Here on earth we touch His hand, we see His face, we hear His voice. "Lo, I am with you alway, even unto the end of the world." And still, as we touch Him, we grow brave and strong and steadfast, and come off more than conquerors. You remember the old story that in the fiery furnace into which the three young men were cast there was seen to be One with them like unto the Son of God; and when they drew them up they found the flames had not kindled upon them, and they had come out of the fiery furnace unscathed? The old story is a parable of universal experience. In our fierce trials we too find we are not alone. We are cast into the furnace of affliction: we are called upon to face sorrow, loss, death. It would be more than we could bear if we were left to ourselves. But we are never alone in the furnace. We are able to triumph over our troubles, our afflictions, our temptations, yea, over death itself, because, in Christ, God has become Immanuel, God with us.

That is the gospel of the Incarnation. God is our Friend, our Helper, our Savior. He is not an awful Being to be feared; He is a Father to be loved. That is what it all means: God is a seeking, loving, redeeming God. He has boundless compassion; He is "full of grace and truth." God with us!—the news has transfigured the world. Fear and dread have gone, and hope and joy have taken their place with us. And yet, to know the fullness of the joy of the gospel of the Incarnation, we must individualize that announcement. He must be God with me. Can we say it? We may every one of us say it. For the High and Holy One who inhabiteth eternity is willing to dwell in the humble and contrite heart. Christ desires to make His home in the soul. All He waits for is to hear us say—

> O come to us,
> Abide with us,
> Our Lord Immanuel.

CHAPTER THIRTEEN

The Positivism of John

We know that whosoever is begotten of God sinneth
not . . . We know that we are of God, and the whole
world lieth in the evil one. . . We know that the Son of
God is come.   —1 John 5:18–20

John's object in writing this epistle has been to confirm and
strengthen faith. He is himself perfectly frank about it. All John's
writings were written with a definite purpose. "These things are
written," he says about his gospel, "that ye may believe that Jesus is
the Son of God, and that believing ye may have life in His name."
"These things have I written unto you," he says about this letter,
"that ye may know that ye have eternal life." The purpose of the
gospel and of the epistle is not exactly the same, and the difference
is accounted for by the difference in the people to whom gospel and
epistle were respectively addressed. The gospel was addressed to a
wider constituency than the epistle. The gospel was addressed, not
to Christians only, but to those who were not Christians as well, and
its object was to quicken faith. The epistle was addressed to those
who already believed on the name of the Son of God, and its object
was to strengthen faith and create assurance.

In this last paragraph John keeps that main purpose of his still in
view. To create the feeling of assurance in the hearts of his readers
he feels moved, before he lays his pen finally down, to remind them
of three great certainties which he shares in common with them,
and which, taken together, furnish a broad and stable foundation for

faith. He introduces each great positive with the phrase "We know." Here they are: "We know that whosoever is begotten of God sinneth not"; "We know that we are of God, and the whole world lieth in the evil one"; "We know that the Son of God is come." Or, as Dr. Findlay paraphrases them—treating them as if they were the apostle's personal creed—"I believe in holiness; I believe in regeneration; I believe in the mission of the Son of God." Only that word "I believe" is scarcely energetic enough. All this was not matter of speculation to the apostle. It was not a case of the balance of probability. He was quite certain of these things. They were facts in his own experience. He was quite certain that the Son of God had come—he himself had experienced His power. He was quite certain that men could be born again—he himself had passed through that mighty experience. He was quite certain that men could live the holy life—he himself and many more had been kept by the power of God unto salvation.

"We know," "we know," "we know." This is the positivism of the apostle John. What a brave, happy, confident note he strikes! And how welcome it falls upon the ear in these days of uncertainty and unrest! "Behold," says the poet, and he expresses the doubtful, hesitant, pessimistic spirit of the age, "we know not anything." But that is not John's note. There is something challenging to an age like ours in the calm, unhesitating way in which he reiterates his "We know" three times over. There may have been some things about which John would have confessed himself agnostic; but, on the other hand, there were some mighty things of which he was absolutely certain and sure. I repeat, absolutely certain and sure. Look at his language—it is almost provocative in its calm dogmatism. What he says is not We suppose, We think, We hope, We should like to believe; but We know, We know, We know. Here is, as Dr. Findlay says, "the genuine apostolic note, the ring of a clear and steady and serene conviction. John speaks as a man sure of his ground, who has set his foot upon the rock and feels it firm beneath his tread."

These three mighty assurances, you may say, constitute St. John's working creed. We are getting, I am thankful to think, beyond that stage when men scoffed at creeds and affected to think that it did not matter what a man believed or what he did not believe. Creed and life stand in the most vital relationship. To live to any purpose at all a man must have a certain amount of positive faith. The faith may be mean and squalid and base, but faith he must have if his life is to accomplish anything at all. His faith, his positives, his beliefs constitute the driving power of his life. No man can live on doubts and negations. The man who is sure of nothing will accomplish nothing. "He that doubteth is like the surge of the sea driven by the wind and tossed." He is the sport and plaything of circumstance— life for him is bound to be without meaning, purpose, or end. It is a man's positives that count, and if he has no positives he will count for nothing. This is true even of our secular lives; it is still more true of the moral life; it is most true of all of the Christian life. If a man is to live the Christian life, there must be certain things which are not mere guesswork to him, but of which he is quite sure,

Well, here are the great positives that sustained John in his life and service. These were the great truths he preached wherever he went. These were the great and mighty affirmations he proclaimed wherever he traveled. There might be many things hidden from him, there might be many things on which he felt constrained to keep an open mind, but he was quite sure of these three things. (1) He knew that, in Christ, God had come into living touch with men. (2) He knew that, through the power of God in Christ, men were reborn, remade, recreated. (3) He knew that, through the same Christ, the regenerate man was kept from falling and made pure and holy. These things John knew. They were not guesses, speculations, perhapses. They were facts of his own soul and his own experience. They were the justification of his faith; they formed the substance of his preaching; they supplied the impulse to his life. It was in virtue of these great positives that John became a Christian man and a Christian preacher.

Now, we live in a perplexed and troubled age. Doubt is in the air. It is not easy to believe. There are many things which our fathers firmly held which we find it difficult, if not impossible, to accept. The long and intricate creeds of fifty years ago impose too heavy a strain upon us today. Well, for our comfort let it be said, there is no need to burden our consciences and souls with a multitude of dogmas. To be a Christian, one need not sign any theory of inspiration, or give in his adhesion to any particular theory of the Atonement. Questions of biblical criticism and doctrinal statement do not touch Christian faith. Here is a brief and simple creed; but, brief and simple though it is, it is amply sufficient. And it has the advantage of being a believable creed. Modern developments have not touched it. Recent discoveries have in no way affected it. On these three great positives a man may build today a strong and vigorous Christian life. Amid all questionings and doubts he can hold on his way serene and untroubled if only he knows these three things: that in Christ the Son of God has come, that Christ can save, and that Christ can keep.

Let me speak briefly of each of these positives of the apostle John. You will notice the order in which he speaks of them. It is the order of experience and not of logic, of practice and not of theory, of life and not of science. John begins with the fact of human holiness and ends with the truth of the Incarnation. He begins with the result and ends with the cause. He starts at the river's mouth and traces it back to its source. He begins with the fruit and argues back to the tree. This is a type of argument that suits well the temper of our age. It is the scientific mode of argument. The scientist starts with his definite, concrete, verifiable facts, and then on the basis of his facts constructs his theory. John anticipates the scientist, begins with the facts of life and history and experience, and then ends with the tremendous truth which, in his belief, accounts for them all. Let us take, then, these great positives in the order in which John names them.

The Positive of Holiness

This, then, is the first. "We know that whosoever is begotten of God, sinneth not." Or, as Dr. Findlay paraphrases it—"I believe in holiness." The fact of Christian holiness—that was the first thing of which John was absolutely certain and sure. He states the fact in his own uncompromising way. A false literalism might easily make nonsense of the apostolic statement. If this is taken to mean that the Christian is absolutely free from sin, that he never does a wrong thing, the apostle is made to say something which is disproved by all the facts of human experience. There has never been any one in the world's history, save Jesus Himself, who did no sin. Men who have been really begotten of God fall into transgression and wrongdoing. Indeed, the holier the man, the more keenly sensible he is of his own sinfulness.

> They who fain would serve Thee best,
> Are conscious most of wrong within.

John recognizes all this himself. In the preceding paragraph he has been writing about the possibility of a "brother" sinning. He

knew sin could manifest itself in the regenerate. He knew that even
a Peter could fall. John nowhere asserts that perfect holiness has
ever been attained by any individual Christian. And yet, I think, he
would say that holiness is possible. At any rate, I am quite sure he
would repudiate, with all the vehemence of his nature, the doctrine—all too popular in our day—that sin is natural, necessary,
inevitable. Sin, according to the apostle's view, ought to have no
place in the Christian life. It is an alien thing, a forbidden thing.
And it is there only because we are imperfect Christians. If only our
union with God were vital and uninterrupted as that of Jesus was,
we should be entirely free from sin. Ideally, that is what a Christian
is—a man who abides in God, and who, therefore, never sins, but
always does the things that are pleasing in God's sight.

But although John would not say that any individual Christian
was perfectly holy, and though this sentence of his must not be
interpreted in that sense, he does say that on the broad scale he
knows holiness to be a fact. "We know that he who is begotten of
God," so the verse might be translated, "no longer lives in sin." Sin
is no longer his element. He is emancipated from its thralldom and
redeemed from its power. John knew that, although no man was
absolutely perfect, Christianity was creating the saint. The good
man was a blessed reality. This was not a matter of guess or supposition with him. It was a fact within his own experience. Paul records
how he had seen the adulterers and fornicators and revelers and
drunkards of Corinth gradually changed into holy men and women,
"washed, sanctified, justified" in the name of the Lord Jesus, and in
the Spirit of his God. And John had seen similar miracles of grace
in Ephesus. He had seen bad men made good and kept good by the
power of Christ.

And we today may be as certain as John was of the fact of
holiness. I know there are some cynical and base men who affect to
disbelieve in goodness. They bespatter even the best of men with
their slanders and insinuations. They tell you that all saints are
hypocrites, and all religion is cant. I agree with Dr. Findlay, that
there is none further from grace than such a man. A man has
touched bottom when he sits in the seat of the scornful. But the
scorner may scoff as he pleases, all history is against him; the
judgment of the world is against him. If there is one thing written
across the front of the history of the past nineteen centuries, it is
this: that holiness is a beautiful and solid fact, that Christ does

create the saint. So much is undeniable. To an extent with which no other religion can compare, Christianity breeds saints. And when I use that word, I do so not in the narrow and unwarranted Roman use. 1 use it in the New Testament sense. The saint is the consecrated man, the holy man, the good man, the man devoted to God. And holy men in this sense are to be found not in the cloister only, but in every walk of life. There have been great saints on the throne like Alfred and Louis; great saints in politics like Cromwell and Gladstone; great saints in business like Samuel Morley and Frank Crossley; great saints in hospital wards like Sister Dora and Florence Nightingale; great saints in the humblest walks of life like John Pounds and Billy Bray. Whatever else may be said about Christianity, this much, at any rate, can be truthfully said: it makes men good. It makes bad men good, and it keeps them good. It delivers them from the sins and passions that once held them captive. It delivers John Bunyan from the habit of profanity, so that from being a blasphemer he becomes a dreamer of holy dreams and a writer of holy books; it delivers the profligate Colonel Gardiner from the tyranny of lust, so that sensual desire has no place in his soul; it delivers J. B. Cough from the enslavement of strong drink, so that not only does he become a sober man, but the instrument also of turning many to righteousness. Take these men, and multitudes of others like them, and of the special sin that bound and shamed them the statement of my text becomes literally true: "We know that whosoever is begotten of God, sinneth not."

Christianity effects a permanent change. The bad man becomes good and keeps good. But the secret of the keeping is not in the man himself. Such an one would be the first to confess it. He keeps good only because he is kept. "He that was begotten of God [i. e. Christ] keepeth him, and the evil one toucheth him not." It is by the grace of Christ he is what he is. It is Christ who enables him to stand in the evil day, and, having done all, to stand. Christ is the secret of his steadfastness and the real source of his goodness. A bedridden old lady, who was being visited by Dr. Jowett, in the course of conversation expressed the hope that she might have grace to "hold on." "Nay," said Dr. Jowett, "it is not a case of your holding on, it is a case of Christ's holding on." That is the secret of security. Christ holds on. That is how bad men become good and keep good. Christ holds on, He strengthens them, He helps them, yea, He upholds them with the right hand of His righteousness. All this, I say, is blazoned in the very front of human history; it is verified by the testimony of innumerable lives. Here is something beyond cavil or dispute. Here is something about which we can say, not I think, or I hope, or I believe, but I know. Holiness is a fact. Christ creates the saint. "We know that whosoever is begotten of God sinneth not."

The Positive of Regeneration

And the second great positive of the apostle is this. "We know that we are of God, and the whole world lieth in the evil one." He knew that a great and mighty and radical transformation had taken place in himself and his brother Christians; that they had been translated from one kingdom into another, from the sphere of death into the sphere of life, so that while the world lay still within the power of the evil one, they were "of God"; they knew that the hand of God had been laid upon them, and that the life of God was pulsating within them. Dr. Findlay paraphrases this into "I believe in regeneration." Only, once again, "I believe" is scarcely emphatic enough to represent the apostle's meaning. He did not simply believe in it as a truth of argument, he knew it as a fact of experience.

What a mighty affirmation this is! If there is one thing that seems blankly impossible it is that men should make such a complete break with their own past selves that rebirth becomes the only word fit to describe the stupendous change. And the wonder of it has not lessened with the years. Our new sense of evolution, of the orderly development of things, of the tendency character shows to set and harden only makes the miracle more amazing still. Long ago men felt the difficulty of believing in regeneration. "Can the Ethiopian change his skin, or the leopard his spots?" asked Jeremiah in a fit of skepticism and despair; "then may ye also do good that are accustomed to do evil." The one seemed just as unlikely and impossible as the other. Nicodemus raised exactly the same difficulty. In reply to our Lord's word, "Except a man be born anew, he cannot see the kingdom of God," he raised his hands with an expression of despair, and said, "How can a man be born when he is old? Can he enter into his mother's womb a second time and be born?" How can a man turn his back upon himself, and become another and a different person, when habits are formed and character is hardened? I know that it sounds absurd! But the amazing thing is this, that this absurd and seemingly impossible thing has been done. It has been done in countless thousands of cases. You would have said it was impossible to get saints out of the adulterers, fornicators, and drunkards of Corinth. But it was done. You would have said it was impossible to get anything good out of Onesimus, the dishonest, runaway slave. But it was done. You would have said it was clean impossible to get a brave confessor and martyr out of a dissolute and flippant young courtier like Henry Barrowe. But it was done. There is a Congregational Chapel at Masbro, Rotherham, whose origin reads like a bit of religious romance. It owes its foundation to a man called John Thorp.

John Thorp was the leader in well-nigh every wickedness in Rotherham. When John Wesley came to preach Throp stirred up the mob to break up his services and assault the preacher. He turned the Methodist movement into ridicule. He made the gospel the subject of ribald jest in the taverns of the town. He would stand up in the bar parlors and preach in blasphemous imitation of Wesley for the amusement of his drunken companions. If any man's case seemed hopeless, John Thorp's was that case. He looked like a man of reprobate mind. But nothing in the way of regeneration is impossible to God. "The wind bloweth where it listeth," and the mighty Spirit of God fell on John Thorp while he was in the very act of mocking Wesley in a tavern parlor, with a mob of evil and obscene men applauding him. And out of that mocker and blasphemer God made a gospel preacher, and the influence of John Thorp, through the church which he founded, works mightily in Rotherham to this day. I am not now concerned to discuss the rationale of conversion. What I am concerned about is just the fact. And about the fact there can be neither hesitation nor dispute. Regeneration happens. Conversion is a solid reality. Men are made anew. Through the power of Christ life is revolutionized, an absolutely new direction is given to it; the change is so radical and profound that the men in whom it takes place are truly described as "new men in Christ Jesus." There may be many things in connection with the intellectual statement of the Christian faith which are perplexing and bewildering. But one thing, at any rate, we know, there is some wonderful power in this gospel of ours that is continually accomplishing the miracle of regenerating men. There is the evil world, and here are men who once belonged to it, and now we know they are of God.

The Positive of Christ's Divinity

And here is the apostle's third and last great positive. "We know that the Son of God is come." Or, as Dr. Findlay paraphrases it, "I believe in the mission of the Son of God." The third positive, it is quite obvious, does not belong to quite the same realm as the two others. The two previous ones move in the region of life; this one belongs to the region of dogma. I am inclined to think that this was the one theological belief that really mattered to the apostle. He returns to it again and again in the course of this epistle. The Christian religion seemed to him to stand or fall with belief that in Jesus the Son of God had come. But while this third great positive partakes of the nature of dogma, it was not by the path of reasoning and logic and argument that John had arrived at it—this mighty assurance of his was also born of experience. "We know that the Son of God is come," he says. We know it. How? Because Jesus was doing God's work in and upon John himself and a multitude of other men. Through Jesus, he and multitudes of others had come into touch with God, and they had gotten to understand God; they had come into fellowship and communion with God, and attained that knowledge which is eternal lives. They had touched God, and the poor, squalid, sinful lives they had previously lived had given place to the life eternal. Christ's divinity was not guesswork with the apostle—he knew it, for Christ had done God's work upon him.

"We know that the Son of God is come." Is come. Not, came, but, is come. The tense implies a permanent and abiding mission. The Son of God is still in the world. He is still busy with His blessed work. And because He is still busy in the world we may still know that the Son of God is come—that, in Jesus, God in very truth entered our world, for He is still doing God's work. He still brings God and man together. In Him men get to understand God. They see God in Him and they touch God in Him. And still He gives to men the eternal life. He transfigures men, recreates them, redeems them from lives which are nothing more than death into lives which are life indeed. Is not that God's work?

The world is poorer for the loss of Professor William James of Harvard, who died last year. Professor James will always be remembered as a great psychologist and the first great philosopher who took into serious consideration the phenomena of religion. But perhaps his greatest contribution to the thought of our age was his championship of what he called "pragmatism." By pragmatism he meant getting a grip on facts. He looked away from principles and theories to results and fruits and consequences. He tested a truth by the way it worked, and if a belief worked well, Professor James claimed that fact as reason for believing that the belief was true. And so he argued for God and immortality from the effects those beliefs produced. Now, I can quite believe that Professor James's philosophical position is easily open to attack. And yet there is a great deal in his contention. That a belief works well is not, perhaps, proof that it is true, but it is a mighty presumption in favor of its truth. After all, men do not gather grapes of thorns or figs of thistles, and a corrupt tree does not bring forth good fruit. Now, the apostle John was very much of a pragmatist. It was not on the lines of abstract reasoning that he had arrived at his belief that in Jesus the Son of God had come. He arrived at it through the facts and experiences of his own life. In Christ he knew God; through Christ he saw men regenerated; by the power of Christ he saw men kept. His assurance that Christ was the Son of God came to him as the result of what he himself had felt and seen and heard. He came to the faith through the facts. And the facts proved the faith. Here was a faith that worked, that proved itself by its results. "We know," says John, as he contemplated these results, "that the Son of God is come."

And we may argue still from the results to the faith. We may find difficulties with the metaphysical doctrine of Christ's divinity. But from metaphysics suppose we turn to the facts of life. I see Him leading men into the knowledge of God, substituting for superstition and fear, trust and filial love; I see Him recreating men, doing this seemingly impossible task, getting clean men out of unclean, strong men out of weak, saints out of sinners; I see Him keeping these changed men faithful and steadfast right through life. There may be a thousand difficulties to explain, but one thing I know—that is God's work. And when I see Jesus doing it, I, too, can say with John, "We know that the Son of God is come."

Here, then, are the apostle's three great positives. I repeat, they are simple, they are credible, and they are sufficient. Here is solid ground for faith. Here is impulse and motive to service. If we know these three things, there is enough in these three certainties to make life as essentially great and noble for us as it was with John. Do we know as much as this? Do we know that whosoever is begotten of God sinneth not? Are we sure of the fact of holiness? Do we know that there are certain men of whom it can be truly said that they are of God, though once they belonged to the evil world? Are we sure of the fact of conversion? Then I say we cannot seriously consider what is involved in these two facts—that Christ converts men and that Christ keeps them, without being constrained soon to say, "We know that the Son of God is come." And to know this is to know everything. "This is the true God and eternal life."

CHAPTER FOURTEEN

To See the End

*But Peter followed Him afar off, unto the court of the
high priest, and entered in, and sat with the officers, to
see the end.* —Matthew 26:58

Acts that to the eye seem sudden would often be found—if we knew everything—to have been long in secret preparation. Europe was startled not long ago by the announcement that in Turkey one of the wickedest and most reactionary of despotisms had been displaced by a constitutional government. The change was so sudden and unexpected that we rubbed our eyes when we saw the astonishing headlines in our newspapers. We could scarcely believe the evidence of our own senses. And yet though the Turkish Revolution startled all Europe by its suddenness, it really was not sudden at all. Behind the Revolution lay years of quiet and persistent propaganda by the Young Turks and the Reform Committees. The explosion that actually shatters the rock and hurls it from its place is the work of a moment; but underground and out of sight men have been for days, and perhaps for weeks, drilling and boring in preparation for it. These cataclysms and catastrophes that startle us by their seeming suddenness have oftentimes a history. If we could only trace their causes we should find they are not nearly so sudden as they seem. The conversion of Saul, for instance, was from one point of view amazingly sudden and unexpected—it was so startlingly sudden that the Christians could not persuade themselves it had actually taken place. But was it really as sudden as it looked? The vision

135

on the way to Damascus was the explosion that laid Saul's Pharisaism in ruins; but who can read the seventh of Romans, with its story of spiritual conflict, with its record of Saul's discovery of the inability of the Law to bring him the righteousness he craved for, without seeing that God had been for years laying the train—preparing Saul for the mighty change? It is very much like that with Peter's fall. From one point of view it is sudden, unexpected, startling. Peter was the last man we should have thought of as likely to betray or deny his Lord. He was in many ways the bravest of the Twelve; he was devotedly attached to Christ, and only a few hours before the denial he had declared himself ready to go with Him to prison and to death. And then in the high priest's hall, at the taunt of a serving maid, a hideous and ghastly collapse took place, and Peter cursed and swore he did not know his Lord. It looks as sudden and unexpected as the Messina earthquake. And yet, it was not so sudden as it seemed. Peter's fall had a history. Many things led up to it. The drilling and boring of Peter's constancy and courage had been going on out of sight for some time. Peter's self-confidence was preparing him for that fall. And his boastfulness was preparing him for that fall. And, above everything else, his neglect of prayer was preparing him for that fall. The ultimate causes of that fall run far back into Peter's life. But, if I want only to discover the immediate causes, I find enough in my verse to account for it all. My text sets forth a whole catalog of blunders which Peter committed, and these blunders led straight to his shameful downfall. Let me call your attention to the mistakes Peter committed as my text sets them forth.

The Line of Communication

I find Peter's first mistake suggested by the first phrase of my verse, "And Peter followed Him afar off." I do not want to be hard upon Peter. I believe it was affection for his Lord that made him follow in the wake of the procession that escorted Jesus to the judgment hall. Like the rest of the disciples, Peter, after that one use of the sword when he smote off Malchus's ear, had been seized with panic and had taken to his heels. "They all forsook Him and fled." All! and Peter and John among the rest. But with Peter and John the panic did not last very long. They recovered courage enough to make them wish to watch developments. And so Peter, instead of running away, began to follow the procession back to the city. I want to do every credit to Peter. Apparently he and John were the only two who had the courage to follow at all. The rest never turned back. It was *sauve qui peist* with them. But Peter followed! It speaks well for his affection and his love. But he "followed Him afar off," and that was his undoing. Peter, shall I say, allowed the lines of communication to be cut. Now, you all know that the efficiency of an army depends absolutely on keeping open the lines of communication with its base. If those lines get broken and the army at the front can receive no supplies either of food or ammunition, there is no prospect before it except either of starvation or surrender. Now, Peter had allowed himself to be cut off from his base of supply. That base was Jesus Christ. There was endless store of strength and power laid up for him in Jesus Christ. At Jesus Christ's side, in touch with Jesus Christ, Peter was brave enough for anything. "Even if I must die with Thee," he had said to Jesus, "yet will I not deny Thee." Granted, that there is a touch of boastfulness about it. Nevertheless, I believe Peter meant exactly what he said. And I believe more, I believe that at that moment Peter would cheerfully have faced death for his Lord. He was in closest touch with Him just then. But in the mean time he had allowed himself to be separated from his Lord. He followed Him afar off. And that put Peter at the mercy of his foes. Peter, plus his Lord, would have been more than a match for all his foes; but Peter, trusting his own unaided strength, went down before the taunt of a servant girl.

And that is the reason for many a defection and fall besides Peter's. Men follow afar off. They do not keep in touch with Christ. They neglect prayer. So long as we keep our hold of Christ no harm can befall us. "I think," said a poor woman, who was about to pass through a terrible operation, to Lady Augusta Stanley—"I think I could go through it if you would let me hold your hand." And so we can go through anything in the way of temptation and trial if we can feel the Christ's hand. For it is a mighty hand, and no one and nothing can pluck us from it. And we can not only face any temptation, but we can accomplish any task, if we keep in close touch with Christ. "I can do all things through Christ who strengtheneth me," said St. Paul. Yes, we are equal to any and every emergency so long as we keep in vital, loving touch with Christ. But if we get out of touch, if we only follow afar off, defeat and ruin are certain. "Such as trust their native strength shall melt away and droop and die." Here are two words which, for our warning, we would do well to lay to heart: "This kind can come forth by nothing save by prayer." "Apart from Me, ye can do nothing."

The Danger Zone

And the second mistake Peter committed was this—he went and deliberately thrust himself into the danger zone. He followed Jesus afar off until he reached the hall or court of the high priest's house. Very likely, as Dr. Morrison says, he "hung about" outside for a season, timidly looking in and wondering if in the dusk and the commotion he might venture in and skulk undetected in some crowd or corner. At length his curiosity and, let me add—to be quite fair to Peter—his affection, won the mastery, and he entered in and sat with the officers. That is to say, he went and sat with the very men who had seized Christ in the garden, and who would very likely be talking over the course of events even when Peter came and sat among them. Peter went and sat in the very midst of those people upon whom he had drawn sword only a short hour or so before. He thrust himself in the way of temptation. He deliberately put himself in the danger zone. And as a result he fell, badly, shamefully, tragically.

And with Peter as my text, I preach again this old lesson: Our safety against sin lies in being afraid of it. There is all the world of difference between foolhardiness and courage. The man who deliberately thrusts himself in the way of temptation, the man who—let us say—boasts that he means to be all his days a sober man, but who yet resorts night after night to the tavern or the drinking club; or the man who, professing to wish to grow up pure and honorable, frequents the company of the profligate and vicious; or the man who, professing to wish to grow up a Christian, makes friends of unbelievers and scoffers—such a man is not a hero, he is a fool. "Lead us not into temptation," our Lord taught us to pray. And the man who really knows himself will pray it constantly and pray it earnestly, for the man who knows himself knows his own weakness. It may be that in the providence of God the path of duty may lead us into the place of temptation. If it does, we may tread it bravely and unfalteringly, with the confidence that God will keep us from falling. If duty takes us into some Caesar's household, God will enable us to live the saintly life even there; if duty fixes our abode in some Pergamum where Satan's seat is, God will enable us to be His faithful witnesses even there. But if we deliberately thrust ourselves into some Pergamum with its fierce temptations, or into some Caesar's household with its polluted atmosphere, we cannot expect divine protection; indeed, by our willful intrusion into danger we in a fashion repudiate divine protection. And that means shame and sin. There is a story told of William of Orange that, as he was watching one of the many battles he fought against the French power, he suddenly found a wealthy London merchant by his side. "What are you doing here, sir?" said the king, "do you not know that you risk your life?" "I run no more risk than you, sire," replied the merchant. "True," answered the king, "but duty brings me here; duty does not bring you"; and the words were scarcely out of the king's mouth before a shot laid the foolhardy merchant dead at his feet. That, you may say, was only a tragic coincidence. But in the moral sphere presumption and penalty follow one another with the inevitability of a law. The man who thrusts himself into the midst of peril does so to his own inevitable loss and hurt. Peter, venturing among the officers, is a lost man. So, give the danger zone a wide berth. Your safety against sin lies in being shocked at it and afraid of it. "Enter not into the path of the wicked, and walk not in the way of evil men. Avoid it, pass not by it; turn from it and pass on." Lot cannot live in Sodom without catching the evil infection of the place. Jehoshaphat cannot make alliance with Ahab without sharing in Ahab's disasters. No man can court the company of the wicked without risking the doom of the wicked. So, keep away from the danger zone. Do not stand in the way of sinners. "The way of the wicked God turneth upside down."

The Weakness of Despair

And the third mistake Peter committed was this—he went into the high priest's palace "to see the end." That is to say, he went there in the spirit of despair. When Peter saw Jesus in the hands of His foes, he thought it was all over with Him and His cause. As far as Peter was concerned, when he saw his Lord marched off in the custody of the soldiers, there was an end to all his hopes of the kingdom. For he knew the high priests; he knew that now they had Jesus in their power they would be satisfied with nothing short of His death. And so all his dreams of crowns and thrones vanished, and his hope in Christ's messiahship perished. If he followed Jesus to the judgment hall it was only because, in spite of disappointment, his old affection still endured, and he wanted to see the end. All of which means that Peter had lost faith and hope, and it was as a hopeless and faithless man he entered the high priest's hall. And this, again, was one secret of his fall. Had Peter retained his faith in the Lord he might have weathered through the fierce temptation that overtook him there. But despair and denial are twin brothers. "We are saved by hope." But when there is no hope and no faith, there is nothing but failure before us. Peter was enfeebled by his own despair. What was the use of risking his life for a Jesus who had come to the end of His career? There was a finish to Him and to His cause—what profit was there in still sticking to Him? Had Peter kept his faith, he might also have kept his constancy and courage. But believing that the end had come, he cursed and swore that he did not know the man!

Despair and denial are still twin brothers. Faithlessness and failure always go hand in hand. No man will dare and suffer for a cause which he believes is a doomed and discredited cause. No man will fight for a Christianity which he regards as played out, or toil and suffer for a Christ who has had His day. A man's enthusiasm for a cause is always in exact proportion to his faith in it. It is a lesson we need to remember in these days. For voices are loudly telling us that while Christianity has served the world well in past centuries, perhaps we need a different kind of religion in these days of ours; and that while Christianity is all right for us here in the West, Buddhism and Confucianism suit them better in the East. Now, once such talk is listened to, then good-bye to earnestness and courage and zeal. Let men believe that possibly a better religion may arise than the Christian, and the world will never see another martyr. Let men believe that Buddhism and Confucianism are as good as Christianity, and the world will never see missionaries like John Williams and James Chalmers, willing to lay down their lives in the preaching of the gospel; or like Griffith John, willing, as he said, to labor for aeons and aeons if only he might save a soul. And perhaps that is one cause of our present-day weakness. We are paralyzed by our doubts and crippled by our fears. We are not quite sure of our Christ. We are not quite sure about our Christianity. We are not sure that Christianity is the absolute and final religion. We are not quite sure that Christ's is the only name. And so we risk nothing, venture nothing, dare nothing for our Lord and His cause. We are not sure that both may not be coming to an end. For our revival and prosperity is a quickening of faith that we want, an unwavering faith in

Christ, an unhesitating faith in our holy religion—that it is not a passing and transient thing, but the absolute, final, abiding religion. According to our faith it shall be unto us.

The End that Never Comes

Peter sat there to see the end. But the end he thought was at hand never came. He cursed and swore he knew not the Man. It did not seem to matter very much at the time, for the shameful death Jesus died seemed to put an end to all His pretensions and claims. When Peter saw Jesus on the cross, and then saw His body laid in the grave, he verily thought that was the last of Him. But it was not the last of Him! On the morning of the third day Peter knew he had denied and betrayed God's own Messiah, for He was declared to be "the Son of God with power by the resurrection from the dead."

And many a time since Peter's day men have sat down to see the end. But the end has always proved to be not an end but a new beginning. The history of Christianity is a rebuke to all faithlessness and fear. Every death of the faith is followed by a Resurrection. Every Good Friday is followed by an Easter Day. Let me remind you for your comfort and good hope, how again and again men have sat down to see the end, and instead of seeing the end they have seen an enlargement of influence and power.

When the chief priest and scribes saw Christ dead upon the cross, when they sealed the great stone that lay on the mouth of the sepulcher with the official seal, they flattered themselves that they had seen the end of Jesus. But in a few short weeks the apostles were boldly preaching that Jesus was alive, and that although they had crucified Him, God had declared Him to be both Lord and Christ.

When, a little later, they laid that strict injunction on the apostles not to teach or preach any more in the name of Jesus, they thought again that they had seen the end of Christianity; but a renewed zeal in preaching was the only result, and the next day the apostles were busy in the temple preaching "the words of this life."

When, some two centuries or more later, the great empire of Rome addressed itself to the last and most searching of all the persecutions, when the prisons were filled with Christian confessors, and the Christian buildings and the Christian Scriptures were ruthlessly burned, so confident were Diocletian and Galerius, the emperors, that they had seen the end of the Christian faith, that to their other titles they added this new one—they celebrated themselves as the emperors who had "destroyed the Christian superstition and restored the worship of the gods." But within eight years of that time the Cross was blazoned on the banners of the victorious Constantine, and a few years later Christianity was the accepted religion of the Roman Empire.

But even that mighty and overwhelming triumph did not persuade all men of the indestructibility of the Christian faith. Again and again, even in comparatively modern times, they have sat down confidently expecting to see the end. I think of the eighteenth century, for instance—the age when a bald and narrow Deism became the fashionable creed. In France, yonder, Voltaire was waging his relentless war against the church. "Crush the monster," was his reiterated appeal, and so confident was he of success that he prophesied the church's speedy overthrow. In England, according to Bishop Butler, things had got to such a pass that it was taken for granted that Christianity was not so much as a subject for inquiry, but was now at length discovered to be fictitious. "This was an agreed point among all people of discernment," says the bishop, "and nothing remained but to set it up as a principal subject of mirth and ridicule." The end seemed very near in those days. But within two years of the date when the bishop penned these words, John Wesley went into the little meetinghouse at Aldersgate Street, where he had his heart strangely warmed, and upon that began that mighty ministry which moved England from end to end, which regenerated thousands, and which made religion more of a reality in England than it had ever been before.

And many a time since then men have confidently predicted that the end was coming. They have positively assured us that the "dear Lord Jesus had had His day," and that Christianity was played out. But instead of the expected end there has been revival and triumph. This Christianity which is supposed to be played out makes its way from land to land, carrying life with it whithersoever it goes. This Jesus, who is supposed to have had His day, amazes the world by staggering and subduing evidences of His saving power. When men—some in sorrow, some in triumph—assemble for the funeral of the faith, instead of funeral they are confronted by a resurrection. The answer to our glooms and fears and despairs comes in the shape of mighty revivals like D. L. Moody's in the seventies; like Evan Roberts's in Wales half-a-dozen years ago; like Gypsy Smith's in America more recently still.

So let us take heart! Amid all setbacks and discouragements let us be of good cheer. Dull and dark days come to us in our Christian service. The days in which we are living would seem to be such. But they will pass as quickly as those days did when Christ lay in the grave and His cause seemed to have come to a final end. "Weeping may tarry for the night, but joy cometh in the morning." We may toil all night and catch nothing, but in the morning our Lord will reveal Himself to us on the shore, and success amazing, stupendous, overwhelming will crown our efforts.

Those who watch to see the end, in the sense of the final defeat of our Lord and the extinction of His holy religion, will wait in vain. But there is an end coming. Would you know what it is? Listen: "Then cometh the end when He shall deliver up the Kingdom to God, even the Father, when He shall have abolished all rule and authority and power. For He must reign till He hath put all His enemies under His feet." That is the end that will come to our Lord and His cause—full, complete and absolute triumph. So let us go on with our service and our labor in that faith! With the courage born of it! With the enthusiasm inspired by it! "Wherefore, my beloved brethren, be ye steadfast, unmovable, always abounding in the work of the Lord, forasmuch as ye know that your labor is not in vain in the Lord."

> Be strong!
> It matters not how deep entrenched the wrong,
> How hard the battle goes, the day how long,
> Faint not! fight on! Tomorrow comes the song.

CHAPTER FIFTEEN

A Study in Depression

And Elijah requested for himself that he might die, and
said, It is enough; now, O Lord, take away my life; for I
am not better than my fathers. —1 Kings 19:4

"Elijah," says the apostle James, "was a man of like passions with us"; or, as the *Twentieth Century Testament* more vividly expresses it, "Elijah was only a man like ourselves." Only a man like ourselves! It is a startling and rather staggering statement. For I imagine that what strikes most men in reading Elijah's story is the difference between him and ourselves. He was not the ordinary type of man at all. He was a man of volcanic force. He was a man of granite strength. He was a perfect Alp of a man. He was one of those men who emerge occasionally in the world's history, who lift themselves far above the common levels of humanity, and are made solitary and lonely by their very size. Only a man like ourselves!—that is almost the last remark in the world I should think of making on the man who on Carmel faced that mob of Baalitish priests and an apostate nation. Only a man like ourselves! That is almost the last remark in the world I should make about the man who, in virtue of some tremendous spiritual energy within, swept along like a whirlwind and outdistanced Ahab in his chariot in that wild race before the storm to Jezreel. Only a man like ourselves! That is almost the last remark in the world I should make about the man who confronted King Ahab at the entrance to Naboth's vineyard and pronounced doom upon him. This man, of courage so splendid, of strength so magnificent, is an extraordinary man; he is almost a superhuman man. He strides among ordinary men like Gulliver amidst the inhabitants of Lilliput. But there is one event in the prophet's life that justifies the apostle's comment. When I see Elijah on Carmel, or at the entrance to Naboth's vineyard, I feel him to be in a class entirely by himself, a gigantic and abnormal man. But when I see him under the juniper tree, I realize that, after all, he was—only a man like ourselves. For it is not the man of superhuman strength I see here. I see a man weak as water, tired, timid, discouraged, depressed, querulous, and fretful, whimpering out in his disappointment, "It is enough; now, O Lord, take away my life; for I am not better than my fathers." And when I see Elijah weak, depressed, fretful, I know, in spite of Carmel and Naboth's vineyard, he was, after all, only a man like ourselves.

Now at first, perhaps, this weakness strikes us as strange in a man of Elijah's build. On a sudden Mr. Valiant-for-Truth seems to have changed places with Mr. Fearing. But, as a matter of fact, these alternations are common enough in actual life. There are ups and downs in the spiritual experiences of men. There are times when men, usually timid, become suddenly brave; and there are times when men, usually brave, become suddenly timid. Mr. Fearing, for instance, so weak and timid at ordinary times, on one occasion, at any rate, showed himself as brave as Great-heart or Standfast or Valiant-for-Truth, or any one of the company. "When he got into Vanity Fair," says John Bunyan, "he wanted to fight all the men of the fair." Indeed, this chicken-hearted man, who could not face the perils of the way in his own strength, grew so hot against the fooleries of the fair, and became so aggressively bold, that he and Great-heart, his escort, were like both of them to be knocked on the head.

And if weak men sometimes suddenly become bold, bold and brave men sometimes suddenly become weak. Abraham was a bold and brave man. He ventured everything at the call of God. He went out not knowing whither he went. It was enough for him that he was under God's guidance and in God's care. But Abraham lost faith and heart and hope and everything in Egypt. Mr. Valiant-for-Truth had become Mr. Fearing.

Peter was a bold and brave man—the Great-heart of the Twelve. When he said to his Master: "I will go with Thee to prison or to death, but I will not deny Thee on any wise," he meant exactly what he said. He would cheerfully have faced death for the Lord that day. But Peter in the judgment hall was a panic-stricken liar and coward. His courage had all disappeared, and weakness and shameful fear had taken its place. Mr. Great-heart had become for the moment Mr. Fearing.

I suppose one of the strongest and bravest men who ever walked earth was Martin Luther. It needed a man of almost superhuman strength and courage to do the work he did. I think of him, for instance, riding to that congress in Worms in face of the warnings and appeals of his friends, saying with a kind of gay and reckless courage that he would go, though there were as many devils in Worms as there were tiles upon the rooftops, and he reminds me of the kind of courage this man Elijah showed when he faced the priests of Baal and an apostate people and a murderous king and queen on Carmel. But I follow Luther to the Wartburg, and in his friendly imprisonment there I find the erstwhile brave and fearless man full of nervousness and timidities, ringing his inkpot at imaginary devils, a prey to depression and weakness and fear. Mr. Great-heart, Mr. Valiant-for-Truth, had become Mr. Fearing.

And side by side with Martin Luther, as possessing that same kind of indomitable courage and strength, I might place John Knox, the Scottish Reformer. "He is not afraid," said some courtiers of him, as he came forth from one of his stormy interviews with Queen Mary. "Afraid?" said the Reformer, who overhead the remark, "I have looked in the faces of many angry men, and yet have not been frightened above measure." That, indeed, was the testimony borne to him by the regent Morton as they laid his body in the churchyard of St. Giles: "There lies he who never feared the face of man." And yet I read of a day when the heart of the intrepid John Knox gave way; when his courage gave place to despair, and he cried, "I cannot win Scotland, let me die." Mr. Valiant-for-Truth had become Mr. Fearing.

And a similar alternation of feeling took place in Elijah. He was Mr. Valiant-for-Truth on Mount Carmel, alone against the world. He is Mr. Fearing when we see him beneath the juniper tree, weak and discouraged, and praying that he might die. Alternations of feeling, therefore, such as we find here are by no means rare. Those who rise high often sink low. Strong, impulsive natures often fall into fits of depression. But these times of depression are usually explainable. They have their ascertainable causes. Elijah's depression and despair are explainable. There were certain reasons for the weakness which is recorded here. I want, if I can, to find out what those reasons were. I want for a few minutes to inquire into the causes of Elijah's depression. The study may not be without its profit to us, for depression is not an unheard-of thing in these days of ours. We, too, get discouraged and despondent, and, like Elijah, are tempted to say that our work is of no use and to abandon it in weariness and despair. Now it is possible that the discovery of the reasons of Elijah's depression may throw some light upon the causes of the depression and discouragement from which we often suffer; and to discover the causes of our malady is to be well on the way towards the discovery of the cure. Well, now, when I turn to the narrative, I find that one cause of Elijah's depression was his physical weariness.

Physical Weariness

He had had to betake himself to a hurried flight in order to escape the murderous wrath of the queen, who had vowed to kill him within twenty-four hours, as the priests of Baal had been slain on Carmel. He had fled first of all to Beersheba, and left his servant there, and then he had gone another day's journey into the wilderness. He was a worn-out, spirit-tired man when he flung himself down under the juniper tree. Now everybody knows that mind and body interact and affect one another in the most intimate and vital way. To have an absolutely sound and healthy mind you must have an absolutely sound and healthy body. It is the recognition of this fact that supplies the substratum of truth there is in Christian Science and faith healing. I have no doubt most of us could quote wonderful instances of the triumph of the spirit over the weakness of the flesh; but, speaking broadly, a man's spiritual condition is largely determined by the state of his physical health. There is no one here who does not know that when we are tired and spent, the very grasshopper becomes a burden. Difficulties and little inconveniences that would not worry us at all if we were fresh and strong become almost more than we can bear when we are weary and worn. There is no need for me to amplify. We know all this by experience. Our spiritual state is affected by our physical condition. Man is not spirit only, he is body also; and, as one of the old Puritans put it, "If you rumple the jerkin, you rumple the jerkin's lining." The penalty for an exhausted body is often a depressed and discouraged soul. It was so in Elijah's case. Physically wearied as he was, the difficulties of his work appeared more than he could bear, and so he fell an easy prey to spiritual depression. From all of which we may learn a simple, practical, but most salutary lesson. The care of the body—the righteous use of the body—is a religious duty. The observance of the laws of physical health is a Christian obligation. When you sin against the body, either by neglect or indulgence, you sin against the soul. For the body is not a tomb, it is a temple of the Holy Ghost.

Loneliness

But while Elijah's depression was in part due to his physical weariness, it was in far larger measure due to his sense of loneliness. There he was in the wilderness, absolutely and utterly alone. And not only physically alone, but spiritually alone also, for he imagined that out of all Israel he only remained true and faithful to Jehovah. Elijah had felt lifted up and elated on Carmel. For after the fire had come down from heaven and consumed his sacrifice, he had heard the people make their confession—"The Lord, He is the God"; "The Lord, He is the God." For the moment he had been a popular hero, and it was easy to be a prophet of the Lord when all the people were on his side. But the favor of the people had been a fickle and short-lived thing; and when Jezebel, the wicked queen, determined to take his life, there was not one out of all the multitude who had applauded him on Carmel to take his part, but Jezebel was able to hunt him as a partridge upon the mountains. And the loneliness of it all well-nigh overwhelmed Elijah's heart, and he cast himself down beneath the juniper tree and prayed the Lord to take away his life.

Loneliness always tends to discouragement and depression. "It is not good that the man should be alone," said the Lord God. And that is more than the justification of marriage. It is the justification of Christian fellowship. "It is not good that the man should be alone." The life of Christian service and discipleship is hard enough at all times. But it becomes ten times harder if you try to live it alone. There is not a young fellow who does not know how terribly hard it is to be true to Christ in the office or the shop when he himself is the only Christian in it. But the whole aspect of things is altered when there is another Christian in the same place of business to sympathize with him and to strengthen his hands in God. Disappointments, difficulties, opposition, mockery—they are not half so hard to bear when we have a friend near to cheer us.

But loneliness is weakening, depressing, heartbreaking. I do not say that there are not men who can pursue, without flinching or fainting, their solitary way. There have been those who have found all the world against them, as Athanasius did, and who yet have never faltered in their appointed task. Nevertheless, it remains true that we are all—even the strongest of us—all the better for sympathy and encouragement and the touch of kindly hands. Loneliness chills and depresses and weakens. One of the few hints of discouragement that we get in St. Paul's letters we find in his second letter to Timothy, where he writes: "Demas hath forsaken me, having loved this present world. Only Luke is with me." The loneliness of it all chilled Paul's soul.

And is it irreverent to say that our Lord dreaded loneliness, and craved for the encouragement of human companionship and sympathy? What is the meaning of His conduct in the garden but this? Why did He take Peter and James and John along with Him into the recesses of the garden, if it was not that He wanted the cheer of their presence? What does that gentle reproach with which He chided His sleeping disciples—"Could ye not watch with Me one hour?"—I say, what does that mean, save that the Lord craved sympathy, and the way was all the harder for Him because He was left to tread it alone?

Loneliness always tends to discouragement and depression. There are two defenses against it. This is the first—to remember God. "Ye shall leave me alone," said Jesus to His disciples, and it came literally true, for in the garden all forsook Him and fled. "And yet," He added, "I am not alone, for the Father is with Me," and in the strength of God He trod the sorrowful way to its bitter end; by the grace of God He tasted death for every man. "At my first defense," writes St. Paul, "no one took my part, but all forsook me." And yet, left alone as he was, Paul did not give way to panic or fear. Men left him, but, he adds, "the Lord stood by me and strengthened me." That is the most effective remedy for the depression that is born of loneliness—to remember God. After all, we are not alone if He is with us; after all, we cannot fail if He is with us. We shall be held up, for He is able to make us stand.

And the second remedy for the depression and discouragement that are born of loneliness is to cultivate the fellowship of the brethren. The Christian life is a social life. It needs fellowship for its vigor and health. I notice that when our Lord sent out His first apostles to preach, He sent them out two and two. Singly they would have been discouraged, and would have lost heart because of the difficulties of the service. But in fellowship they found the encouragement they needed. They went forth two and two, and each strengthened the other's hands in God.

I notice in John Bunyan's allegory that he does not make the pilgrims travel to the Celestial City alone. They have company on the way. Christian has Faithful for his companion on the first stage of the journey, and Hopeful for his companion in the later stages, while Christiana and her children make the journey in the midst of a great caravan of pilgrims. That is only John Bunyan's way of setting forth the advantages of fellowship. "As iron sharpeneth iron, so a man sharpeneth the countenance of his friend." Why, I wonder sometimes whether Christian would ever have got out of the dungeon of Giant Despair alive had it not been for Hopeful; and I wonder whether he would have crossed the river in safety had it not been for that same helpful friend. It was Hopeful who kept his head above water. It was Hopeful that cheered him with that word, "Be of good cheer, Jesus Christ maketh thee whole," which at last enabled Christian to take courage and win his way to the other side.

The cure for depression is fellowship. It is not good that a man should be alone. And I pass on to you the old advice: "Forsake not the assembling of yourselves together." Cultivate the fellowship. It is not a good sign that we are reducing the number of times we gather ourselves together with the people of God. Once-a-week Christians are not, as a rule the most hopeful and cheerful and robust. Cultivate the fellowship. It is a tonic for low spirits. I know that again and again when I have been a little discouraged and depressed, to meet at the Lord's Table with my fellow Christians, to gaze into their faces, to realize that they are all living the same life, pledged to the same Lord, engaged in the same service—the realization that I am not alone, but one of a great host, has knit thews and sinews of strength in my soul.

Failure

And yet another cause of Elijah's depression was his sense of failure. Elijah had had one great object in life, and that was the winning of Israel back from the vile worship of Baal to the worship of the one true God. It looked at Carmel as if his work was to be crowned with success. But any emotions created there were as fleeting as the early cloud or the morning dew. As soon as the excitement was over, Israel fell back into the old ways. All Elijah's work seemed to have gone for nothing. Utter and irretrievable failure seemed to dog his steps. He felt he had accomplished nothing. All his labors had been in vain. And the sense of his failure well-nigh broke his heart. "It is enough," he cried; "Lord, take away my life."

And failure, or apparent failure, is still a frequent cause of despondency and depression. We start with great ambitions and vast plans, but we find the world is too strong and stubborn for us; and gradually the realization that we have failed comes home to us, and with the realization of the failure comes depression and despondency. You remember, perhaps, how the poet describes the disenchanted king—

> He walked with dreams and darkness, and he found
>   A doom that ever poised itself to fall,
> An ever-moaning battle in the mist,
>   Death in all life and lying in all love.

And the reason for our depression is the apparent failure of our manifold efforts. Our churches have for successive years reported decreases in membership. They are staggering and sobering statistics. And they only reveal a state of things many of us were quite conscious of even before they were published. And that is what they seem to spell—failure. And many, in face of them, are sadly and sorely discouraged, and are almost tempted to give up the work. Now, I do not want to minimize the significance of statistics like these, and I do not want to encourage a delusive and unwarranted cheerfulness. But there are two things I would have us ever bear in mind in these dark and troublous days. This is the first: If it is failure, it is high failure. And high failure is infinitely better than low success. The work is worth the doing if we see no results of it. "I am sure I shall like his way of fighting and being beaten," writes Burne-Jones of a politician still happily left to us; "he would not discourage me a bit—what discourages is a shabby victory." And we may take that encouragement to our hearts—fighting even a losing fight in certain causes is better than winning a shabby victory in others.

And the second thing is this: After all, the failure is only apparent. Elijah discovered, to his amazement, there were seven thousand in Israel who had not bowed the knee to Baal. And so, too, our Lord's work may be making progress of which we do not dream.

church statistics do not tell the whole tale of the progress of our Lord's kingdom. I do not, of course, minimize their importance; but I repeat they do not tell the whole tale. Christ has followers of whom the churches take no account. His influence is spreading in ways that cannot be tabulated or expressed in denominational year books. By all means let us examine ourselves to see wherein we have fallen short of our duty. By all means let us humble ourselves for our neglects and failures. But let us beware of supposing that the cause is lost or that Christ has failed. Momentary setbacks and reactions there may be, but Christ cannot fail. It may be, indeed, that the years which record such grave and startling loss, if we knew everything, would prove to be years of great gain. For in various directions I can see the influence of Christ spreading. In various directions I can see signs of a turning to the Lord. In the growing belief of scientists in the reality of the spiritual; in the evidence we see on all hands of the hunger of the soul for the Infinite; in the ever-growing homage to Christ and the appeal to Him as Master of Conduct and Lord of Society, I see signs of promise and hope. Take the wider view and you will gain courage, for Christ has not failed.

> Say not, the struggle naught availeth,
> The labor and the wounds are vain,
> The enemy faints not nor faileth,
> And as things have been, things remain.
> If hopes are dupes, fears may be liars;
> It may be, in yon smoke concealed,
> Your comrades chase e'en now the fliers,
> And, but for you, possess the field.
> For while the tired waves, vainly breaking,
> Seem here no painful inch to gain,
> Far back, through creeks and inlets making
> Comes silent, flooding in, the main.

CHAPTER SIXTEEN

The Whitening Harvest

*Say not ye, There are yet four months and then cometh
the harvest. . . . Lift up your eyes, and look on the fields,
that they are white already unto harvest.* —John 4:35

And unless I am sadly and utterly mistaken, our Lord uttered
these words with overflowing emotion and exaltation of spirit. And
what was it that stirred Him to this unwonted emotion? He saw in
the distance a procession of the inhabitants of Sychar eagerly making their way across the plain to Him, led by the woman with whom
He had spoken by the well. And the sight moved Him to something
like rapture, as did the request of the Greeks to see Him on a
subsequent occasion. It was a prophecy of the rich fruitage that
would yet result from His travail and sorrow.

The disciples had, apparently, been discussing the harvest prospects. The green blade had just begun to appear in the fields. In four
months, they had been saying, the whole plain would be a golden sea
of waving corn. But while they were thinking of crops, their Lord
was thinking of men. While they were thinking of the harvest of
grain, Jesus was thinking of the harvest of souls. There were four
weary months to wait for the one; the other was ready even now to
their hands. "Lift up your eyes and look on the fields," our Lord
said—and He pointed to the crowd of villagers who were eagerly
hastening towards them,—"that they are white already unto harvest."

Now, as I have suggested, I believe that the harvest the disciples
had been talking about was the corn harvest. That was the harvest

of which there were as yet but scanty signs, and for which the
farmers would have to wait four long and tiresome months. But I
am also persuaded that the antithesis in my text between the "four
months" of the disciples and the "white already" of Jesus, is meant
by Him to represent the difference between the disciples' ideas of
the possibilities of Samaria and His own. Where the disciples saw
scarcely a promise of harvest, the Lord saw fields already white.

The Harvest in Unlikely Places

Take this very case of Sychar. What did the disciples see in
Sychar, and indeed in Samaria in general? Barren soil! They did not
look for any recruits for the kingdom in Samaria. All they wished
was to pass through it as quickly as possible. They never imagined
that Jesus would think it worthwhile to stop and preach in Samaria.
Samaria, as the disciples thought of it, was hard ground, barren soil,
from which no harvest could be gathered except by infinite toil and
after long and weary waiting. And what did Jesus see in this same
Samaria? Fields white already unto harvest. And this is not an
isolated instance. It is characteristic of Christ. In the most unlikely
and, humanly speaking, impossible places He saw the promise of
fruitage and harvest.

In ancient prophecy, you remember, it had been foretold that with
the coming of Messiah the most unexpected places would become
teeming and fruitful. Let me just quote two illustrations: "I will open
rivers," says Isaiah, "on the bare heights; I will make the wilderness a
pool of water; I will plant in the wilderness the cedar, the acacia tree,
and the myrtle and the oil tree. I will set in the desert the fir tree and
the pine and the box tree together." What a marvelous transformation
all that represents! I have read in some of the newspapers that there is
a scheme on foot for afforesting the Black Country. The Black Country, with its smoke and grime and heaps of unsightly refuse! There
are some people sanguine enough to hope that they may clothe the
Black Country with some of the leafy beauty of our own New Forest.
And that is, according to the prophet, the prospect that the Messiah
beholds in the moral sphere. He sees the cedar and the myrtle growing in the wilderness; He sees the fir tree and the pine flourishing in
the desert. He sees all the potency and promise of the beauty of a
New Forest in the Black Country of a man's soul.

"There shall be abundance of corn in the earth," says one of the
psalmists, "upon the top of the mountains." Abundance of corn on

the top of the mountains! What an unlikely place! The top of the mountain is usually a bleak and sterile place. The top of Cader Idris, or the top of Snowdon—that is the last place in the world where we would look for a harvest. The air is too biting cold; the soil is too hard and rocky for grain to spring up and grow. But when Messiah comes harvests shall be gathered from places as unlikely and impossible as a mountain summit. "There shall be abundance of corn in the earth on the top of the mountains."

And the anticipations of prophets and psalmists were more than fulfilled when Jesus came. He saw harvests where no one else saw anything but barren soils. He saw the abundance of corn on the tops of the mountains. He saw the fir tree, and the oil tree, and the box tree, and the pine, growing in what to every other eye was a desert waste. "Why eateth your Master with publicans and sinners?" the Pharisees asked His disciples one day. "Why does your Master company with them? Why does He waste time upon them? They are barren soil. This people, that knoweth not the law, is accursed." But where the Pharisees saw only an accursed people, Jesus saw "stormers who were taking the kingdom of God by force"; and where they only saw barren soil, He saw fields already white unto harvest; and Matthew and Zaccheus are, shall I say, two of the sheaves He gathered from that seemingly sterile and hopeless field.

"This man if he were a prophet," said Simon, in pious horror, "would have perceived who and what manner of woman this is which toucheth Him, that she is a sinner." Sinner—that was what Simon saw in the sobbing woman—a woman whose very touch was defilement, a moral derelict, an irrecoverable, barren soil. But where the Pharisee only saw the sinner—the hard and barren soil— Jesus saw the field white already unto harvest. "Her sins, which are many, are forgiven, for she loved much!"

And so it was with the Samaritan woman in this story. "The disciples," I read, "marveled that He talked with a woman"—and a Samaritan woman at that! They never imagined that any good could come out of it. I question very much whether they thought such a person could be saved at all! But Jesus knew what He was about. He saw in this sinful woman—miserable and unhappy in her sin—a field white already unto the harvest.

I say this is characteristic of our Lord. He is always seeing leafage and fruitage where others see only the wilderness; He is always seeing harvests where other people see only sterile ground.

He sees seven thousand who have not bowed the knee to Baal when Elijah fancies he is the only worshipper of Jehovah left in the land. He sees much people in the city of Corinth when Paul is moaning over the seeming failure of his efforts.

Now, I want to know whether this may not be so at the very present moment? We are living in anxious and troubled times. It has been often said of late that these are bad times for religion. I wonder what Jesus thinks of these times of ours and this land of ours. It may be that while we are moaning and complaining over the sterility of the soil and the poor promise of fruit, He sees fields white already unto harvest. And that is what I want to do in this sermon. I want to speak about some of the tokens of harvest, some of the signs of the times that are full of encouragement for the future of religion. I want to speak, if I can, a heartening and cheering word. For a disheartened and discouraged church is always a weak and ineffective church. And there is a good deal of depression and almost despair abroad among Christian people just now. They keep on doggedly with the work, but there is no dash or enthusiasm about it. They work oftentimes like men who have lost heart and hope, and that very loss of heart and hope dooms them to impotence.

Discouraging Signs

Now, I do not deny that there are many things in the present religious condition of our land to depress and discourage us. Take, to begin with, the vast and appalling spread of religious indifference. I suppose there never was a more general disregard and neglect of religion among our people than there is today. The vast masses of our people are outside the churches altogether. Organized religion seems to have little or no hold upon them. We sometimes congratulate ourselves that the old aggressive, blatant atheism that used to trumpet itself forth from various halls of science up and down our land is dead and gone. So to a large extent it is. But I am not sure that the inert and stolid indifferentism that has taken its place is not more heartbreaking than the old vehement and almost blasphemous antagonism. The present generation does not seem to possess conviction enough to believe or to disbelieve. It simply does not care. It neglects religion altogether. It treats it as a thing of no importance. And this indifferentism is not confined to any one class. We speak of the lapsed masses, as if the religious problem lay mainly at the lower end of the social scale. Alas, it is only too true that, somehow or other, the church has lost its hold on the toiling millions of our land. They turn to the Labor Club and the Socialist meeting rather than to the Christian church. But the classes are lapsed just as much as the masses. Indeed the lapsed classes are a bigger and harder problem than the lapsed masses. For if the masses have left the church, it has only been to betake themselves to something that seems to hold out to them a better gospel. There is aspiration and moral passion and lofty idealism still to be found among the masses, although they may never darken a church or chapel door. But the lapsed classes have not only lapsed from religion, they have lapsed from all idealism. They have given themselves up to luxury and pleasure; to Sundays spent in motoring and bridge playing. And there is nothing in the world like luxury and pleasure for stifling and destroying the soul. That, then, is one of the depressing facts we have to face—the bulk of our people pay no heed to religion at all.

And then a second cause of anxiety and foreboding is the unrest and unsettlement within the churches themselves. Indeed, I do not think I am going beyond the facts when I say that many good Christian people are far more troubled about the "new theology" than they are about the prevailing indifferentism. They worry themselves more about the vagaries of heterodoxy than they do about the fact that there are at their very doors scores of people who have no theology, either new or old, no religion of any kind at all. So that altogether, what between theological unrest and popular indifferentism, we do seem to be living in a bad time for religion.

But that, after all, is only one side of the picture. There is another side to it—a bright and hopeful side, and we must see that bright and hopeful side if we are to work with any enthusiasm and zeal. The criticism I should pass upon the churches at large is this: that they have allowed the dark and discouraging signs to practically engross their attention to the exclusion of every bright and hopeful sign, with the result that the hands hang down and the knees are feeble, and a desponding, pessimistic spirit is abroad. What we need is to see the bright as well as the dark, the cheering as well as the depressing. I do not wish to live in a world of make-believe, I do not want to work up a sham cheerfulness by ignoring or minimizing the hard and unpleasant facts, but what I do want is that we should note the encouraging signs that surround us on every hand. For, while perhaps we are moaning and complaining over the slow progress of the work and the poor prospects of it, our Lord is saying to us, as He said to these disciples of His, "Lift up your eyes and look on the fields, that they are white already unto harvest." Now let me mention some of the signs of the times which are full of encouragement to all Christ's people, and which tell them there is a great spiritual harvest on the point of being ingathered.

Encouraging Signs

First of all I will mention the practical abandonment of scientific materialism as a theory of the universe and of life. It is only about thirty years ago since Professor Tyndall, in his address at Belfast to the British Association, resolved everything into matter. He did not except even life itself. "I discern in matter," he said, "the promise and potency of all terrestrial life." For a time "materialism" held the field. Mr. Froude could even say that scientific men had gone over in a body to the "materialistic" camp. They left no room for spirit anywhere, and the majority of them left no room for God.

But that was thirty years ago. Things have changed much and moved far since then. Science itself has found the materialistic theory untenable and has abandoned it. Professor Tyndall reduced everything to matter. Sir William Crookes, a recent president of the British Association, took exactly the opposite view and found everything shading off into the spiritual. Science in our day is coming round to the religious view of the world. In America, Professor William James made it his business to insist upon the reality of religious phenomena; here, at home, Sir Oliver Lodge—on the whole our most influential scientist—is emphasizing the spiritual interpretation of the universe, and bidding us believe with a simpler faith in God and the efficacy of prayer. In a word, science has ceased to be the antagonist of religion, and is becoming its ally and friend. And surely it is an encouraging sign that scientists in our day should be preparing the way of the Lord.

And the second encouraging sign that I will mention is the obvious unrest and discontent of men and women as reflected, let us say, in the pages of our literature. I have said that the great majority of our people are outside all the churches, and apparently indifferent to religion altogether. Now, if it could be said that the people were quite content and happy in their indifferentism, I confess the prospect for religion would seem but poor. But the striking and unmistakable fact is that they are not happy and content in it. You cannot take up the literature of the day without seeing on all hands evidence of human restlessness and woe. Take Thomas Hardy's novels, for instance. What grimly powerful books they are! Yes, and what unhappy books they are. It needs no stretch of imagination to hear the sob and cry of a burdened and unhappy humanity go sounding through their pages. Contentment? There is contentment nowhere. It is true that it looks as if the people had forsaken God, the fountain of living waters, but they are bitterly conscious that the cisterns they have hewn for themselves are broken cisterns which can hold no water. It is quite true that the people, like the prodigal son in the parable, have turned their backs on the Father's house; but it is also true that they have, like the prodigal, found the far country a hard place to live in, and, like him, they are in want, sick, and faint, and ready to die. And this consciousness of need, this sense of discontent, is a sign full of encouragement. The only people I despair of are the people who say they are rich and increased with goods and in need of nothing. But there is hope for people who realize that they want something, who know they are wretched, miserable, poor, unhappy. To all such Christ's call will come as a veritable gospel—"Come unto Me, all ye that labor and are heavy laden, and I will give you rest." This disillusioned and unhappy age may be driven by its very disillusionment and unhappiness to take refuge in Christ, saying—

> Thou, O Christ, art all I want,
> More than all in Thee I find.

And the third encouraging sign that I see is this—that wherever I look I see a hunger and a hankering after the spiritual. It is not simply a case of discontent and unhappiness in the mere worldly life, but I see everywhere positive signs of a hunger after spiritual things. I see these signs even in movements that we sometimes reckon hostile and menacing. Two movements that have attracted no little notice during recent years have been the Theosophical and the Christian Science movements. Now, I grant at once that these are not Christian movements. In some respects they are anti-Christian. But we are simply purblind if we do not recognize this—that both Theosophy and Christian Science are a testimony to man's hankering after the spiritual. When I was a student, Mrs. Besant was an out-and-out atheist of the aggressive and materialistic type. To-day Mrs. Besant is the leader of the Theosophist movement. What a vast change the change from atheist to Theosophist implies! Look at the very words: atheist—without God; Theosophist—wise in God. The great transition has really been made. Mrs. Besant found the soul could not do without God. Atheism is impossible. She has turned Theosophist, and by that mere act illustrated the unappeasable hunger of the soul for the divine. And who knows but that before the end she may, like G. J. Romanes, make the full circuit, and find that the truest way of being "God-wise" is to sit at the feet of Christ and learn of Him.

The rise of Christian Science illustrates the same thing. Christian Science is full of absurdities and superstitions and falsities, but it, too, is an illustration of the demand of the human heart for the Infinite. Christian Science has spread mainly among the leisured and wealthy classes. From one point of view you may say that Christian Science is the nemesis of skepticism. Unbelief often issues in credulity. But it is not the rights and wrongs of Christian Science that I am concerned with just now, but just this simple fact—the vogue of Christian Science among the leisured and wealthy classes is but an illustration of the truth that the world, with all its pleasures and delights, cannot fill the infinite abyss of the human heart. It cries out for God, the living God, and if it cannot get the God and Father of our Lord Jesus Christ, it takes refuge in a god of its own making. It is not only a discontented world we see before us. We see a world hungering for the spiritual and the infinite and the eternal; a world ready for the proclamation of the gospel; a field already white to the harvest.

And, fourthly, it is a token of infinite encouragement that, though the masses of the people seem indifferent to the organized churches, they are by no means indifferent to religion. Even the hubbub about the New Theology has not been without its compensating encouragements. It caused, no doubt, a good deal of distress and fear to pious folk, but, incidentally, it revealed this—that religion, as distinguished from ecclesiasticism, was still a topic of vital interest to the people of this land. The newspapers were full of it; wherever men congregated they talked of it. The excitement was in a way an index to the Englishman's soul. It showed that, though he perhaps never entered a church, he was by no means indifferent to religion.

And the present Social movement demonstrates exactly the same thing. We are living in momentous times. The probability is we are on the eve of great social developments. Now, whatever we may think of the Socialist movement—and I for one think that, as advocated by its leaders, it is open to damaging criticism and absolutely. Ignores human nature—common fairness demands that we should recognize that its ideals of a regenerated society are Christian ideals. They were in the New Testament long before they figured on any Socialist program. For the prophets spoke of a new order, when righteousness and peace should flourish; and Jesus Himself came to found a kingdom of God; and the Bible closes with a vision of that kingdom actually realized. The Socialist is no doubt making his blunders. He is cutting himself off from all his spiritual sanctions. He is adopting a false reading of what equality means. He is proposing to adopt futile and impossible methods of realizing his ideal. But again I say we are purblind if we do not see that the modern Social movement represents a mistaken but passionate desire for the kingdom of God which is righteousness and peace and joy in the Holy Spirit. This very ferment which, from one point of view, seems to threaten and oppose the church, from another point of view is a challenge to the church. I see the multitudes of our land ignoring the church, but in their own groping way all eagerness for the kingdom, and I see in it all the church's opportunity. I seem to hear our Lord say, "Lift up your eyes and look on the fields, that they are white already unto harvest."

White already! After all, it is not to a heedless, callous, satisfied world we have to carry our message. It is to a burdened world, and a dissatisfied world, and a world that craves for God—a world all aflame with desire for the kingdom. It is ours to interpret to the world its own need, and to show how Christ meets and satisfies it all. After all, our time is not a bad time for religion. It is a good time. It is a time full of hope and promise. We have encouragements on every hand. For in every movement of our day I seem to see an indication of the world's hunger for Christ. So let us strengthen the weak hands and confirm the feeble knees, and let us say to him that is of a fearful heart, "Be strong, fear not." Away with despondency and fear—despondency and fear which paralyze our energies and sterilize all our labors! Let us go on with our work with brave hearts and cheerful courage—with the courage that comes of the conviction that our labor is not in vain. The world needs our Christ.

He is the one answer to its bitter cry. The revival for which we long may be at our very doors. It is not a case of "four months and then"— a long and weary wait before the harvest comes. It is here, at our doors, waiting for an ingathering. It is the day of the church's opportunity if only she will rise to it. We have about us a people not only in need of salvation, but ripe and ready for it. "Lift up your eyes, and look on the fields, that they are white already unto harvest."

CHAPTER SEVENTEEN

The Glorification of Christ

And Jesus answereth them, saying, The hour is come,
that the Son of man should be glorified.   —John 12:23

Our Lord, according to all the commentators, uttered these words with an exaltation of spirit amounting to rapture. There were two occasions in our Lord's life when He was moved to something like exultation and triumph. The first occasion was when Peter made his great confession and declared that Jesus was the Christ, the Son of the Living God. The second was when Andrew and Philip came to tell Him of the desire of these Greeks to see Him. In the first instance He rejoiced over His disciples' faith. In the second, He rejoiced at the prospect of His own glorification. "The hour is come," He cried, "that the Son of man should be glorified." At last the hour had struck when His real and essential glory was to flash out upon a startled and astonished world. Up to this point Christ's glory had been veiled. It had been veiled in the lowly birth at Bethlehem; it had been veiled during those humble and laborious years in the carpenter's shop at Nazareth; it had been veiled during those two years when, clad in His seamless cloak, He had gone about the cities and villages of Galilee teaching and preaching the kingdom of God. Glimpses of the glory had been given to a chosen and favored few. "We," says John, "beheld His glory." And when he penned that sentence he remembered the first flash of the glory at the wedding feast in Cana of Galilee, and the fuller revelation of it he had received when, with Peter and James, he beheld his Lord in shining raiment talking with Moses and Elijah on the Holy Mount. But as to the people at large, they had seen no hint of the exceeding glory. "A prophet, or as one of the prophets," was their verdict upon Him.

It was to win faith in Himself as God's Messiah that Jesus came into the world, and there must have been something infinitely disappointing to Him in the fact that the people did not recognize Him or receive Him. And yet all suggestions prematurely to disclose His glory our Lord steadfastly opposed and set aside. His brothers one day urged Him to set all reserve aside and publicly to declare His claims. "If Thou doest these things, manifest Thyself unto the world," they said, and they urged Christ to go up to one of the Jewish feasts which was then nigh at hand and assert Himself openly. But Jesus would not be hurried. "I go not up yet unto this feast," He replied, "because My time is not yet fulfilled." He longed for recognition, for acceptance, for faith. He longed for the time when men should in very truth behold His glory. But He never attempted to hasten the appointed hour. He waited the Lord's leisure. But the coming of these Greeks told Him God's hour had struck. The veiled and hidden glory was to blaze out upon the world. The great consummation to which He had looked forward and for which He had lived had at length arrived. "The hour is come, that the Son of man should be glorified."

"The hour is come, that the Son of man should be glorified"— and what event was it, the prospect of which stirred Jesus to this rapture of spirit? The very word "glory" suggests outward splendor and pomp and magnificence. For instance, perhaps I may be allowed to say that the day of our king's coronation was the day of his glorification. When, amid the booming of guns and the plaudits of the people, King George passed in his splendid robes of state into the abbey of Westminster, where all the rank and wealth and talent of this land and the Britains beyond the seas were already assembled together, and there had the orb and scepter placed in his hands and the royal crown placed on his head, while the assembled multitude did homage to him—by that series of symbolic acts the glory of the king as lord of the mightiest empire the world has ever known was manifested and revealed. Was something like that going to happen to Jesus? Were the leaders of the people about to establish Him upon the throne of David His father? Was He about to exchange the lowly Nazarene cottage for a palace, and the seamless cloak for the royal robe?

Or, again, the word "glorification" suggests the idea of vindication. That is surely a day of glorification when a man who has been misunderstood and slandered and wronged is restored to public confidence and esteem. Here is an incident, for instance, from the life of John Calvin. For the strictness of his rule in Geneva, the city cast him out and exiled him in the year 1538. They called him "despot" and "tyrant," and bade him begone. But in 1541 Geneva was begging Calvin to come back again. It sent a formal embassy to him in Strasbourg, entreating him to come back. And when, in the September of that year, he actually did return, all the people of Geneva turned out into the streets to acclaim and welcome him. The day of John Calvin's triumphant return was the day of his vindication and glorification. Was something like that going to happen to Jesus? He had been the despised and rejected of men. Were they now about to acknowledge that He was the chiefest among ten thousand and the altogether lovely? Priests and Pharisees had called Him a gluttonous man and a winebibber; they had charged Him with being in alliance with Beelzebub the prince of the devils—were they now going to make humble confession that they had been wrong, and that Jesus was in reality the Son of the Most High God? Was it some public vindication of this kind, some national mark of honor that Jesus looked forward to and which moved Him to this exultant cry, "The hour is come, that the Son of man should be glorified"?

No, that is not how I read. Well, then, what was the "glorification" to which Jesus looked with such eager anticipation? The context will help us to our answer. "The hour is come," He said, "that the Son of man should be glorified." And then He added: "Verily, verily, I say unto you, Except a grain of wheat fall into the earth and die, it abideth alone; but if it die, it beareth much fruit." And die! It was of dying Jesus was thinking! It was not David's throne but the bitter Cross that loomed up before His vision. That was how Jesus was going to be glorified—by dying. He was looking forward, not to an hour of vindication, but to an hour of rejection; not to an hour of acclamation and applause, but to an hour of awful and deadly shame; not to being led into Jerusalem to sit on David's throne, but to being led out of Jerusalem to suffer on Calvary's hill. And yet as the Lord thought of that shameful Cross and that ghastly death, He was stirred to exultation and triumph. "The hour is come," He cried, "that the Son of man should be glorified."

It seems a strange thing to glory in—a cross! It seems a strange hour to look forward to as the hour of His glorification—an hour when He would be the object of all Jerusalem's insult and reviling and contempt. And yet, strange as it was, our Lord was right. The hour of His outward humiliation was the hour of His eternal glorification. The Cross which the Jews meant for shame has become His throne of power and glory. "God forbid," cries Paul as he thinks of it, "that I should glory, save in the cross of our Lord Jesus Christ." An infinitely glorious and splendid thing—that was what the Cross was to Paul. And that is what it is also to me. If I were asked where Christ's glory is most splendidly and subduingly displayed, I should not point to Cana, where He turned the water into wine; nor to the Holy Mount, where He was so transfigured that His raiment became white and glistening; nor to Palm Sunday, when He rode in lowly triumph into Jerusalem while the crowds sang Hosanna; I would point to that day when, on a cross on Calvary's hill, with a robber on His right and a robber on His left, while all Jerusalem mocked and scorned, He suffered without the gate.

Now, I want to ask in what respects is it that Christ is glorified in the Cross? In other words, I want for a few minutes—though it seems almost a desecration to do so—to analyze the glory of the Cross.

The Glory of Christ's Character

First of all, then, I want you to notice the glory of Christ's character as it shines forth upon us from His Cross. After all, a man's real glory is not in what he has, but in what he is; not in any outward pomp or splendor, but in spiritual qualities; not in inherited wealth or titles but in character. Our own king's glory does not consist in his state robes and manifold titles, but in his character as a man of simple tastes and honorable life. Now, Christ's glory is in His nature. And the qualities that made that nature of His so perfect shine in their fullest splendor in His Cross. I am only going to mention two of them, though perhaps they are the two chief—our Lord's obedience to the will of God and His measureless love for men. Both these qualities find their "glorification" in the Cross.

Take first the quality of obedience to the will of God. Obedience is, according to our Lord Himself, the test of the genuineness of religion. There can be no obedience, of course, without faith and love. And the proof of faith and love is to be sought in obedience.

Now, obedience is the great characteristic of our Lord's life. When a mere boy He declared that He must be about the Father's business. When a man He said it was His meat to do the Father's will and to accomplish His work. Christ lived in such close fellowship and complete harmony with the Father that His own will and His Father's were absolutely one. Now, there are times when we find it comparatively easy to obey. When God's voice summons us into the green pastures and by the still waters we find no difficulty in listening to it. But what about those times when He summons us to climb some steep ascent or to tread some Via Dolorosa? Now, the duty to which God called His Son, and the path along which He bade Him walk, was hard and toilsome from the start. The Devil sought to persuade Him to take an easier way. He offered Him the kingdoms of the world and the glory of them if He would only pay a little homage to him by adopting worldly methods and consenting to unholy compromises. But Christ's reply to the Devil's temptation was simply a declaration of His unfaltering allegiance to the will of God. "It is written," He replied, "thou shalt worship the Lord thy God, and Him only shalt thou serve." And in that great resolve of His, made in the wilderness, our Lord never faltered. The will of God led Him along a painful way.

> Privations, sorrows, bitter scorn,
> The life of toil, the mean abode,
> The faithless kiss, the crown of thorn,
> These were the consecrated road.

Heart and flesh cried out against them. "Father," He said in His agony, "let this cup pass." But when He knew it was the Father's pleasure He should drink it, He drank it to its last bitter drop. He obeyed His Father all the way through. And He did not falter in His obedience when God asked of Him the last and uttermost sacrifice. "He became obedient unto death, even the death of the cross." His dying is the glorification of His obedience. He left nothing undone which the Father gave Him to do.

Take next that other quality of love to men. Once again Jesus loved men all the way through. "Jesus," says our old hymn, "Thou art all compassion, pure, unbounded love Thou art." And every act of His life is a proof of it. Bethlehem is a proof of it. He emptied Himself and took upon Him the form of a servant—for love. Nazareth is a proof of it. He

served those years at the carpenter's bench—for love. Galilee is a proof
of it. He went about preaching the Gospel, healing the sick, comforting
the sad, befriending the outcast, all—for love But if you want the
uttermost proof of love you must go to the Cross.

> There on the Cross 'tis fairest drawn,
> In precious blood and crimson lines.

Now, love is measured by the lengths to which it is prepared to go
in the way of sacrifice. The Cross is the measure of the length of the
love of Christ. I am not going to enter upon any discussion of the
rationale of the Atonement; I will content myself with this broad
and simple statement—He died for love of us. "Greater love hath
no man than this," said Jesus, "that a man lay down his life for his
friend." That is the uttermost reach of love, and our writers have
delighted to give us stories of love that did not shrink from that final
sacrifice. "*A Tale of Two Cities*," Mr. Chesterton says, "stands alone
among the works of Dickens in dignity and eloquence." And that
great and moving story culminates, as you all remember, in the
sacrifice of Sidney Carton, who went to the guillotine to save the
life of the husband of the lady whom he, too, loved. Life was
pleasant to him, and to face death while still young was a hard and
bitter experience. But for love's sake he did it. Sidney Carton had
given expression to his love many a time, but to see his love in its
glory we must see him die. And it is so with the love of Christ. He
gave expression to His love in many a beautiful word. He gave
expression to it in many a gracious deed. But if you want to see
Christ's love at its noblest and best you must see Him die. For He
died for love. It was not the high priests and Pilate who put Him to
death. He laid down His life of Himself. He died for love. Only the
love of Christ was a mightier and stronger thing than the love of
Sidney Carton; for while Sidney Carton died for a friend, Christ
died, the just for the unjust, that He might bring us to God.

> Oh, 'twas love, 'twas love, 'twas wondrous love,
>   The love of Christ for me,
> It brought the Savior from above,
>   To die on Calvary.

Love, we say, is the greatest thing in the world. It is the very nature of God Himself. Measured by this test of love, Christ is at His greatest and divinest when He hangs upon the cross. It is no paradox to say that when He is weakest, then is He mightiest; when He is the sport and derision of men, then is He most divine. All the experience of the centuries bears witness to the fact. It is when men see Christ on the cross that they are moved to "crown Him Lord of all."

"Is it not strange," Keble says in his hymn on Good Friday—

> The darkest hour
>> That ever dawned on sinful earth
> Should touch the heart with softer power
>> For comfort than an angel's mirth?
> That to the Cross the mourner's eye should turn,
>> Sooner than where the stars of Christmas burn.

No, it is not strange. Christ is greatest, noblest, tenderest, dearest upon that cross. His love is mightiest in the Cross. From the Cross He rules a world. It is in His Cross we see His matchless glory. And so our Lord, knowing the issues and results of that Cross, welcomed it with a solemn joy—"The hour is come, that the Son of man should be glorified."

The Glory of Christ's Triumph

And, in the second place, I want you to notice not simply that the Cross revealed the glory of Christ's character, but that by means of it Christ was given the name which is above every name. Godet says that what is principally in Christ's mind is the exaltation of His person to heaven. Westcott says that what Christ is thinking of is His victory through death over death. They are simply two aspects of the same truth. The Cross did more than reveal the beauty of Christ's character; it gave Him His supreme place. In one of the preceding paragraphs I made a sort of antithesis between the Cross and the throne. It was not to David's throne Christ was looking, I said, but to a cross between two thieves. I withdraw the antithesis. It is as false as false can be. Christ's Cross was His throne. It gave Him the name which is above every name. You remember how Paul couples His Cross and His glory together. "He became obedient even unto death," he says, "yea, the death of the cross. Wherefore God highly exalted Him and gave Him the name which is above every name." The humiliation led straight to the exaltation.

Death was for Him the pathway to glory. For it was by dying and rising again Christ was declared to be the Son of God with power. It was a dark and lonesome way to tread, but our Lord knew it would bring Him to the right hand of God the Father Almighty. Rejection, humiliation, suffering—they were coming to their end; after death would come the glory which He had with the Father before the world began. And so He hastened to the Cross. "The hour is come, that the Son of man should be glorified."

And notice, further, that, as Westcott says, it brought Christ the glory of a great triumph. When Christ died and went down to the grave He fought the last and final battle, and on the morning of the third day He emerged victor. Through death, as the writer of the epistle to the Hebrews puts it, He destroyed him that had the power of death—that is, the Devil; and delivered them who, through fear of death, were all their lifetime subject to bondage. Up to Christ's day the grave had always been the victor, never the victim. Generation after generation had been swallowed up by its ruthless maw, and still it yawned unfilled, unsatisfied, until men cowered in speechless fear before the black and awful terror of the grave. But Christ, the Son of Man, went down to the grave and took death and captivity captive. He broke death's power. He robbed the grave of its terror, until its one-time prisoners can make a mock at death and laugh at the grave. "O death, where is thy sting? O grave, where is thy victory?" Christ's resurrection has changed the entire outlook. Men who are appointed to die give Him praise for robbing death of its power to terrify the heart and darken the day. This triumph is Christ's great glory. You have noticed how in the case of great soldiers who have won mighty victories for us, the title a grateful country confers is associated with the scene of their victories, so that the name and the triumph are for ever coupled together, and the one derives its glory from the other. So Nelson was made Earl Nelson of Trafalgar; and Lord Roberts, Lord Roberts of Kandahar; and Lord Kitchener, Lord Kitchener of Khartoum. And in exactly the same way Christ's name and His triumph are associated together. You remember how He announced Himself to the seer on Patmos: "I am the first and the last, and the Living one; and I was dead, and behold, I am alive for evermore, and I have the keys of death and of Hades." "I have the keys of death"—that is it. Christ's name and His triumph go together. He is the Conqueror of death. And so Christ welcomed the hour of His death. He knew it would be the hour of His victory. "The hour is come," He said, "that the Son of man should be glorified."

The Glory of Redeeming Power

And lastly, and in just a word, I want you to notice how, in the Cross, Christ was glorified as Savior and Redeemer. Once again, I am not going to enter upon any theological discussion. I mean simply to stick to the facts of experience. And the fact to which all experience testifies is this, that Christ crucified is the power of God. I am not for the moment concerned to explain it—though I think we can get glimpses into its meaning. I content myself just now with the statement of the fact—the redeeming, regenerating, saving power of the Christian faith is in the Cross. Nothing has power to cleanse and purge like the Cross. Nothing has such power to breed holiness and courage like the Cross. It is at the Cross—like Bunyan's Christian—men lose their burdens and find restoring grace. Banish the Cross out of your teaching and preaching and you sacrifice your power. Reduce your Christianity to a mere ethic, and you fling away its regenerating force. Unitarianism has its message and its work, but it is useless to redeem a sinful world. Every one knows who has tried it, that when we really set about trying to save men from their sins, the Cross is our only effectual weapon. "By this conquer." Jesus knew it, too. He knew that it was from His death men would derive life. "If it die," He said, "it bringeth forth much fruit." And so He died that He might have the glory of being a Savior and a Redeemer.

For what glory could anyone have—even Jesus Himself—more exalted than this—the glory of being a Savior? The glory of saving men's souls from death? You remember the old story of Cornelia and her boys. Some Roman matrons were conversing with Cornelia about their possessions, and the talk ultimately turned upon their precious stones. The visiting ladies talked much about their diamonds and pearls, and then they turned to Cornelia and said, "And what jewels have you?" Whereupon she sent out of the room to fetch her two young sons, and, with a hand upon each, she presented these boys to her friends, saying, "These are my jewels." And the men and women whom He has saved are the jewels, the gems, the ornaments, the orders, the glory of the Lord Jesus. And the thought of saving them made Him hasten to His Cross. You may remember what Dickens says about Sidney Carton's end: "They said of him, about the city that night, that it was the peacefullest man's face ever beheld there. Many added that he looked sublime and prophetic." Sidney Carton thought of his love and her husband, and her child and her father, and his death became to him a glory. And Jesus, too, thought of the multitudes who would be set free from the law of sin and death, and who would be loosed from their sins by His blood, and He, too, gloried in His dying. "He sang a hymn," we read, as He passed out of the Upper Room to face the spitting and the scourging and the Cross. And the hymn was no doleful minor chant either, but a song of exultation and triumph. "Return unto thy rest, O my soul, for the Lord hath dealt bountifully with thee." Dealt bountifully? Yes. For our Lord saw the multitude which no man could number, of all kindreds and peoples and tongues, who would wash their robes and make them white in the blood of the Lamb, and at the thought of that multitude He sang. Death was not defeat, but glory. "For the joy set before Him He endured the cross, despising the shame." He welcomed the hour of His sacrifice. "The hour is come, that the Son of man should be glorified."

That is how Christ is glorified in the Cross. It is the proof of His obedience; it is the revelation of His love; it proclaims Him the victor over death and the Savior from sin. And just because Christ is thus glorified in the Cross, because it reveals Him as the lover of my soul, the Savior from sin, the Deliverer from death, I, too, will glory in the Cross. For this is the Christ I need. I need the love, the uttermost love there shown. I need to be saved from my sins. I need to be delivered from fear of death. And the crucified Lord will do all this for me. There is comfort and good hope for lost and dying men in the Cross. "God forbid that I should glory, save in the cross of our Lord Jesus Christ."

CHAPTER EIGHTEEN

Individuality

*And Saul clad David with his apparel, and he put an
helmet of brass upon his head, and he clad him with a
coat of mail. And David girded his sword upon his
apparel, and he assayed to go; for he had not proved it.
And David said unto Saul, I cannot go with these, for I
have not proved them. And David put them off him.*

—1 Samuel 17:38–39

You remember all about this old Scripture story. It was only after
much persuasion that Saul consented to let David go and fight
against Goliath at all. But when once he had given consent, his next
care was that David should be properly equipped for the encounter.
Now, Saul had only one notion of a soldier's equipment, and so he
produced for David the coat of mail and the helmet of brass which,
apparently, he himself was accustomed to wear, and the heavy
sword which he himself was accustomed to wield. But when David
put them on, he found Saul's armor an encumbrance, and not a
help. It did not fit him. It impeded and hampered his movements.
He could not fight in it. So he had the courage to lay aside the
helmet and the coat of mail and the heavy sword and to say frankly
to the king, "I cannot go with these; for I have not proved them";
and he issued forth to his encounter with Goliath in his simple
shepherd's dress, and with only one weapon in his hand—that sling
which he so well knew how to use.

Now, it is not about Saul and David and this historic combat that

173

I wish to speak in this sermon. Saul and David are types. Saul stands, shall I say, for the desire for uniformity. David stands for the assertion of individuality. And it is about the necessity of resisting the tendency to uniformity and insisting upon our own individuality if we are to be successful workers and fighters that I want to speak for a few minutes.

The Passion for Uniformity

Look first at Saul's action in the story. Saul had the notion that there was practically only one method of fighting, and that was·the one to which he himself was accustomed. He thought there was only one equipment for war, and that was the regulation equipment of helmet and coat of mail and heavy sword. He thought that Goliath could be fought only by the use of one set of weapons, and those were the weapons he himself employed. And so he sought to dress up David in his own armor. No doubt he did it all in good faith, but it was a foolish thing nevertheless. For what he was really trying to do was this—he was trying to repress David's individuality, and attempting to convert him into a second Saul.

And in this respect Saul stands for the prevailing tendency and temper of human society. "The virtue in most request in society," says Emerson, "is conformity. Self-reliance is its aversion. It loves not realities and creators, but names and customs." And Emerson has not stated the case a whit too strongly. All the facts of life and experience confirm what he says. The whole tendency of society is to destroy individuality and to produce a level and monotonous uniformity. Every child who comes into this world from the hand of God is a unique, an original. But from the moment of his birth all the forces of social life set to work upon that little child to destroy his individuality and turn him out a copy of the approved and recognized type. Society has its forms and conventions and standards, and these it seeks to impose upon every living person. In dress, in speech, in thought, it seeks to reduce men to a common level. Every one knows how society dislikes the man with new ideas, new methods, new phrases. It distrusts the innovator. It fears the man who dares to be original and individual. The man it loves is the correct, respectable, orthodox person, who respects traditions, worships convention, and falls in with established customs and ways.

Now, up to a certain point, respect for the usages and customs and traditions and beliefs of society is right and admirable. For these customs and usages and beliefs are the result of the accumulated experience and knowledge of the centuries. But a blind acceptance of them is fatal to all individuality and to all progress. Illustrations occur to me of attempts which are made even to this day to secure certain kinds of uniformity, with quite disastrous results.

(1) There is often an attempt made to secure a certain uniformity of religious experience. We expect all people to pass through the same processes of religious development, and if they do not pass through what we consider to be the normal and recognized experience, we are more than half inclined to think they are not Christians at all. For instance, a great many think the one and only method of becoming a Christian is by means of the penitent form, and through that tremendous and radical change which we speak of as conversion. And so the attempt is often made to force people through this process. They are swept into the inquiry rooms at special missions, and are often made to confess to experiences which they do not really feel. It is only by passing through these various experiences that we think they can be soundly saved.

But surely there is more than one way of coming to Christ and winning the kingdom, and it is foolish and absurd of us to try and insist upon one stereotyped method. Here are two hyacinths in full and perfect bloom. But they came by their perfection and beauty in different ways. One grew in earth, the other in water. Here are two Christian men, both obviously living consecrated lives; one came to Christ, like Paul, through a startling and overwhelming experience; the other came, like Timothy, through the gracious ministries of the home. One son wanders far before he really settles down in the Father's house, another never leaves home at all. In face of the facts of life it is absurd to try to limit the methods of God's working. The Spirit bloweth where it listeth. Our way into the kingdom is not the only way. There are on the north three gates, and on the south three gates, and on the east three gates, and on the west three gates, and by any one of these the redeemed may enter. And we sin against the plain teaching of Scripture, and we may do grave and irreparable wrong to souls by insisting upon a uniformity of religious experience. And just as there are different methods of entering the kingdom, so there are different types of religious life, and we make a fatal blunder when we expect the spiritual life in every one to express itself in the same way. What Saul tried to do in this story was to put a giant's armor upon a boy. We make the same mistake in another sphere when we expect the man's religious experience from the youth. Youth has its own type of religion; manhood has another; old age has yet another; and they are each beautiful in their place. But it is foolish and wicked to expect the grown-up person's religion in the child. Buoyancy and strenuousness are, or ought to be, the marks of a young man's religion; a certain wistful waiting for the beyond is often a touching characteristic of the religion of the old. I can understand the old saint saying—

> I'm kneeling at the threshold,
> A-weary, faint and sore.

But I do not want to hear a young man talk like that. When the young man adopts the phraseology of the old Christian, that is cant. "Rejoice, O young man, in thy youth." There can be no uniformity of religious life, and we simply destroy its naturalness and beauty when we try to run the experience of young and old into the same mold.

(2) It is equally foolish to try to impose the forms of truth accepted in one age upon another. We would never dream of doing this in the realm of secular knowledge. You could not, for instance, make this early part of the twentieth century talk in the scientific language current in the beginning of the nineteenth. We have outgrown the nineteenth. New tracts and continents of knowledge have been discovered as the result of the unremitting researches of scientists, and multitudes of the ideas and beliefs of a hundred years ago have been cast into the lumber room of exploded superstitions. So rapidly, indeed, does scientific knowledge advance, that even in a score of years a book becomes out of date. But if we refuse to attempt to make the twentieth century speak the scientific language of the nineteenth century, why should we try to compel it to speak the theological language of centuries long gone by? For religious knowledge enlarges and grows just as certainly as scientific knowledge does. Our Lord Himself said that the Spirit would take of His things and would reveal them unto His people. "The Lord," said our own John Robinson in a golden sentence, "hath still more light and truth to break forth from His Word." And the new light and larger knowledge will inevitably express themselves in new speech. It is nothing less than absurd and foolish to expect the twentieth century to speak the religious language and think the religious thought of the fourth century or the seventeenth. Has the Spirit of Christ not

been with us through the centuries that have since elapsed? And has He not been leading us into fuller and larger truth? Calvin was a great and subtle theologian, but it is foolish, and worse than foolish, to try to make men speak today in the language of Calvin's Institutes. The Westminster Confession is a great and notable document; valuable as an expression of the Puritan faith, and useful even now for spiritual purposes, but it is futile to try to make men speak the language and propound the belief of the Westminster Confession. John Wesley was one of God's greatest gifts to England, but it always seems to me, as an outsider, foolish and absurd to try to make modern Methodists speak the eighteenth-century language of Wesley. We should have been spared many a weary controversy and humiliating heresy hunt if we only realized that knowledge constantly grows from more to more. Creeds are invaluable as marking the successive stages of theological development, but to try to make English religious thought of today speak the language and propound the beliefs of the Westminster Confession is as foolish as Saul's attempt to dress up David and send him forth to fight in an armor that did not fit him.

(3) There is, once again, the attempt which is often made to insist upon uniformity of method. Saul thought there really was only one way of fighting. The bare idea of fighting with a sling and a few smooth stones scandalized him. There was one orthodox method of fighting, and Saul wished to compel David to adopt it. Now, a great many cherish a similar passion for uniformity in Christian work. They feel there can be only one right way of working, and that is the way to which they have been accustomed, and that particular method they would like to constrain every man to follow. History abounds with illustrations of this attempt to enforce uniformity and destroy individuality. In Elizabeth's reign, and again in the reign of Charles II, Acts of Uniformity were passed, the whole object of which was to try to constrain the people of this land all to worship and work in the same way.

Wesley and his first helpers were all of them members of the established church and had no wish to leave it. But when they started their great revival and took to open-air preaching and society meetings, the members of the established church did all they could to thwart and strangle the movement and drive Wesley and his friends back into the old grooves, the respectable, recognized methods of religious work.

And we need not even go back to the beginnings of the Methodist movement, for in General Booth's experience we have an illustration of very much the same kind of thing. William Booth was a New Connection minister. He did not wish to leave the Connection. But the Connection had no room for him. With its veneration for rules and traditions it wished to make this man, whose soul was all aflame with a great passion for evangelistic work, tread the humdrum path of the circuit ministry. It wanted no individuality, and so William Booth came out and founded that marvelous Army which has won such triumphs in every quarter of the world.

And may I not add that this is the tragic mistake that the churches are making in their several attitudes towards each other? There is an astonishing veneration for uniformity—uniformity of method and organization. "Master," said one of His disciples to Jesus one day, "we saw one casting out devils in Thy name, and we forbade him because he followeth not with us." The man was doing good work, holy work, saving work, but that disciple wanted to stop him simply and solely on a point of method—"because he followeth not with us." And is not that typical of what the churches are doing to one another? I do not desire to speak bitterly—it is not matter for bitterness, but rather for sorrow and regret—but is not that exactly what the Romanist does to the Anglican? He pronounces his orders invalid; he says he has no right to teach and preach—and all because "he followeth not with us." And, in turn, is that not exactly what the Anglican does to the Free churchman? It is all very pitiable and very deplorable, and utterly mistaken and false. Jesus refused to forbid that irregular and unorthodox worker. Uniformity was no idol of our Lord's. He knew there were diversities of operations, but the same spirit. And it is foolish, and worse than foolish, to try and insist upon uniformity of method and organization today. Men have their individual temperaments and tastes. One man finds himself happier with the more elaborate organization of the Episcopal church; another finds himself more at home in the freer life of these churches of ours; one man worships best by the aid of a liturgy; another finds our own simpler order more helpful to him. You are not going to help the kingdom by trying to bring about a forced uniformity of method and organization. Let each man work and worship in the way that suits him best. It will be the same Lord all the time that worketh all in all.

It would have been quite easy to prove that this attempt to enforce a rigid uniformity of thought and belief and method has been the greatest barrier in the way of human progress, but I pass that by in order to be able to dwell for just a moment upon the need for the assertion of individuality.

Assertion of Individuality

David declined to be an imitation Saul. Had he gone forth in Saul's heavy and unwieldy armor, you may be quite sure of this, there would have been no victory over Goliath. But he had the moral courage to refuse to be a feeble copy of Saul, and just to be himself. He put Saul's gorgeous armor aside, saying, "I cannot go with these; for I have not proved them." And David put them off him. And when he went forth to face Goliath it was with those weapons in his hand which were his own, and which he knew how to use. "And he took his staff in his hand, and chose him five smooth stones out of the brook, and put them in the shepherd's bag which he had, even in his scrip; and his sling was in his hand, and he drew near to the Philistine." And David won his great fight that day just because he dared to be himself.

And that is what I would say to all who desire to be efficient workers and valiant fighters for the Lord—be yourselves. Give your individuality play. "Whoso would be a man," says Emerson in that great essay to which I have already referred, "must be a nonconformist"—nonconformist, I need scarcely say, not in the ecclesiastical sense, but in this sense—that no matter what the world may think or say, he will speak his own language, think his own thoughts, work on his own lines, and generally be himself. Be yourself! Be the man God meant you to be.

Work in your own way. We recognize in secular affairs that in choosing a calling or business for a boy, consideration should be had to the bent of his own mind. The same principle holds good in higher things. It is not what the world—even the religious world— counts the correct way that matters; what matters is that every man should work in the way best suited for him. It matters little whether it is counted correct or orthodox. It is his way—let him work in it. Think what would have happened if certain men we know of had allowed themselves to be coerced into orthodox ways of work. If Francis had been coerced into recognized ways of service, there would have been no revival in Italy. If Luther had been coerced into living and working in orthodox monastic fashion, there would have been no Reformation in Europe. If John Wesley had been coerced back into the respectabilities of Anglicanism, there would have been no evangelical revival or Methodist church. If William Booth had allowed himself to be bound down by the red tape of Connexionalism, there would have been no Salvation Army. They did their great work because they dared to be themselves. Let every man follow their example. Be yourselves. Don't copy. Don't imitate. Work according to the law of your own being.

And think your own thoughts and believe your own beliefs. Hast thou faith? Have it to thyself before God. To thine own self be true. This is axiomatic—no man can fight effectively in the Christian warfare with borrowed weapons, with secondhand opinions and beliefs. The man who wants to speak effectively and work effectively in Christ's cause must have convictions which are his own, beliefs which he himself has proved. There is more power in the proclamation of one personal conviction than in the repetition of a score of borrowed and orthodox beliefs. David fared better with that sling of his and the five smooth stones from the brook—it looked a poverty-stricken equipment, it is true—but he fared better with it than he would have done had he gone into the fight clad in a complete panoply which was borrowed and not his own. It is much like that with our religious beliefs. The world is ready to supply us with a complete creed ready made. But such a borrowed creed will not be of much service. I feel myself oftentimes I should like to have a complete theology, and I have textbooks on my shelves ready to supply me with one. But then I remember that the only beliefs which are worth preaching are the beliefs which are part and parcel of my own experience; the only truths which are worth proclaiming are the convictions of my own soul. And so I turn away from the ready-made systems of the textbooks. "I cannot go in them; I have not proved them." Beliefs which are to be effective are not borrowed; they are discovered, they are hammered out in life and experience. It is not the length of a man's creed that tells, but the conviction with which he holds it. And so I say, let every man think his own thoughts, believe his own beliefs, speak his own words. Let him be a voice and not an echo. Let him speak that which he knows, and testify what he himself has seen. All history tells us there is power for men, progress for the race, victory for the kingdom only when men rise clean above all fear of what the world may think or say and dare to be the men God meant them to be, to work in the way God meant them to work, and to speak the word God meant them to speak.

The Success of Individuality

Notice, in the last place, and in a sentence or two, what blessings followed David's assertion of his own individuality. I dare say Saul smiled when he saw David go forth with his sling and five stones. We know how Goliath mocked him and insulted him when he saw him approach. But we also all know the end of the story. David won a notable victory for Israel that day. And he won it by being David and refusing to be an imitation Saul. What we need to realize is that God wants all types of men in His service. He does not want all men to be of one type. He wants all types. He wants Saul to be Saul. He wants David to be David. Look at the circle of the apostolate. What varying types you have there—Peter, the man of impulse; John, the man of strong enthusiasm; Andrew, the man of common sense; Matthew, the man with literary gift; Philip, the man of affairs; Thomas, the man of gloomy but devoted heart. Our Lord did not try to convert them all into men of one type. He wanted Peter to be Peter, and John to be John, and Andrew to be Andrew, and so on. He needed the individuality of each. There was opportunity and work for each. And so it is still. Christ wants you and me—as we are, with our individual capacities and gifts. We rob and impoverish God when we become feeble copies and imitators of somebody else. He has work for us, and He wants us as we are. Yes, even though we seem to have but little to offer him. Even though, like David, our only equipment be a sling and five smooth stones. God can do the most amazing things with weak and unpromising tools. Think of D. L. Moody—he was the manager of a Chicago boot store, without any education worth the name. He heard God call him, and he gave himself to God as he was. He gave his life to the service of his Lord and began to speak for Him. He never went to college; he never belonged to what is known as the regular ministry. I have no doubt many wished he had been trained and had taken holy orders. But supposing D. L. Moody had done the orthodox thing and gone to college, the world might have gained an indifferent minister and lost the greatest evangelist of modern times. But he gave himself to God as D. L. Moody, the Chicago boot manager—with what many would think his very imperfect equipment—and God used him to quicken religion in two continents. It is as we are God wants us. With our poor sling and five stones, let us offer ourselves to Him. He can put His treasure in earthen vessels. He can and will repeat His ancient miracle; He will use the weak things of the world to put to shame the things that are strong, and the things that are not to bring to naught the things that are.

CHAPTER NINETEEN

The Beauty of the Lord

And let the beauty of the Lord our God be upon us.
—Psalm 90:17

"The beauty of the Lord our God." It was Charles Kingsley, was it not, who was overheard in his last illness murmuring quietly to himself, "How beautiful God is! How beautiful God is!" Perhaps the phrase, "the beauty of God," strikes us as just a little inappropriate and incongruous. We do not often apostrophize God as Augustine did—"O beauty, so old and yet so new, too late I loved Thee." And yet it must be true that God is beautiful. He is indeed the supreme and absolute beauty. The old Greeks put into their statues and representations of their gods their highest conceptions of human beauty; into their Aphrodite, all they knew of womanly charm; into their Apollo, all they knew of manly grace; into their Zeus, all they knew of royal majesty and dignity. The instinct that made them thus identify the divine with the beautiful was altogether right. It was only the mode of expression that was wrong. It was physical beauty they attributed to their deities, and they did this because their conception of deity was material and anthropomorphic. But the Godhead is not like unto silver or gold graven by art and man's device. God is a Spirit, and the beauty that characterizes Him is moral and spiritual beauty. You cannot express this beauty on canvas or in stone, but you can always feel it with the worshipful and believing heart.

From this point of view—that is, from the standpoint of beauty of character—how beautiful God is! You could guess as much from glancing at His works. I remember a friend of mine, after reading a chapter from, I believe, one of John Ruskin's works, remarking to me, "What a beautiful mind the man has!" And so exactly when I look out upon the works of God's hands I always feel moved to say, "What a beautiful mind God has!" Take the glory of the springtide. The earth in springtime fills anyone who has any sense of beauty with a perfect exhilaration of delight. It is full of light and fragrance and life and color. I look upon the trees dressed in their new robes of fresh and vivid green; I look upon the fields, decked as they are with innumerable white-eyed daisies and yellow buttercups; I look at the wealth of color in our gardens; I listen to the joyous song of the birds; and when I remember that God is the Author and Giver of all this color, fragrance, glory and song, I am constrained to cry, with Kingsley, "How beautiful God is! How beautiful God is!"

"Nature," as our hymn puts it—

> With open volume stands
>   To spread her Maker's praise abroad;
> And every labor of His bands
>   Shows something worthy of a God.

But it is not in Nature that I find the highest revelation of the beauty of the Lord. For that I turn to the gospel. You remember that passionate psalm in which the singer expresses his love for God's house—"One thing have I desired of the Lord," he cries, "that will I seek after, that I may dwell in the house of the Lord all the days of my life." And why did he desire this perpetual abiding in God's house? He himself supplies the answer: "To behold the beauty of the Lord." That was the attraction, the compelling fascination of the sanctuary—in it, as nowhere else, the psalmist beheld the pleasantness of the Lord, the delightsomeness of the character of God in all its perfection and completeness. And to the psalmist there was no vision comparable to this vision of the divine pleasantness; everything else was dust and ashes compared to this; like St. Paul, he counted all things but loss if only he could gaze upon God, and so he would fain dwell in the house of the Lord all the days of his life, that he might behold the beauty of the Lord. For it is in the sanctuary that the "pleasantness," the "beauty" of God's character is most clearly revealed. The heavens declare the glory of God—yes, but

His Holy Word declares it more plainly still. And it is declared most plainly of all in the Incarnate Word—in Jesus Christ. If you want to behold the "beauty of the Lord," you can do better than study the book of nature; come and study Jesus Christ, for in Him dwelleth all the fullness of the Godhead bodily, and He and the Father are one.

Wherein the Beauty Consists

Now, I am going to ask the question wherein the beauty of the Lord, as revealed in Jesus Christ, consists. For beauty is itself always a product. It is not itself a single quality or characteristic; it is the result of a combination of qualities and characteristics. It is so even in the matter of physical beauty. I cannot discuss beauty as an artist could. But this I know, that regular features by themselves do not create beauty; and a fair complexion by itself does not create beauty; and a graceful carriage by itself does not create beauty. Beauty is a complex thing. It takes regularity of feature, brilliance of complexion, grace of carriage, and, above everything else, pleasantness of expression to create the impression of beauty. It is like the ray of light. The ray is really not single, though it seems such. It is complex. Let it fall upon a prism and it splits up into its constituent colors. It is a combination of violet and orange and green and blue that produces the purity and beauty of the white ray. And moral and spiritual beauty is also a complex thing. It is never the result of one quality, but always of a combination of qualities. Beauty, in a word, is something that can be analyzed. You can see some of the necessary constituents of moral and spiritual beauty in most men's characters. But no human life ever lived on this earth has ever created the impression of perfect beauty. The combination is never complete. Some element or other is always lacking. There is ever some defect, some flaw, some fault. The only perfect and flawless beauty is the beauty of the Lord. Now, I want to inquire what are the elements that go to make up the divine beauty. What are the constituents which, blended together, create the impression of the divine pleasantness? I am not going to mention all of them, for every good we know of is in God. I will confine myself to two qualities—contrasted qualities almost—which, blended together, go far towards creating the impression of the ineffable beauty of God.

(1) And first I will mention God's holiness. There can be no moral beauty without holiness. It is in a very real sense the basal,

the foundation quality of all moral character. When a man's life is smudged and stained with sin, the beauty of his character is wholly gone. Now, the Bible is full of an awestricken sense of the holiness of God. "The Lord our God is holy"—it was the first truth about the character of God that the Israelites were taught to learn. The contents of the law and the awe-inspiring circumstances that accompanied the giving of it were all meant to grave upon their hearts the truth of the holiness of God. God is absolute, awful purity, that is almost the main lesson of the Old Testament. Before Him even the cherubim veil their faces in their wings and continually do cry, "Holy, holy, holy, is the Lord God of Hosts." So absolute is the holiness of God, that, compared with Him, even the whiteness of the angel's wing seems stained and soiled. And this quality of holiness is a permanent element in the beauty of the Lord. In Jesus Christ, He revealed Himself as the Holy One. Our Lord was the chiefest among ten thousand and the altogether lovely, and the basal element in His beauty is His holiness. "He did no sin, neither was guile found in His mouth." Perhaps in these days we are tempted to overlook, if not to ignore, this element in the divine beauty and glory. But there would be no beauty in God, He would indeed cease to be God, if He were not holy. The most striking feature in Swiss scenery, the glory and boast of Switzerland, is the vision of its mighty mountain peaks clothed ever in their mantles of snowy white. Take the snow mountains away, and you have destroyed the beauty of Switzerland. And in much the same way you destroy the beauty of the Lord if you forget His holiness. The basal thing in God's character is His awful purity. We need to lift our eyes to these shining and snow—lad peaks of the divine holiness if we are ever to be moved to say, "How beautiful God is!"

(2) And the second quality in the character of God that I will mention is His grace. I have been saying that holiness is the basal element in moral beauty. I want to go on now to say that holiness in and by itself would not produce the impression of beauty. For the word "beauty" carries with it the suggestion of charm. Indeed, the word that is translated "beauty" might, perhaps, be more correctly translated "pleasantness." It is winsome and attractive beauty. It is not something that commands your admiration simply, it is something that constrains your love. Now, holiness, in and of itself, would scarcely constrain love. Nobody would think of describing those snow-clad peaks of Switzerland as pleasant—they are grand,

if you like; majestic, if you like; awe-inspiring, if you like. And in the same way holiness by itself is not pleasant; it is too high and majestic and austere; it does not charm and win us; it awes us, it subdues us—I might almost say it terrifies us. "Woe is me, for I am a man of unclean lips," is the heartbroken cry of the prince of the prophets. It was a cry wrung from him by a vision of the holiness of God. "Depart from me, for I am a sinful man, O Lord," is the bitter cry of the chief of the apostles. It was a cry wrung from him by a vision of the holiness of God. There is something more than holiness needed to create the beauty that wins and charms and attracts. And that something more we find in God's grace. The holiness of God would compel our reverence and awe; but the grace of God wins our love.

That was what struck the disciples most about the character of Jesus. "We beheld his glory," says John; "glory as of the only begotten from the Father, full of grace." It was this characteristic of Jesus that gave Him His charm. Publicans and sinners, we read, came together for to hear Him. It was His grace that attracted them. "The common people heard him gladly." It was His love that drew them. The grace of Christ—the stooping, condescending, love of Christ—how it shines forth in the gospel story! Read the account of the wedding at Cana—what delicate considerateness Christ showed. Read the story of His visit to the house of Zacchaeus—what infinite compassion and beautiful hopefulness He displayed. Read the narrative of His dealings with the woman who was a sinner—what a depth of tenderness and forgiving love He revealed! And these are the things that lent charm and winsomeness to the character of Jesus. No wonder the common people delighted to hear Him; no wonder publicans and sinners hung on His lips and followed Him from place to place. He was full of grace. Mere holiness would not have drawn them. Righteousness is apt to be hard and repellent. You remember what Paul says: "Scarcely for a righteous man will one die"; there is not much about the righteous man to command enthusiastic love. The righteous man is often harsh and austere. "But for a good man," he says, "some would even dare to die." When righteousness is blended with love to produce goodness, then men's hearts are won to such enthusiastic devotion that they will even dare to die. And that is what you find in Jesus—love has joined hands with righteousness to produce goodness. And Jesus Christ in this is but the picture and expression of God. God is more than infinite holiness; He is also boundless love. He is more than the pure God who cannot behold iniquity; He is the loving God who gave His Son to die to save the sinner. And that constitutes the beauty, the pleasantness, of the Lord; in Him mercy and truth have met together, righteousness and peace have kissed each other.

The Beauty of God a Human Possession

And now, having spoken thus briefly about the beauty of the Lord, I want to call your attention to the prayer the psalmist utters in the text. He prays, "Let the beauty of the Lord our God be upon us." He prays, in a word, that the divine beauty and glory may become the possession of all God's people. This is a daring prayer. Is it a possible prayer? Is it a prayer that can be answered and realized? Yes, surely it can. It was one of the best-beloved of our modern mystics who said in his own quaint way, "The Christian ought always to be good-looking." Beneath the quaint phrase there lies a great and blessed truth. The Christian ought always to be good-looking. He ought to share in the perfect beauty of God. "Let the beauty of the Lord our God be upon us." It is no vain and impossible wish. It is no foolish and unwarranted prayer. Men have shared in the glory of God. There have been men on whom, visibly and unmistakably, the beauty of God has rested. The apostle tells us that all who steadfastly gaze upon the glory of the Lord are transformed into the same image from glory to glory. And the apostle's statement is confirmed and ratified by the facts of experience. Men have been so changed and transformed. "And they took knowledge of them," I read about Peter and John, "that they had been with Jesus." They had caught from their Master some of the beauty of the Lord. "And all that sat in the council," I read about Stephen, "fastening their eyes on him, saw his face as it had been the face of an angel." Stephen had caught some of the beauty of the Lord. "From henceforth let no man trouble me," says St. Paul; "I bear in my body the marks of the Lord Jesus"—the marks of the Lord Jesus, not simply in the scars and wounds he had suffered in his Christian service, but even more in his consecration and devotion and absolute self-sacrifice; and all this was Paul's share of the beauty of the Lord.

And to come from those early days down to these days of ours, there are men and women in our midst who are invested with this heavenly beauty. "I have seen God in you," a famous novelist makes one of her characters say of another; "I have seen God in you." The human life was glorified with some of the beauty of the Lord. No, this is no wild, extravagant and impossible prayer. The beauty of the Lord is a beauty in which we may all share. The New Testament quite clearly contemplates our sharing in this beauty: in the beauty of holiness, to begin with, for St. Peter says, "Like as He which called you is holy, be ye yourselves also holy in all manner of living, because it is written, Ye shall be holy, for I am holy"; and in the beauty of love, for St. Paul says, "Let this mind be in you which was also in Christ Jesus," and the mind which was in Christ Jesus was, as the apostle proceeds to show, the gracious, unselfish, loving, and self-sacrificing mind illustrated in the Cross. The grace of the Lord Jesus Christ is to be with us.

The New Testament clearly contemplates our sharing in the holiness and love of God. The beauty of the Lord our God is to be upon us. But is it? Do we share in it? Have we some of the holiness of God? Do we participate, to some poor degree, in the divine purity? And have we the loving mind of Christ? And does the combination of holiness and love make people feel that the beauty of the Lord our God is upon us? I repeat once more, we may share in the very beauty of God; but, I am bound to add, it is not a beauty easily or cheaply won. This is a costly beauty, and it is not to be acquired without paying the price.

Holiness is costly. Every one who has sought to acquire it knows this. It costs struggle and agony and blood and tears. "We wrestle," says the apostle, "not against flesh and blood, but against the principalities, against the powers, against the world-rulers of this darkness, against the spiritual hosts of wickedness in the heavenly places"—that terrific struggle is the price of holiness. "If thy hand cause thee to stumble, cut it off, it is good for thee to enter into life maimed rather than having thy two hands to go into hell; and if thy foot cause thee to stumble, cut it off; it is good for thee to enter into life halt rather than having thy two feet to be cast into hell. And if thine eye cause thee to stumble, cast it out; it is good for thee to enter into the kingdom of God with one eye, rather than having two eyes to be cast into hell." And this maiming and cutting, this lopping off of the hand and the foot, this plucking-out of the eye, represents the price and cost of holiness.

And if holiness is costly, so also is the grace of love. See what it cost God. It cost Him His only Son. Calvary stands for the cost of love to God. And Calvary stands forever as the type and illustration of the costliness of love. For love implies a cross and a crucifixion. Love implies the crucifixion of self, the absolute putting away and annihilation of self. Therefore Jesus said, "Whosoever would come after Me, let him take up his cross, deny himself daily and follow Me." The Cross—that is the price of love. Yes, without doubt, this is a costly beauty. But it is worth the price. All other beauty is like a fading flower. Age wrinkles the fairest brow, takes the color out of the brightest cheek, bends the straightest and most graceful form; but age cannot wither the beauty of the Lord. It grows ever more and more beautiful as the years pass. The only change is a change "from glory to glory." And it ends in the perfect and complete beauty of heaven. "We shall be like Him, for we shall see Him as He is." I ask, once again, do you possess this fadeless and heavenly beauty? Physical beauty is beyond the reach of many of us; but the beauty of the Lord our God may become the possession of us all. If we commune with Christ, if we take up our cross and follow Christ, we shall be transformed into His image from glory to glory.

The Effect of the Beauty on the World

In the last place, notice the effect of the divine beauty upon the world. If only the beauty of the Lord our God is upon us, the world will be startled, charmed, subdued. There is no such apologetic for Christianity as a beautiful Christian life. A holy and loving character is the most potent and effective of all sermons. Perhaps that is why Christianity has made such slow progress—there has been so little of the beauty of the Lord our God upon us. There has been so little holiness; there has been so little love. There has been so little difference between us and men of the world. We have been selfish, grasping, loveless, as they are. The world is so indifferent to the charm of Christianity because it has seen so little of it. But whenever people see Christian folk with some of the beauty of the Lord upon them, they are subdued and won.

I read about the members of the early church, in the spirit of love, selling their goods and contributing to one another's needs, continuing steadfastly in the prayers and taking their simple food with gladness and singleness of heart, praising God; and the result of it all was "they found favor with all the people." All Jerusalem was impressed by the vision, in the characters of these first Christians, of the beauty of the Lord. I read about a young Glasgow engineer who joined a Glasgow church, and who, when asked what it was that had won him for Christ, replied that it was the impression produced upon him by the life and character of the foreman in his shop. He had been won by the beauty of the Lord in a human life. And that is what I believe is most sorely wanted in order to conquer the world for our Lord—that the beauty of the Lord our God should be upon us all.

A significant sentence follows this one of the text: "Let the beauty of the Lord our God be upon us: establish thou the work of our hands upon us; yea, the work of our hands, establish thou it." That is a striking sequence—first the "beauty of the Lord," then "the established work." First the Christian character, then the success of our labors. We cannot have the second without the first. There can be no triumph for the Christian church until all Christians are clothed in the beauty of the Lord. But if only the beauty of the Lord were upon us, our work would be speedily established. "If those who call themselves Christians only lived the Christian life," said Charles Kingsley, "the world would be converted to God in a day." We long to see our work established; we long to see church and school crowned with success; we long to see the kingdoms of the world becoming the kingdoms of our God and of His Christ. But there is a prior prayer we need to offer. The secret of the slow progress is in ourselves. We are such unlovely Christians. We do not commend the gospel we profess. Let us ask God to do His work first upon us to purge us of our littlenesses and selfishnesses and sins, to make us holy and pure and loving. Yes, let us pray that, whatever the price and cost, the beauty of the Lord our God may be upon us; then will God also establish the work of our hands upon us; yea, the work of our hands He will establish it.

CHAPTER TWENTY

John and Jesus

John the Baptist is come eating no bread nor drinking
wine . . . The Son of man is come eating and drinking.
—Luke 7:33–34

The passage from which the two sentences of my text are taken
has for its subject the obstinate and unreasoning perversity of the
Jews as illustrated in their treatment of John and Jesus. They were
like sulky children, Jesus says, who peevishly refused to join in
when their little companions suggested they should play at weddings, and who, with equal peevishness, refused again when, to
please them, their companions offered to change weddings for fu-
nerals. John and Jesus represented contrasted types of teaching and
preaching. The natural expectation would be that if one type of
teaching did not suit the Jews, the other would. But neither John nor
Jesus pleased them. They criticized and rejected both alike. They
objected to John because he held himself so completely aloof from
the common life of men; they objected to Jesus because He condescended to share in it. They criticized John for his asceticism, they
criticized Jesus for His geniality. "John the Baptist is come eating
no bread nor drinking wine; and ye say, He hath a devil. The Son of
man is come eating and drinking; and ye say, Behold, a gluttonous
man, and a wine-bibber, a friend of publicans and sinners!" All of
which, of course, shows that the Jews' rejection of John and Jesus
was not due to any honest difficulty or doubt, but was due to the
perversity of their own hardened and evil hearts.

It is not, however, about the perversity of the Jews that I desire to speak. It is the difference between John and Jesus, as our Lord here describes it, that has attracted my attention, and it is upon some thoughts suggested by that difference that I wish to speak. John and Jesus, we may say, were absolutely one in aim. They were both God's servants. They were both intent upon winning the people back into holy ways. They were both eager to bring in the kingdom of God. Indeed, so identical in spirit and aim were John and Jesus, that the New Testament continually speaks of John as the Lord's forerunner, making straight His paths and preparing His ways; and of Jesus, again, as John's successor and fulfiller, taking up John's work and carrying it out into larger and fuller issues.

But though Jesus and John were one in aim and purpose, it is impossible to conceive a greater contrast than that between the Baptist and the Christ. The phrases of my text flash the whole difference upon our minds. It is all the difference, to use our Lord's own illustration, between a wedding and a funeral; between merry peals and the passing bell; between joyous sunshine and sepulchral gloom. John is the stern and rather forbidding ascetic; Jesus is the genial friend of men, sharing in their joys and sorrows. John makes his home in the bleak, bare wilderness; Jesus moves in and out among the busy haunts of men. John scorns to join in the pleasures of the people—he would scarcely, indeed, have added to the gaiety of a feast; Jesus, on the other hand, is a welcome guest at the festal meal, and multiplies the joy of the wedding feast at Cana by sharing in it. John came eating no bread and drinking no wine, holding so far aloof from men that he did not even share their common food; Jesus came eating and drinking—taking His part, that is to say, in the common life of men, so that His enemies said of Him, by way of reproach—little realizing that thereby they were paying Him the highest and finest compliment—that He was the friend of publicans and sinners. John was an austere preacher of repentance; Jesus was full of grace and truth.

And yet they served the same God and labored for the same kingdom. All this tempts me to pause to remark—using the apostle's words—that "there are diversities of gifts, but the same Spirit. And there are diversities of ministrations, but the same Lord. And there are diversities of workings, but it is the same God who worketh all in all." Jesus is the Prince of the eternal kingdom. But there is always room for John in it. Indeed, Jesus has need of John, just as

John is incomplete—a mere torso—without Jesus. There is a sense in which, to this very day, John must always go before the Lord to prepare His way. What does John stand for? What the old Scotch preachers used to call "law-work." And law-work must still precede the gospel. Confession and conviction of sin must always precede the proffer of pardon. The call to repent must always precede the preaching of grace. "He showed me all the mercy," says the dying girl in Tennyson's poem, "for He showed me all the sin." There you have John and Jesus at work together. "He showed me all the sin"—that was John's stern law-work. "He showed me all the mercy"—that was the Lord's beautiful gospel of grace. The two must always go together. They must go together really in every preacher. "No man," says Dr. Forsyth in one of his latest books, "can heartily say, "My God," till he has humbly said, "My guilt." That is to say, no one can truly and deeply realize the gladness of Jesus' gospel who has not first had his heart subdued and broken by the preaching of John.

And surely I may broaden the application of all this and say, not only that there is room for John, but that there is room in the service of the kingdom for men who differ as widely in temperament and method as did John and Jesus. It is not one type of mind, it is not one type of character, that God wants. He wants every type. We men have a passion for uniformity. We try as far as we can to cast all men into the same mold. We are inclined to insist upon recognized and stereotyped methods of service. That is why some churches make so much of what they call "orders"; that is why we are all of us inclined to look askance at work that adopts unconventional methods. But God loves variety. Variety is His mark in this outward and external universe. And variety is also the mark of His spiritual kingdom. He can make use of the man of the ten talents and the man who has only one. He can make use of Peter and Thomas; of Dr. Pusey and Charles Spurgeon; of Canon Liddon and Billy Bray. He can use the ornate and stately liturgy of the established church, and the brass bands and hallelujahs of the Salvation Army. There is no gift He cannot use. He has a place in His kingdom, and He has need in His work of every variety of gift and method. And so the field of service is open to every one of us. "Whosoever will may come" is the legend I read. "Even I," every one of us may say, "in fields so broad, some duties may fulfill." Yes, and make sure of this, that if we bring our gift and do our best, that—

> Neither man nor work unblest,
> Will Christ permit to be.

But all this is by nature of parenthesis. It is not about the variety of gift as illustrated in the differences between Jesus and John that I wish to speak. The differences suggest to me a deeper and still more vital truth. The two little phrases I have quoted as my text do a great deal more than flash light upon the personal habits of John and Jesus. Habit is really a revelation of character. Study a man's habits and methods, and you will discover his determining opinions and beliefs. It is so in the case before us. If you will look closely at these two phrases which describe for us the habits of Jesus and John, you will find that they furnish a clue to the minds and the hearts of Jesus and John. They reveal to us two views of human life, two contrasted beliefs about the world. The personal habits of Jesus and John were the expression and result of their personal beliefs. They differed in habit, because profoundly and radically they differed in belief. We move on the mere surface of things if we simply notice the external difference, if we simply notice the asceticism of John and the geniality of Jesus. This outward difference of habit is a symptom, an index to a deep and radical difference of view. Why did John shun the world? Why did Jesus, on the other hand, share freely in its life? In a word, because John despaired of it, while Jesus hoped for it.

Two Views of the World

That, then, is what I find in the two phrases of my text—two absolutely contrasted views of the world. The difference in habit and method is only important as it points to this deeper difference of view.

(a) Notice first John's attitude to the world as indicated by his personal habit. "John came eating no bread nor drinking wine." No one ever saw John familiarly walking along the streets and lanes of Judean villages or towns. No one ever saw John in the marketplace or the synagogue. No one ever saw John a guest at a dinner or wedding feast. John cut himself clean off from the great world. He held himself aloof from the common life of men. He went and lived in the wilderness apart, alone. Now, why did John act like this? Not surely from idle whim. It was not from mere caprice that the greatest man born of woman turned his back upon the world. There must be deep and serious reason for action like this. What was it? I think you will find the reason in John's haunting and overwhelming sense of the world's corruption and sin. There are some shallow people in the world who turn a blind eye to all the world's sin and sorrow, its agony and shame, and then prate about everything being as it should be in the best possible of worlds. And they think that is being optimistic. It is not being optimistic. It is simply being silly. That is the tragic mistake Christian Science is committing. In its protest against morbidity it has done the world a service. But when it goes on to tell us that disease and sickness and sin have no real existence, it is simply trying to live in a world of fatuous and silly make-believe. Stevenson says somewhere that a cheerful man is better than a five-pound note; that his coming into a room is like the lighting of another candle. I agree. But I refuse to call him a cheerful man who keeps up his cheerfulness only by ignoring all the tragic facts of life. The cheerful man I want to meet is the man who can be cheerful in spite of them and through them. In other words, the only optimism that is worth a straw is the optimism that has taken full account of all life's tragedies and sorrows and sins. Genuine optimism is calm and strong, but it is never gay and irresponsible. It does not ignore the bitter facts of life, but it believes that even out of the bitter, good will come. If it were not paradoxical to say so, the optimist arrives at his optimism by way of pessimism. No man has a right to the title "optimist" who has not had his heart crushed and well-nigh broken by the sins and sorrows of the world, and yet has come to a strong, calm faith that all things work together for good. The man who has never looked into the abyss, who has never felt the ache and burden of the world's sin, who has known nothing of a bleeding and broken heart, and who comes to us in his gay and irresponsible way and says, "Let's be cheerful; this is a good world," is not an optimist. He is simply an ignorant fool.

Now, John had looked into the abyss. He saw how terribly and fearfully wrong the world was. He saw how far men had wandered from God's ways. For him the whole head was sick and the whole heart faint. He saw the open and unabashed sin of publicans and sinners. He saw the no less terrible, though hidden, sin of scribes and Pharisees. He saw the very religion of the people turned into a huge hypocrisy. And the awful, desperate tragedy of it all well-nigh broke John's heart. Far from thinking the world the best possible of worlds, John thought its case desperate and past mending. The iron entered his soul. As he thought of its misery and shame, the world to John seemed beyond hope of redemption. His message to men was, "Escape from the wrath to come." He severed himself from society, with all its corruption and sins. He left the world because he despaired of it.

He is not the only one who has turned pessimist at the vision of the world's sin. Elijah fled to Horeb and wanted to die because he felt Israel was hopelessly lost to God. The monks and hermits of the early centuries who, in their thousands, fled to the sandy deserts of Egypt and the caves of Asia Minor, did so because they wished to escape the corruptions of a society which they despaired of redeeming. Savonarola betook himself to a convent because the wickedness of his day was so great that it seemed hopeless to contend against it. "The whole world is overset," he cried; "there is none that doeth good, no, not one." And the same pessimism—a far nobler and deeper thing than much that passes for optimism—had entered John's soul. He came eating no bread nor drinking wine. He cut himself off from the world because he despaired of it.

(b) Now, let me ask you to notice Christ's view of the world as indicated by His personal habit. "The Son of man is come eating and drinking." His habit was the precise opposite of John's. He lived and moved not in the solitary wilderness, but amid the busy haunts of men. He frequented the synagogue. He joined the crowds of pilgrims on their way to Jerusalem to the feasts. He was no stern ascetic; He was the genial friend and lover of men. He shared their joy; He participated in their sorrows; He took part in the common life of every-day men. "The Son of man came eating and drinking." And this difference of habit runs down to a difference of belief and view. John despaired; Jesus hoped. John saw a corrupt world; Jesus saw a redeemable world.

Do not, however, imagine that Jesus was one of those shallow and flippant optimists who preserve their cheerfulness only by ignoring the hard and bitter side of life. There are three stages in men's views of the world. The first is that stage of gay and irresponsible optimism of which I have already spoken—that is the stage of ignorance. The second is that of a deep and brooding pessimism—a pessimism created by the overwhelming vision of the world's misery and sin—that is the stage of realism. The third is that of a calm and sober and reasoned optimism, which ignores not

one of the hard facts, and yet believes that good is at the end of it
all—that is the stage of triumphant faith. Now, John stopped at the
second. But Jesus reached the third. He saw as plainly as John did
how terribly wrong the world was. He felt far more keenly than
John could the awfulness of its wickedness and sin. And yet He did
not despair. He looked deeper than John, and even in sin-stained
man He saw possibilities of better things. He looked higher than
John, and He knew that God could make the very wrath of men to
praise Him. And so Jesus hoped for the world. Nay, He did more
than hope. He had a calm and confident assurance that the world
was a salvable world, that all its relations could be redeemed. And
so Jesus did not turn His back upon the world. He lived in the midst
of men to help and bless them. He lived in the midst of the world to
cleanse and save it. "The Son of man came eating and drinking."
He did not ignore the sin; He did not overlook the corruption. He
did not look at the world through colored spectacles. He looked
squarely at the wickedness, the depravity, the tangled and ghastly
wrong that had made other men despair, and He said, "This world
can be redeemed; it is not the Devil's world. It is God's world." So
it was in the midst of men that Jesus was found, laboring to bless
them, toiling to purify human life, working for the new earth wherein
dwelleth righteousness. "The Son of man is come eating and drinking."

The Redeemable World

Which of the two was right? John or Jesus? There is scarcely
need to put the question. The history of nineteen centuries, the
experiences of our own souls, all unite to attest that Jesus was right.
The world is a redeemable world. John was a great man. The Lord
Himself said that a greater man was never born of woman. And yet,
He added, the least in the kingdom of God, the most insignificant
disciple who has entered into God's purposes, who shares in the
Lord's faith, who is certain that sin is not going to triumph, but even
now lies under sentence of death—the least in the kingdom of God
is greater than he. The world a redeemable world—that was our
Lord's faith, and it must be the faith of every one of His disciples.

Every man a redeemable man! It is a sore strain upon faith
sometimes to believe it. But Jesus believed no less, and so He called
the chief publican a son of Abraham, and the woman who was a
sinner a daughter of the great King. And we must believe no less.

There are no hopeless cases. There are no incurables. He can save even to the uttermost. The most hopelessly lost may be found; the most desperately foul may be cleansed; the most abjectly sunk may be uplifted and saved. Every man a redeemable man!

And every duty a redeemable duty, and every relation a redeemable relation! Every man redeemable, and the whole of life redeemable, too, so that there shall be nothing mean or profane in it, but that every relation shall be sanctified, and every common duty transfigured into divine service, and that over the whole life, from beginning to end, shall be written, "Holiness unto the Lord"; and that whether we eat or drink, or whatsoever we do, we shall do all to the glory of God. And, cherishing that same faith, where shall our place be? Not in the desert or the convent cell, out of reach and sight of the world's sins and sorrows. You can never save the world if you despair of it. You can never help it if you leave it. If you believe, with Jesus, that the world is a redeemable world, then it is your business to be in it. That is surely what our Lord Himself contemplates. He never thinks of His people leaving the world as sailors leave a sinking ship. He thinks of them as in the very midst of it. "Ye," He says, "are the light of the world." Where the darkness is thickest, there the light is most wanted. Where men throng and crowd, it is there the lamp is needed most. Men do not light lamps away in unpeopled solitudes; they light them in busy streets. "Ye are the light of the world," said Jesus. It is in the midst of the world we must let our lights shine. "Ye are the salt of the earth," He said again. The salt! The preservative against corruption! It is where the corruption is rankest that the preserving salt is most sorely needed "Ye are the salt of the earth," said Jesus. It is not our business to leave the world to rot. We are to supply the preservative, the antiseptic. It is in the world our influence is needed most. "Ye are the salt of the earth."

In the world—that is our place; in the very midst of men, like Jesus Himself, seeking to help and bless and save them. "I am become all things to all men," said the apostle, "that I may by all means save some." We must take our share in the ordinary duties and relationships of life. We must enter the world's business, and show men—as our Lord did in the carpenter's shop—that the labor and traffic of the common day can be converted into the Father's business. I know business life is difficult. I know that men sometimes in their despair are tempted to say that no man can be a modern businessman and a Christian. But business is not to be handed over to the Devil. The Christian is to take part in it with the confident belief in his soul that business can be redeemed, and that he can buy and sell, build and plow, all to the glory of God.

And we must take our share in the innocent gaieties of life, going, as our Lord did, to the festal meal, and showing that the very laughter and recreations of life can be redeemed. The pleasures of men do not belong to the Devil. They have been soiled and stained in many ways by unholy hands. But they are redeemable. The very pleasures of life can be sanctified, so that, like St. Carlo, we may play our games to the glory of God. We must take our share in social and national duties, rendering to Caesar the things that are Caesar's, taking part in politics and doing our duty by the state. Politics are mixed up with much that is immoral and unconscientious and dishonest. But the Christian is not to shun them. He is to go into them to purify them. For even politics can be sanctified and the vote transfigured into an instrument for the promotion of the kingdom of God.

The world is a redeemable world. In the United States they have some districts reserved for the Indians. There is in this world of ours nothing "reserved" for the Devil. There is nothing surrendered to sin. Every man and every duty is redeemable. Therefore, like our Lord, it is in the world we must be found. Like Him, we shall be the friends of publicans and sinners. Like Him, we shall be found where the need is keenest and the woe is direst and the sorrows are deepest and the sin is blackest—laboring there with the courage born of a holy confidence, a blessed confidence, our Lord's confidence in a redeeming God, and able therefore, like Browning, to say—

> My own hope is, a sun will pierce
>   The thickest cloud earth ever stretched
> That, after last, returns the First
>   Though a wide compass round be fetched;
> That what began best can't end worst,
>   Nor what God blessed once prove accurst.

CHAPTER TWENTY-ONE

The Christian Life as a Partnership

Partakers of the divine nature. —2 Peter 1:4

Partakers of Christ's sufferings. —1 Peter 4:13

Partaker of the glory that shall be revealed. —1 Peter 5:1

That is a great and notable saying of Augustine's with reference to the Incarnation, that the divine became human in order that the human might become divine. Christ shared our lot in order that we might share His. That was how our redemption was accomplished—Christ shared our lot; the divine condescended into the human; the Eternal Lord submitted to the conditions of space and time; the Son of God became a man. I am not going to stay to discuss the reason for all this. I am not going to try to answer Anselm's question, *"Cur Deus homo?"*—why did God become a man? I am satisfied for the moment just to accept the fact. There was a divine "must needs" about the Incarnation. Christ had to stoop low in order to lift us up high. He had to empty Himself in order that we might be enriched. He had to become a man before He could become men's Redeemer. And He did not shrink from the sacrifice. "Since then the children are sharers in flesh and blood, He also Himself in like manner partook of the same." He shared our lot. He partook of our nature. And the partaking was real and the sharing absolute. Christ was a true man. He was born; He grew; He acquired knowledge; He labored; He was tempted; He suffered; He died. There was no make-believe about Christ's humanity. "He also Himself in like manner partook of the same." He was as real a man as you or I. He was made in all things like unto His brethren. In no other or cheaper way could redemption be achieved. The divine became human; the Son of God partook of our nature; He shared our lot. And that is why the divine became human, that the human might become divine. He shared our lot, that we might share His. This was the means of redemption—the Son of God living as man in the midst of mortal men. This is redemption itself—mortal man living in Christ.

Harold Begbie's *Broken Earthenware* has passed now into the category of familiar and popular books. You will remember it tells the story of the work of a Salvation Army Corps in one of the wickedest and meanest of London's mean streets. The little band was led by a fair, refined woman adjutant, whose goodness was so obvious and so radiant that even the vile dwellers in that vile street spoke of her as an angel. Day after day she marched at the head of the little band through this wretched quarter. Night after night she held meetings among the thieves and criminals and prostitutes and outcasts who made that awful street their home. She spent her life in that wretched street and among those dreadful people. What for? To lift those creatures who had almost ceased to be men and women back to that pure and happy and blessed life which she herself enjoyed. She shared their lot in order that they might share hers. She would have felt she had shared in the life of that vile street in vain if she had not been able to help some of its wretched inhabitants to sit down in the heavenly places with Christ Jesus. But she felt that the desire of her heart was given her when she saw the Puncher and the Tight Handful, and that ghastly creature who was known as Old Born Drunk, entering into possession of her secret, sharing with her the life which was life indeed.

That woman adjutant was but treading in the footsteps of her Lord. He, too, "emptied Himself." He stooped to the lost and the last and the least. He became the friend of publicans and sinners. And He, too, will feel that He became poor in vain unless He can make the men and women to whom He stooped eternally rich. He, too, will feel that He shared in our misery and woe for naught unless He can make us share in His own blessedness and peace. But it will be reward sufficient for Him for stooping to partake of flesh and blood if He sees flesh and blood partaking of the life divine. For that is salvation, that is regeneration, that is redemption, when the human is lifted up into the divine, and mortal man lives the eternal life.

The Life of Partnership

That is what being a Christian means, according to the New Testament, sharing in the very life of Christ. We are not to understand the Christian life to mean an external imitation of Christ, taking Christ as a kind of copybook pattern, but rather having Christ Himself living again in us.

> Thy nature, gracious Lord, impart;
> Come quickly from above.

We sing, "Thy nature, gracious Lord, impart." That is what being a Christian really means. It means partaking of Christ's nature. It means, not having Christ outside of us as a model, but having Christ within us as a power. The *imitatio Christi* may be nothing better than a more exacting and burdensome legalism. We are in the region of the gospel—of the glad, genial, gracious gospel—only when we share the very nature of Christ, when we partake of His very life. That is how the Christian life is represented consistently in the New Testament—it is a participation, a fellowship, a vital communion. That is how Christ Himself taught us to think of it. "Abide in Me," He said to His disciples, "and I in you. Apart from Me ye can do nothing." The Christian life is not possible to man unaided and alone. It is only possible to man plus Christ, or rather to man possessed and informed by Christ, to man inhabited by Christ.

And that is exactly what the Christian life was in the actual experience of the saints. Take that mightiest of all the saints—the apostle Paul. How does he explain the life he lived? Listen to him: "I live, yet not I, but Christ liveth in me." Christ liveth in me—he was conscious of a participation, a fellowship, a vital communion. It was as if the natural and original principle of life within him had been changed for a nobler and a greater. "I live, yet not I, but Christ liveth in me." Nor was this conception of the Christian life confined to the apostle Paul. Paul had at Antioch to withstand Peter to the face because he allowed himself to be led astray. But whatever sharp differences the two apostles may have had as to the place and function of the Mosaic Law, Peter agreed absolutely with his beloved brother Paul in declaring that the Christian life was a fellowship, a participation, a vital communion. That is what being a Christian meant from first to last, from beginning to end, according to Peter—sharing Christ's lot and life. Look at the three clauses which I have culled from various passages in Peter's writings and brought together to form my text. The word that lends a certain unity to these three passages is the word *partaker*. A partaker is a man who has certain things in common with another. He is a sharer, a partner. And if we take the three clauses together, they will serve very well as Peter's picture of the complete Christian. What is a Christian? A Christian is a man who has a nature in common with Christ. He is a man who has sufferings in common with Christ. He is a man who at the last will share an infinite glory in common with Christ. Or take the phrases in the order in which I have taken them, and they become a picture of the Christian life in its beginning, its course, and its great and blessed end. Here is the Christian life in its source: a man becomes a partaker of the divine nature. Here is the Christian life in its course: a man becomes a partaker of Christ's sufferings. Here is the Christian life in its consummation: a man becomes a partaker of the glory. At the start and the finish and all the way between, the Christian life is a participation, a fellowship, a vital communion. I want briefly to speak of this vital fellowship between Christ and the Christian, taking these three clauses as my guide.

The Divine Nature

First, then, notice, here is the Christian life in its origin, at its source, at its very fountainhead—a man becomes a partaker of the divine nature. That is how a man becomes a Christian—by changing his very nature; the human gets transfigured into the divine; he becomes a partaker of the divine nature. But perhaps some one will take me up sharply at this point and ask me whether, as a matter of fact, the divine nature is not in every man born into the world. Does not the old Book say that God breathed into man the breath of life? Does it not go further and say that God made man in His own image? To talk, therefore, of becoming a partaker of the divine nature is to convey a false impression. Participation in the divine nature is every man's birthright.

Now, let us look at this objection for a moment. Of course, there is an element of truth in it. There is a spark of the divine in every man. Original goodness is as much a fact as original sin. If there were no original goodness in men, no bit of the divine to which we could appeal, preaching would be an absurdity. We might as well close our chapels and cease our meetings for worship and let the dust gather thick about our Bibles. They could effect no good. Preaching would have about as much effect upon men devoid of the instinct for God as music would have upon a man stone deaf. In that limited sense, let me freely admit that the fact that we preach at all is due to our belief that every man is in a measure a partaker of the divine nature.

But now, having made that admission, let us look at the matter, not from the high theoretical and logical point of view—let us look at it from the plain, practical point of view. To illustrate the point I want to make, let me turn to the usage of our common speech. We say sometimes of persons, "He is of an optimistic nature," or, "He is of a melancholy nature." Now, what exactly do we mean by statements like these? What we mean is that in the one case optimism, and in the other case melancholy, is the man's prevailing disposition, the bent and bias of his mind. That is not to say that the optimistic man does not occasionally have his dull days, or that the melancholy man does not occasionally see a bit of blue in his sky. But, speaking broadly, the one man has an eye for the dark cloud and the other for the silver lining. And we characterize them by their dominant moods, by their prevailing dispositions. In other words, when we say a man is of such and such a nature, we mean that such and such a quality is preeminently characteristic of him.

Now, using the word *nature* in that sense, will anyone tell me that the preeminent characteristic of human nature, as we see it, is its divineness? Is there anyone who will assert that the conduct of the average every-day man strikes him as divine? Why, we give the whole case away, we confess the tragic truth, in our very use of the term *human nature*. We use it apologetically. We use it to excuse faults and failings and sins. We hear of some acts of revenge, of some selfish conduct, of some deed of lust and passion, and we say, "Ah, well, it's human nature!" In other words, we confess that human nature, as we know it, is selfish, greedy, revengeful, passionate. I admit frankly that is not human nature as God made it. But it is human nature as we know it—human nature as we see it defiled, debased, depraved by sin. I do not want to slander this human nature of ours, but a vast amount of unreal cant is being talked about it in these days. All this talk about the native and inherent divineness of human nature is very fine—but it is not true. Human nature, as I see it, is not so much divine as broken, marred, guilty, rebellious. It is not the rosewater view, but the tragic view of human life that is the truest. It is the tragic view of humanity that the Bible takes from first to last. There is no talk here about the divineness of human nature. There is no suggestion here that the race can elevate itself by its own waistband. Human nature, as the Bible sees it in actual fact, is antidivine. It has received a twist. Its natural bent is towards sin and evil. Listen to some of the Bible's plain and unvarnished statements. "The natural man receiveth not the Spirit of God." "He that is in the flesh cannot please God." "The works of the flesh are these: fornication, uncleanness, lasciviousness, idolatry, enmities, jealousies, drunkenness, and such like." "The flesh lusteth against the Spirit." "The carnal mind is enmity against God." I need not multiply passages. That is the Bible view—goodness is not natural to us. Left to ourselves, it is not towards holiness and purity we would incline. If we allowed ourselves to drift, we would drift, not into saintliness, but into lives which are earthly, sensual, devilish. Our bias is towards evil. If we follow the broad and easy road of our own instincts and appetites, we end in destruction; it is only by agonizing to enter through the strait gate and climbing a steep and narrow way that we end in life. That is the Bible representation of the facts about human nature, and everyone carries the verification of that representation in his own breast. We know that the instincts and passions of human nature would sweep us into sin and shame; it is only by crucifying the flesh with the affections and lusts thereof that we keep straight at all.

And that is why the Bible insists, as the first step in the Christian life, that we must become "partakers of the divine nature." There is no chance for us so long as the old nature is dominant. We must be "born again," as Jesus said. We must be "renewed in the very spirit of our minds," as the apostle Paul puts it. We must "put off the old man," we must "put on the new man." Every phrase used in the New Testament to set forth conversion, to describe the first step of the Christian life, indicates a change which is radical, revolutionary, profound. We are changed at the very core and center of our beings. We get a new principle of life. We get new hearts, as the psalmist expresses it. We "renew" our strength, or rather we *exchange* our strength, as Isaiah puts it. Leave human nature to itself, and what will it live for? Self. Self is the dominating principle. But when a man becomes a partaker of the divine nature, what does he live for? Love. "God is Love." That is what God is essentially and in His inmost being; and when a man becomes a partaker of the divine nature, that is what it means—love and not self becomes the animating principle of his life. And that is conversion, redemption, salvation, when we share the divine nature. "Every one that loveth is born of God and knoweth God." And God is equal to this mighty miracle of changing a man at the very core and center of his being. The first story in *Broken Earthenware* is that of the Puncher, as he was familiarly known. He was a prizefighter, the terror of his neighborhood; he was a thief; he was a drunkard; he terrorized men into giving him drink. If ever a man was earthly, sensual, devilish, the Puncher was that man. But the grace of God laid hold of him and transformed him. And the man whose one passion at the beginning of the story was the passion for drink, at the end of it has still one passion, the passion for souls. That is Christianity in its beginning and at its source when we become "partakers of the divine nature," when we are born again, when we live not in the flesh, but by the Spirit.

The Sufferings of Christ

In the second place, here is the Christian life in its course—a man becomes a partaker of Christ's sufferings. I said a moment ago that that is what the divine nature is at its very core and essence— love. Now, love is in its very nature sacrificial. It involves the ideas of suffering and sacrifice. Love means nothing if it does not mean self-impartation, self-surrender, self-abnegation. "God is Love," says John. Love is the ruling principle of the Divine life. And how did that love show itself? It showed itself in sacrifice and suffering. "God so loved the world that He gave His only begotten Son, that whosoever believeth in Him should not perish, but have everlasting life." God saw men estranged from Him by their sin and wicked works, and to make a way for them, He Himself—if I may borrow a phrase of Dr. Jowett's "filled up the gap." He filled up the gap with the sufferings and death of His own Son, whose sufferings and sacrifice were, after all, God's sufferings and sacrifice. That is how His love showed itself: He suffered and died in order to fill up the gap and make it possible for men to be reconciled once again to Him. You remember how Paul in a familiar phrase links together the two ideas of love and sacrifice. "The Son of God," he cries, "loved me, and gave Himself for me." Loved and gave Himself. All the suffering and sacrifice of the Incarnation and the Cross were implicit in the love. Because He loved, He gave Himself. Because He loved, He bore the Cross. Because He loved, He filled up the gap by the sacrifice of Himself. Holy love, like that of Christ, in a sinful world is bound to be a suffering love. Redeeming love is bound to be a sacrificial love.

Well, I want to go on to say that as soon as a man becomes a partaker of the love which is the divine nature, he is bound to become a partaker of those sufferings which love always involves. And so it comes about that the man who starts by becoming a partaker of the divine nature finds that the Christian life for him means that he becomes a partaker of the sufferings of Christ. I know well that, from one point of view, the sufferings of Christ are unshared and unshareable. Our Lord's Cross is solitary. He offered the one full and perfect oblation and sacrifice. In His atoning work not one of us can share. And yet from another point of view, we not only may, but we must share Christ's sufferings. It is the condition of discipleship. "Whosoever doth not take up his cross and follow after me, he cannot be my disciple."

Let us assume that a man is a genuine partaker of the divine nature, that he really shares in the Spirit of Christ—what will follow? This will follow, to begin with: he will take the sin and wickedness of the world onto his own heart. He will feel the shame and burden of it. It is impossible for a man to walk heedless and unconcerned amid the misery and evil of this world if he really has the Spirit of Christ. Do you remember the story Dr. George Adam Smith tells about Henry Drummond, how, after one Sunday night's meeting with the students, he was found with drawn and haggard face, leaning over the fire, leaving his supper untasted? And when his friends urged him to eat, he moaned, "Oh, the sins of these men!" He had been hearing the stories of their reckless lives, and the recital had filled his soul with shame and pain. Sharing in the very spirit of Christ, he shared also in the sufferings of Christ in the face of human sin. Yes, it is impossible for a man who is a partaker of the divine nature to be unconcerned in the presence of sin. Just as Jesus, in sheer agony of soul, wept over Jerusalem, so the Christian will "sigh and cry for the sin of the city."

This second thing will follow upon a genuine participation in the divine nature: like Christ, the Christian will want to stand in the gap. He will want to share in his Lord's redeeming and saving work. Look at Paul. He had no sooner found Christ for himself, he had no sooner become a new creature in Christ, than he wanted to be by his Lord's side in the gap. "Straightway in the synagogue he proclaimed Jesus that He was the Christ." As soon as Paul received the divine gift of love, he was ready to share Christ's toil and suffering for the sake of others. You remember how in that great passage of the epistle to the Philippians he links the two things together: "That I may know Him," he says, "and the fellowship of His sufferings." That I may know Him—that is the participation of the divine nature. What next? And the fellowship of Christ's sufferings—he wanted to be with Christ in the gap. And so you see Paul spending himself in his missionary labors, and suffering untold things in the process—stoned at Lystra, scourged at Philippi, fighting with wild beasts at Ephesus, shipwrecked at Malta, put to death in Rome; and looking back on all he had endured and suffered in his Christian service, he declared in a great and solemn word that he had been "filling up on his part that which was lacking of the afflictions of Christ for His body's sake, which is the church."

And everyone who shares in Christ's nature is bound to share in Christ's sufferings. For he will want to stand with Christ in the gap. He will be consumed with the passion for souls. He will want to bring this sinning and weary world back to righteousness and peace. And that inevitably means suffering. Do you not think that the missionary, and the preacher and the Sunday school teacher, and the Christian worker know what suffering means? I do not mean simply physical suffering. I do not mean the physical hardships the missionary has to endure; I do not mean the outbreaks of violence which sometimes take place even in this land when Christianity becomes aggressive; I am not thinking of the bodily outrages the Eastbourne mob inflicted upon the Salvationists. I am thinking of the disappointments, the delays, the heartbreaking failures every Christian worker has to face. "More sufferings, Lord; more sufferings," cried Xavier. There is no need to cry for suffering and trial. They come inevitably to us if we are filled with the Spirit of Christ. You cannot be a partaker of the divine nature and share in Christ's seeking love, but inevitably you become a partaker of Christ's suffering.

The Divine Glory
And here is the end of the divine life—a man comes a partaker of the glory that shall be revealed. That is how Peter comforted

himself amid all the sufferings and trials of his apostleship and ministry: he thought of the glory which was to be revealed. The glory would compensate for all the hardness and suffering of the service. And the glory and the suffering went together. "If we suffer with Him, we shall also be glorified together." "Our light affliction worketh for us a far more exceeding and eternal weight of glory." As for Jesus, so for the disciple—the cross was the way to the Crown. And that is how the Christian life ends—we share in the glory. There is probably not one of us who does not want to share in the glory. But what about sharing in the sufferings? There is only one way to the glory that shall be revealed, and that is first of all to become partakers of the divine nature, and then to become partakers of the sufferings of Christ. I put it to those of you who profess to be Christ's people: are you with Him in the gap? Have you got the passion for souls? Are you ready to lay down your lives for the brethren? Are you bearing the cross? It is stark and cruel and ugly, but it ends in the crown.

> O Cross, that liftest up my head,
>   I dare not ask to fly from thee;
> I lay in dust life's glory dead,
>   And from the ground there blossoms red,
> Life that shall endless be.

CHAPTER TWENTY-TWO

Christ As Mediator

*For there is one God, one mediator also between God
and men, Himself man, Christ Jesus, who gave Himself
to be a ransom for all.* —1 Timothy 2:5

I want to discuss briefly in this sermon the work of Jesus Christ as
Mediator. The commentators tell us that the actual word is only to be
found in this passage; but the idea of mediation runs right through the
Bible. The Old Testament is full of mediation. There is a great deal
said about the ministry of angels in the older books of the Bible.
Angels again and again appear to men, bringing with them divine
messages of comfort or of warning. They were mediators, go-betweens,
between God and men. And not angels only, but men also were
called to this high office and mission. Moses, for instance, was the
mediator between God and the people of Israel; he pleaded in the
name of the people with God; he spoke as the representative and
mouthpiece of God to the people. And not Moses only, but all priests
and prophets were mediators, or at any rate it is true to say there was
a mediatorial element in all their work and service. But all these
mediators were imperfect, and their mediatorial service but partial.
Paul brushes them all aside, as if they were scarcely worth reckoning,
and fastens our exclusive attention on Christ: "There is one mediator
also between God and men, Himself man, Christ Jesus." One mediator! Neither priests nor prophets, neither Moses nor angel could accomplish a full mediatorial work. Their relation to Christ was that of
the candle to the sun. As Tennyson puts it—

> They were but broken lights of Thee,
> And Thou, O Lord, art more than they.

Christ, and Christ alone, has achieved a perfect mediation. There is one mediator between God and man, Himself man, Christ Jesus.

Now, if I were going to discuss this matter of mediation in any exact and theological way, there are many great New Testament terms which I would have to examine, for the idea of mediation connects itself with other great ideas such as atonement, reconciliation, propitiation, redemption. But what I have in mind is not an exact discussion of a theological theme, but a plain and simple talk about a certain broad aspect of the work of Christ. The word μεσιτης, which is here translated "mediator," means literally "one who stands in the middle"—middleman, as we might say. But he is one who stands in the middle for a special purpose; he is one who stands in the middle for the purpose of drawing two together in a pact or covenant, or else (and here we touch the very marrow of the Pauline use of the word) he is one who stands in the middle in order to bring about a reconciliation where there has been division or enmity. So that *mediator* is almost equivalent to *reconciler* or *peacemaker*. And when I think of it, it begins to appear to me as if no title could better describe the work of Christ than this word *mediator*. He is the great Middleman, drawing estranged parties together into concord and peace. Throughout the centuries He has been busy at His reconciling work, filling up gulfs of distrust and hate, bridging great chasms of difference, pulling down middle walls of partition, and everywhere making peace. In every sphere He has been carrying on His mediatorial activities—in the individual soul, on the field of history, between man and God. And the hope for the individual and for the world lies here—that He has not abdicated His functions. The Middleman is still at His work. And He will not cease from it till our peace shall be like a river and our righteousness like the waves of the sea.

Now, I seem to recognize three great spheres within which Christ carries on His mediatorial work. First of all there is the sphere that Paul mentions in my text—He is the Mediator between God and man. He is the great Middleman bringing God and man together. This is the sphere within which Christ does His mightiest mediating work, and in that sphere He stands alone. He is the One Mediator. But that is not the only sphere in which our Lord discharges the gracious office of the mediator. He mediates between a man and himself; He makes peace between a man and his conscience. And then, finally, He mediates between man and his brother; He is the Middleman who draws Jew and Gentile, freeman, bondman, black and white together, and binds them in indissoluble bonds of affection and love. I am quite prepared to be told that Christ's mediating work in these two last respects is but a consequence and corollary of His mediating work between God and man. I am not in the least concerned to deny it. Still, as a matter of fact, we can in thought distinguish between them. So for clearness sake, let me talk of Christ as Mediator (1) between man and God, (2) between man and his own conscience, and (3) between man and his brother.

The Mediator Between God and Men

First of all, then, let me speak of Christ as the Mediator between God and men. The very fact that a mediator was necessary proceeds on the assumption that man was sundered far from God. The fact that man is alienated from God is regarded as axiomatic in the Bible. You may agree or you may disagree with the Bible account of the origin of that alienation, but about the fact there can be no dispute. All life and experience bear it out. The Bible traces this alienation back to a single cause. It declares it roots itself in sin. And at bottom the Bible position is unchallengable. Sin is the ultimate root of it all. But possibly for clearness sake we may say that there are two main causes of alienation from God—ignorance and sin. To disarm any criticism let me at once admit that in the last resort ignorance is the result of sin. That is one of the most disastrous effects of sin—it blurs the moral vision; the god of this world always "blinds the eyes of the unbelieving." Had men kept morally straight, they would not have gone intellectually so far astray. The pure in heart always see God.

Still, let me take the fact as we see it, without tracing it back to its cause. Multitudes in our world are sundered far from God by sheer ignorance. That is the condition of the pagan world at this very moment. That was the condition of the entire world before Christ came. By its wisdom it knew not God. It could only grope after God if haply it might feel after Him and find Him. And to that wandering and alienated world Christ came. And by His coming He became the Mediator between God and men. He introduced men to the Father. When Jacob lay down to sleep at Bethel, he dreamed he saw a ladder stretched from heaven to earth, and the angels of God ascending and descending upon it. The angels were the only mediators he had ever heard of. But the ladder that really stretched between heaven and earth, the link that really bound God and men together, was just the Lord Jesus Himself. "Henceforth," our Lord said, "ye shall see the angels of God ascending and descending upon the Son of man."

The Gnostics were conscious of the vast distance that separated Almighty God from mortal man, and they tried to bridge the gulf by imagining that there was an almost endless chain of spiritual beings, the first link in the chain being a being only a little lower than God, the second a little lower than the first, other successive links descending in spiritual excellence by subtle shades and gradations until a being was reached who was only a little better than man. That was how the Gnostic tried to mediate, to introduce man to God—by these endless genealogies of his. Paul, perhaps, has these Gnostic speculations in his mind in this passage. He brushes them almost contemptuously aside. They are vain imaginations. For the multitudinous aeons of Gnosticism he substitutes the One Mediator, the man Christ Jesus. In this historic person God had come to men; in that same person men had gazed upon the very face of God. He mediated to them the knowledge of God. In Him they saw the Father.

This is, shall I say, the prophetic aspect of Christ's mediatorial work. He did the work of the middleman, He brought God and man together by revealing to men the character of God in His own words and life. And in this respect He is the One Mediator. If Jesus was not the revelation of God, if He was not Himself God manifest in the flesh, then God is still a God who hides Himself. Apart from Jesus we have no right to speak of God as Father. History does not reveal the Father. Nature does not reveal the Father. "No man cometh to the Father but by Me." That is our Lord's own imperious and challenging claim. Leave Christ out of account, and God will be a God afar off, and we shall be back in the night of ignorance and fear. It is Jesus who has made the difference. It is Jesus who has brought us nigh. In Him we touch God and see God, and realize we belong to God. In Him we cease to wander in some far country; we become members of the family of God, and receive the spirit of sonship by which we cry, Abba, Father.

Now, let me pass on to speak of the separation caused by sin—

which is the separation Paul has in his mind in my text. If you will turn to the old story which tells us of the entrance of sin into our world (and whatever you may think of the story, the essential truth it teaches remains permanently valid), you will find that the immediate effects of sin were fear and estrangement. Adam and Eve went and hid themselves from the presence of the Lord, That is the invariable effect of sin. Now, as then, sin results in fear and estrangement. That was the solemn truth Isaiah proclaimed to the Jews in exile: "Your iniquities," he said, "have separated between you and your God." Do you remember how St. Paul describes the condition of the sinner? This is how, for instance, he describes the condition of the Ephesians in their pre-Christian days: "Ye were at that time separate from Christ, alienated from the commonwealth of Israel, and strangers from the covenants of promise." Notice the words—*separate, alienated, strangers*—every one of them expressive of the breach sin has made between man and God. He uses even stronger words to the Colossians: "You," he writes, "being in time past alienated, and enemies in your mind in your evil works." *Alienated, separate, strangers, enemies!* I know of no group of words that could more vividly set forth a complete severance. And that is what sin has done for men; it has alienated them from God; it has separated and estranged them from God; it has made them the enemies of God. Do you say that this is an exaggerated statement? I reply that it is confirmed and verified by all the facts of life and experience. The sinner, the man who is conscious of wrongdoing, is conscious also of this separation and alienation and estrangement. Let a man have sin upon his soul and he becomes afraid of God and seeks to shun God, and, like Adam of old, tries to hide himself from the presence of the Lord.

Now, let me go on to say that the estrangement is mutual. I mean this, that sin alienates man from God and alienates God from man.

(a) It alienates man from God. Sin destroys all desire for God's fellowship. It is not the sinner who says, "My soul is athirst for God, for the living God." The sinner, like Dame Quickly in Shakespeare's play, shrinks and shudders at the bare mention of God's name; for God to him, instead of being a Friend, has become a dreadful fear. And it is not mere alienation that sin breeds; alienation in countless cases deepens and darkens into hostility. "Alienated," says Paul, "and enemies in your minds in your evil works." Enemies! That is a severe indictment, but is it not a true one? Do not narrow the reference of this word down to the handful of men among us who openly repudiate God's name. "Love of the world," says John, "is enmity against God." The man who clings to the sins and follies of life is at enmity with God. Mr. Live-Loose, and Mr. Love-Lust, and Mr. Malice, and Mr. Hate-Light, and all other dwellers in Vanity Fair, are at enmity against God. Illustrations of this alienation often present themselves to us. Here is one. Quite recently I saw a working man in one of our public streets take his cap off his head, and addressing himself to other working men standing by, I heard him say, "Gentlemen, I am happy to testify that I have taken Jesus Christ as my Savior." And at that those other men began to boo and to jeer. They somehow did not want to hear about Jesus. They did not want to be reminded of God. They were "alienated in their minds."

(b) But sin also alienates God from man. You may think this is a hard saying. For the popular idea of the alienation caused by sin is that it is all on one side. But if there is one thing the Bible makes abundantly clear it is this—sin has its effect upon God as well as upon man. It grieves God, it offends God, it alienates God. If God were not so grieved and offended and alienated, He would not be the Holy and Righteous God we know Him to be. But the God the Bible reveals is a God who hates sin, who loathes sin, who is a consuming fire of wrath against sin. Listen to words like these: "God is angry with the wicked every day." "The eyes of the Lord are upon the righteous, the face of the Lord is against them that do evil." "The wrath of God is revealed from heaven against all ungodliness and unrighteousness of men." You must write a new Bible, you must forever get rid of the words *anger, wrath, consuming fire* from the descriptions of God's attitude towards men, if you are to maintain the position that alienation is only on one side. Sin affects not only man's feelings towards God, it affects also God's feelings towards men. And all this is not only true to the facts of spiritual experience, but is in no way at variance with the foundation truth that God is love.

But without staying to prove that statement, I come now to the blessed truth that Christ mediates between sinful man and that God who has been so justly displeased. He stands in the midst of order to bring about a reconciliation. He makes peace between them. Those who once were far off are brought nigh. That is, indeed, the very core of the Gospel message. Paul calls it somewhere "the word of reconciliation." It is just the good news that the alienated ones have been brought together again—man brought back to God, and God brought nigh to man; and Jesus is the Middleman in whom they clasp hands and meet. And this is how Christ became the Mediator—"He gave Himself a ransom for all." Throughout Scripture the mediation of Christ is connected with His death. It was by dying that Christ brought man back to God, and brought God's favor and grace to men. The reconciliation, like the estrangement, is twofold.

(a) He reconciled man to God by His Cross. For it is seeking, stooping, sacrificial love men see there. "He gave Himself a ransom for all." I am not going to discuss the implications of that word *ransom*. But at any rate this much is suggested to us by it—in some wonderful way Christ took our place; He gave Himself to death that we might go free.

> In our place condemned He stood,
> Sealed our pardon with His blood;
> Hallelujah.

That is a love to melt the stoniest heart. And it is God's love, for God was in Christ. There is a story told of John Wesley, that one of his preachers by some action of his grievously offended him. Meeting this erring preacher one day, John Wesley asked him to apologize for his fault and beg his pardon. The man stubbornly and obstinately refused. "Well," said John Wesley, "if you won't beg my pardon, I'll beg yours." And at that the man broke into tears. That the man against whom he had sinned should stoop to this in his desire for peace melted and subdued him. And it is something like that with us and the God whom we see on the Cross. In the Cross God stoops to the very death to rescue and save those who had rebelled against Him. "He who might the vantage best have took, Himself found out the remedy." He gave Himself a ransom. And the vision of that mighty love changes alienation and hate into passionate devotion. We are subdued, conquered, and won by the love of the Cross. There the rebel becomes a friend. We who once were far off are made nigh in the blood of Christ. We are reconciled to God by the death of His Son. "Lord," we cry—

> Thy love at last has conquered,
> Grant me now my soul's desire,
> None of self and all of Thee.

(b) And, secondly, Christ reconciled God to man. And this also He did "by giving Himself a ransom." That God Himself provided the ransom makes no difference to the fact that the ransom had to be paid before man could be set free. That God Himself was "in Christ reconciling" makes no difference to the fact that the reconciliation had to be made before God could bestow on man His forgiving and restoring grace. And Christ, again, was the Middleman. In the Cross He represented God to man, revealing Him as a God of infinite and uttermost love; in that same Cross He represented man to God; He offered to God the sacrifice of perfect obedience, and by bearing in His own person the pain and penalty of sin, confessed in man's name that God's law was holy, just, and good. I am not going to discuss the Atonement; but this much, at any rate, is true: the Cross was more than a display, it was a sacrifice; it was more than a revelation of the divine love, it was a propitiation for the sins of the world. By the sacrifice which Christ—Himself man—offered there, God's holiness and righteousness have been vindicated and satisfied. He can now be Himself just and the justifier of all those who by faith in Christ make that sacrifice of His their own. "There is one mediator between God and men, Himself man, Christ Jesus, who gave Himself a ransom for all." In Christ God and man meet. In the Cross man is able to say, "Father," and God says, "My Son." Christ came and stood in the yawning gap between God and man, and in Him they clasp hands.

"I know, oh, now I know," cried poor John Bunyan to his wife, after living in misery and torment for long, weary months, "I know, oh, now I know! I must go to Jesus the Mediator of the new covenant, and to the blood of sprinkling that speaketh better things than that of Abel." And thereupon John Bunyan emerged out of his wretchedness and woe. "Christ," he writes, "was a precious Christ to me that night; I could scarcely lie in my bed for joy and peace and triumph." And many another beside John Bunyan has had that same blessed experience. Many have gone to Him who gave Himself a ransom; they have gone to the blood of sprinkling that speaketh better than that of Abel, and they have left unrest and fear and despair far behind. They have found Christ an effectual Mediator. They have found peace with God through Jesus Christ.

> Peace, perfect peace, in this dark world of sin?
> The blood of Jesus whispers peace within.

The Mediator Between Man and His Conscience.

I have left myself little space in which to discuss the other two spheres of Christ's mediatorial activity. The briefest of sentences must suffice. In the second place, Christ mediates between a man and his own conscience. Sin does more than create a breach between man and God. It creates a breach between man and his own better and truer self. Sin means civil war, a divided and distracted heart, and a divided and distracted heart means misery and pain. If you want to see what I mean by civil war, a divided and distracted heart, read again that tragic seventh of Romans, with its record of inward conflict and pain. "The good which I would I do not: but the evil which I would not, that I practice." "I delight in the law of God after the inward man: but I see a different law in my members, warring against the law of my mind." And then for the pain in which such civil strife always issues, read the cry with which the chapter ends. "Wretched man that I am! who shall deliver me out of the body of this death?" It is because sin inevitably means a discordant heart that the Bible utters that stern old word, "There is no peace, saith my God, unto the wicked." That is not a threat, it is simply a statement of spiritual law. The sinner sins against his own best nature, and that is to lay up pain and misery for himself. The unrest and pain and misery of sin—who does not know it? The haunting fears that follow wrongdoing—who has not experienced them? "Duncan hath murdered sleep," moaned Macbeth. No, it was not Duncan who had done it; it was just his own outraged conscience. But once again Jesus mediates between a man and his conscience. He blots out these sins that haunt us and terrify us. "He gives the guilty conscience peace." And then He reconciles a man with his better self. He reunites him to his better nature. He sets him once again on the upward path. He sets a Zaccheus on the path of self-sacrifice and a Mary on the path of purity and an Onesimus on the path of honest service. He takes the discord and strife and unrest clean away. He reconciles them with their best and truest selves. He unites their hearts to fear God's name.

Christ the Mediator Between Man and Man.

And, in the last place, Christ is the great Mediator between man and man. He has stood in many a gap in the course of the centuries and closed it up. He has played the part of the Middleman, and in Him differences have been solved, divisions have been done away with, and people long sundered have been united in the bonds of a common love.

He has mediated between individuals. What marvels of reconciliation He has accomplished! Have you ever stopped to think of this simple fact—simple but tremendous in its significance—in the circle of Christ's disciples you could find at one and the same time Matthew the publican and Simon the zealot? Matthew the Jew, who had entered the pay of the Roman government; and Simon, to whom every such Jew was a renegade, and who, in his furious hatred of Rome, would not have shrunk from plunging his dagger into such a renegade's heart. In his old pre-Christian days Simon would have spat upon Matthew, and Matthew would have paid back Simon's hate with interest. But Christ laid one hand on Matthew and another on Simon, and in Him the Jewish patriot and the Roman servant became friends. And Christ has been Mediator between men sundered by antipathies as deep as those which separated Simon and Matthew. Listen: "There is neither Jew nor Greek, there is neither bond nor free, there is no male and female, but all are one in Christ Jesus." He is the Middleman between men of differing tastes and classes and colors and tongues. A common love to Him unites them to one another. He has been doing this mighty mediating work, reconciling men to one another, all down the centuries. And when I think of the mighty achievements already wrought by Him, I can believe that before the end of the day all separations will be brought to an end, and all differences will be settled, and brotherhood will become a blessed fact, and peace and goodwill our abiding possession.

And He has mediated not only among individuals, but among nations too. There is One Mediator between nation and nation, and that is the man Christ Jesus. He is the hope of the world's peace. In the long run all national jealousies and suspicions and hates will go down before Him. It is not between America and England only that peace will be established, but all the nations will dwell together in amity and concord, and men shall learn war no more. Christ is the Center of Unity, the great Reconciler, the mighty Mediator. Men cannot love Him without being constrained to love each other too. It is said that in a certain picture gallery an old man was gazing one day at a picture of the thorn-crowned Christ. Involuntarily, almost, the expression broke from his lips, "Bless Him, I love Him!" A stranger standing by heard the remark, clasped the old man's hand

and said, "Brother, I love Him too," and a third and a fourth made the same confession and joined hands with one another, and soon there was round that picture a little group of men who had been strangers to one another a few moments before, but who had been made one by their common love for the crucified Lord. And that is a parable of what is going to happen throughout the world.

The world just now is full of suspicions; there are wars and rumors of wars; the very lifeblood of the European nations is being drained out of them as they pile up their crushing armaments one against another. But when the love of Christ gets shed abroad in human hearts, all this kind of thing is going to vanish and disappear. Armies will cease to be; guns will be allowed to rust; Dreadnoughts will be consigned to the scrap heap; the money now wasted on munitions of war shall be spent, not to spread death, but to enrich and gladden life. Judah shall not vex Ephraim, and Ephraim shall not envy Judah. England shall not fear Germany, and Germany shall not distrust England. England shall say, "Bless Him, I love Him!" and Germany will respond, "English brother, I love Him too." And war shall not be named among us, as becometh saints. But

> Peace shall over all the earth,
> Her ancient splendors fling,
> And the whole world send back the song,
> Which now the angels sing.

CHAPTER TWENTY-THREE

Speech to the Weary

The Lord God hath given me the tongue of them that are taught, that should know how to sustain with words him that is weary (RV). Know how to speak a word in season to him that is weary (AV). —Isaiah 50:4

The passage from which my text is taken may be regarded as Isaiah's account of the qualifications necessary for the making of a prophet, and so perhaps it may be fairly regarded as an account of the ideals he cherished for his own ministry. Indeed, it is not too much to say that he is the prophet whose training and ministry he describes in this great and glowing passage. And it is no wonder at all that, with such ideals of the prophet's office as are here set forth, Isaiah should have become the greatest prophet of pre-Christian times.

For this is what Isaiah says about the prophet in this and the preceding chapter. The function of the prophet, he says, is to be a voice for God. He is no mere rhetorician or lecturer, making the passing topics of marketplace discussion his theme; he is God's mouthpiece, making eternal things his theme, and judging all the events of everyday human life from the divine standpoint. He is not a fore-teller, in the sense that his main concern is with future events; he is a forth-teller, bringing God's will to bear upon the present and the now. That is essentially and fundamentally what the prophet is—and the modern representative of the prophet is the preacher—he is God's voice to men. The preface to his message is ever this: "Thus saith the Lord."

But if the message of the prophet is to be effective, if it is to strike home to the hearts and consciences of men, then behind the voice, as Dr. George Adam Smith says, there must be a life. Behind Isaiah's own message there was a consecrated life. From the very womb Jehovah had called him; from his earliest years he had lived the dedicated life. And that consecrated life lent power to his speech. What a man says, or rather the effect of what a man says, always depends upon what he is. They used to say of the elder Pitt that there was more in the man than in anything he said; while, on the other hand, they used to say that a certain flippancy and insincerity of character robbed the brilliant efforts of Sheridan of half their influence and effect. Speech apart from character, speech which is not the expression of the life, is no better than sounding brass or a tinkling cymbal. There are some men who must be known if their power is to be understood. I think of a preacher of my own acquaintance. In print, his sermons are almost dull, as they are certainly lacking in literary style. But when you come into his presence, the transparent honesty of the man, the obvious saintliness of the man, lend to his words compelling and subduing power. "I cannot understand your minister's power," said a visitor to a friend of mine who was a member of a Midland church, to which a man ministered who was not a great preacher, perhaps, but who was a great saint, "I cannot understand your minister's power," he said; "I do not see very much in him." "Ah," replied his host, "you see there are thirty years of holy life behind every sermon." "A man blossoms through his lips," says Dr. Smith, "and no man is a prophet whose word is not the virtue and the flower of a gracious and consecrated life."

But there is at least one other requirement which must be fulfilled before a man becomes a prophet. Before even a good man can speak for God he must listen to Him. That is the point emphasized in the passage from which my text is taken. "My Lord Jehovah," writes the prophet, "hath given me the tongue of the learners: He wakeneth morning by morning, He wakeneth mine ear to hear as the learners." Morning after morning Isaiah sat at the Lord's feet like a learner; morning by morning he listened to what the Lord God had to say, and then, having listened, he went forth and delivered his message to his countrymen. And men recognized in the words he spoke—as, indeed, we recognize to this day—the accents of the voice divine. No man can speak for God without first of all listening to Him. Communion is the condition of effective speech.

As Dr. Smith says (to whose commentary I am much indebted), our Lord's healing of the deaf and dumb man is full of instruction for us upon this point. The first command Christ issued was not "Be loosed" to the tied and halting tongue; but "Be opened" to the closed and stopped ears. Then when his ears had been opened, the bond of his tongue was loosed and he spoke plain. First the opened ear, then the loosened tongue. First the listening, then the speaking. And no man can be a prophet who does not first of all listen. If he ceases to listen he will begin to spin little talks about little topics out of his own little brain, and men will miss the deep, profound, divine notes that reach the depth of the soul.

And, if I may interpolate a remark just at this point, it is to say that I wonder sometimes whether in these days we listen enough. I venture to think that Martha, careful and troubled about many things, represents the prevailing spirit and temper of our day. We are practical folk, and we believe in being busy. And so we like our ministers to be much in evidence, and to rush about from one little meeting to the other. We think that kind of thing represents pastoral efficiency. As a matter of fact, our ministry would be infinitely more efficient if our ministers spent less of their time in the public eye and more of it in private communion; if our churches insisted less upon public appearances, and thought more of giving their ministers opportunity for quiet with God. For, after all, it was Mary who sat at the Lord's feet and heard His word, and not Martha who was cumbered about much serving, who chose the good part; and our ministers will preach all the better if they imitate Martha less and imitate Mary more. For before a man's tongue can be loosed about divine things he must first of all have his ears opened, and before he can effectively speak for God he must first of all listen to Him.

Now, all this and more Isaiah says about the prophet. He is a voice for God; he is a voice whose words are enforced by a holy life. He is a voice speaking what first of all he has received in communion with God. And all this Isaiah was himself. He was God's voice to the exiles. He lived what he preached. And he said nothing which first of all he had not received from God Himself. To the people he was a teacher; in his relation to God he was a learner. And among other things he had learned from God was this: he had learned how to succor with words him that was weary. He had learned how to cheer the despondent and encourage the hopeless.

Isaiah was a comforting preacher, a heartening preacher, a hope-inspiring preacher. That is how he begins his prophecies, you remember: "Comfort ye, comfort ye, my people, saith your God." He strikes the keynote of his ministry in his opening sentence. It was a discouraged, listless, hopeless sort of congregation that Isaiah had to preach to. The exiles in Babylon were broken in spirit and bankrupt in hope. And it was Isaiah's business to breathe new courage into their fainting souls, to tell them they were not doomed to perpetual exile, but would yet come with singing unto Zion, and with everlasting joy upon their heads. And his ministry in this respect was not in vain. Hope and courage did spring up again in the hearts of the exiles. Taught by the Lord, the prophet knew how to sustain with words him that was weary.

The Ministry of Comfort

Now, if I were preaching to a congregation of students for the ministry, I would tell them this: that the ministry of comfort makes up a large, if not the larger part of the Christian minister's service, and unless a man has learned how to sustain with words him that is weary he can never, in the fullest sense, be a Christian minister at all. I do not say it is the whole of the Christian minister's duty. There are other things besides comfort that are necessary.

There is a ministry of intellectual enlightenment to be discharged. There are mental difficulties that have to be explained, and baffling mysteries that have to be, if possible, unraveled, and dark Scriptures that have to be expounded. Our Lord discharged this ministry Himself. Men went to Him with their doubts and difficulties, and He opened to them the Scriptures. The Gospel stands for enlightenment, and no minister makes full proof of his ministry who does not seek to help his people in their intellectual perplexities and doubts.

Then there is a ministry of rebuke. The minister must not be always saying soft things. There come times when his words have to be as sharp and stern as his Lord's always were in the face of hypocrisy and sin. No minister makes full proof of his ministry who does not speak to his people as plainly as Paul did to Felix about sin and self-control and a judgment to come.

No, comfort does not make up the whole of the work of Christian ministry. There is a season for everything, and as the Authorized Version puts it, it is "in season" the Christian minister has to learn to speak his word to the weary. But the season, after all, is pretty nearly every season, for the weary, the broken-down, the burdened, the bankrupt in hope, are always with us. The remark that struck me most in reading the story of Ian Maclaren's life was a remark he himself made to a body of American students. His own ministry had been, to all appearance, brilliantly successful. He had built up in Sefton Park one of the greatest churches of the Presbyterian order. He had a loyal and devoted people. Crowds hung upon his lips. But, looking back upon it all, he said: "If I had to live my life over again, I would make my ministry a more comforting ministry." We ministers are very apt to think that the philosophical and theological problems that interest us are of equal interest to our people. And so we occupy our Sundays with discussing the latest question started in the pages of the *Hibbert Journal*, or what the latest German critic has said about the book of Habbakuk. And all the time, if we only knew it, our people are wishing we would leave the critics and the *Hibbert Journal* alone, and tell them something that shall help them bear their troubles and face their temptations and bind up again their broken hearts. These—the troubles and sorrows and dark griefs which every day brings—these are the things that vitally concern them. And so, while not for one moment making light of the value of intellectual discipline, the ministerial gift I covet most for myself is that of being able to sustain with words him that is weary; to comfort the man who has breaking sorrows to bear, so that faith fail not; to strengthen a broken man to face temptation once again with the hope of triumph in his heart; to say some word that, amid perplexing providences, shall help a man to preserve his trust in the love of God; to establish the hope of the dying so that they may walk through the valley of the shadow without fear, because they know that God is with them. Let others covet for themselves the gifts of eloquence and learning—the gift I most desiderate, in order that I may be a good minister of Jesus Christ, is that of knowing how to sustain with words him that is weary. Now, all this and more I would have said if I had been addressing a gathering of ministerial students, but, speaking to men and women engaged in the everyday pursuits of life, the point I wish specially to emphasize is this—that this ability to sustain the weary is the distinguishing characteristic of the Christian faith. If the Christian minister is able to sustain with words him that is weary it is because there is something in the faith he preaches that exactly meets the needs of the burdened and the broken and the bankrupt.

Christianity's Message to the Weary

That is the decisive test of a religion that claims to be universal, and that professes to meet the needs of a world—what message has it for the weary? For the weary, after all, form the majority of mankind, and a religion that cannot minister to them cannot pretend to be a religion for the world. For by the "weary" I do not mean the physically tired and worn. That is not what the prophet means. The weary whom he has in mind are the people who are weary in soul. In his particular case they were those exiles who had clean lost heart, who despaired of a return, and who believed they were doomed to exile for ever. And these are the weary, I too, am thinking of— the people who have lost heart; the people who feel life's load too heavy for them; the people whose spirits are wounded and crushed by sorrow. And the weary in this sense—the people who are worn and burdened by sorrow, by temptation, by sin, by fear—are everywhere. I venture to say again, they constitute the majority of mankind. At one time or another we all find ourselves enrolled in their ranks. And the real test of a religion, of its value and worth, is this: Can it do anything for the weary? Can it minister to the diseased mind? Can it bind up the broken in heart?

It is easy enough to speak a message of cheer and good hope to the vigorous and strong. Plato, Confucius, Buddha all have a message for the noble and the good. Plato, for instance, can build his ideal republic if you will allow him to select his material as a dyer does his wool. Let him have cultured, refined, virtuous, wellborn people to work with, and he can create what he believes would be an ideal state. But it is only the fit he wants. Plato has no use for the poor and the ignorant and the vicious and the sinful. The weary folk—he can do nothing with them. Indeed, it was very much like that with Judaism also. Judaism could make use of the morally righteous; it could make room for the respectable Pharisee in the kingdom, but it had no message to the broken and the outcast; it could do nothing with publicans and sinners; it abandoned them to their fate—"This people," it said, "that knoweth not the law, is accursed."

Platonism, Buddhism, Judaism—they do not appeal to us in England here. Our interest in them is purely theoretical. They do not offer themselves to us as rivals of the Christian faith. But there are certain things in England here that offer themselves to us as substitutes for religion. Over against the appeal of Christ, these things cry to us as Madam Bubble did to Standfast: "Come, live with me, and I will fill your life with dainties." Pleasures, business, the world, they all make their appeal to us. Now, I do not deny that in our days of health and strength these things may look as if they could satisfy our souls. But what can these things do for the weary? What will happen when the heart is crushed and strength fails?

Pleasure, for instance, can speak to the young—speak with seductive and almost resistless power. But what can pleasure do for you in the day when sorrow comes, and the blinds are drawn? And what can your boon companions do for you in those days when the very grasshopper shall be a burden, and the silver cord is loosed, and the golden bowl is broken, and the pitcher is broken at the fountain, and the wheel broken at the cistern? No, Epicureanism will never do for a philosophy of life. It is impotent to sustain us in the days of our weariness.

And business can speak to the vigorous and the strong. It speaks to them of success and fortune. But what can business say to the weary? Business has no use for the weary. What is this one hears? "Too old at forty." Business does not succor the weary; it casts them adrift.

And life in general can speak to the healthy and the youthful. It seems to give us, with its manifold interests, practically everything we need. But life in that sense—all these temporal and mundane interests of ours—they pall upon us in the days of our weariness. When age comes, or sickness comes, or loss comes, the world becomes dull, flat, stale and unprofitable, and of our days we are constrained to say that we have no pleasure in them. It is of no use talking about pleasure to a man who is broken by sorrow, or about business to a man who is facing eternity, or about life to a man whose dearest hopes are shattered. But it is the glory of our Christian faith that it can minister to the weary, that it can succor with words the tired and the broken, that it can breathe new hope into the bankrupt and the despairing.

Dr. Matheson, in his book, *The Portrait of Christ,* puts it this way: "Christianity," he says, "is a regressive religion. It goes back to gather up the lost things—the things which have fallen by the way and been left behind. It is the glory of Jesus that He goes back to the forest of humanity to seek the children that have lost their way. All the rest are pressing forward. Brahmin, Buddhist, Parsee, Greek, Roman—all their messages are for the strong. Jesus alone has a message for the weak." That is it exactly. Other religions preach the rather heartless doctrine of the survival or the fittest. Jesus preached the survival of the unfit. He came to preach good tidings to the poor. He was the friend of publicans and sinners. He gathered up the outcasts of Israel. The men and women who had fallen out on the march and been abandoned by their fellows— Jesus breathed new hope into them, and helped them to run in the way of God's commandments. He made Zacchaeus believe he could yet be a son of Abraham; He made the woman who was a sinner believe that she could yet be a King's daughter, all glorious within; He made Simon—plagued by his own weakness and impulsiveness—believe he could yet become Peter the rock; He made Martha and Mary—the light of whose lives had gone out with the death of Lazarus—realize that life did not end at the grave, but that their brother, though lying in the rocky tomb, was alive unto God. He knew how to succor with words him that was weary.

He is still master of that gracious secret. And that is what makes him a Savior for the world. He still makes the old appeal: "Come unto Me, all ye that labor and are heavy laden, and I will give you rest." The people who labor and are heavy laden, the weary folk— what a multitude of people they are! What are the chief causes of weariness? Well, perhaps these: trouble, sin, death.

"Man is born to trouble," says the old Book, "as the sparks fly upward." And beneath the burden of it men stagger and faint. Read the story of Job, it is the story of a man weary with trouble. But Jesus knows how to succor with words him that is weary. What is the trouble? Is it sickness? Afterwards it yields the peaceable fruit of righteousness. Is it loss? "Be not anxious," He says, "what ye shall eat or what ye shall drink—your Father knoweth." Is it bereavement? "Fear not," He says, "in my Father's house are many abiding-places." And many a weary soul, succored by the words which the Lord has spoken, has lifted up his head.

And there is sin. And what a source of weariness this is! At bottom, it is the one source of weariness. This is what really constitutes the ache and pain and burden of life—the consciousness of guilt and shame. This is what embitters our present and makes our future a dread. This is what makes us conscious of being at enmity with ourselves and at enmity with God. The weariness of sin! The crushing, heartbreaking weariness of sin! John Bunyan has much to say about it in his *Grace Abounding*. And men and women feel it still. They come to tell me about it sometimes—this awful weariness which is more than they can bear. But Jesus is able to sustain with words him that is weary. He has a message for the sinner; it is the message of forgiveness and restoration and a Father's love. There is no sinner for whom He has not His word of comfort to speak. Let none say he is too low or base or vile as to be beyond the comfort of the Gospel of Christ. "The blood of Jesus Christ, God's Son, cleanseth us from all sin." From all sin! The heaviest load of sin rolls off the heart at the foot of Christ's Cross. The despairing publican, smiting upon his breast and crying "God be merciful," becomes transfigured, as he listens to the words of Christ, into a rejoicing saint.

And then there is death. In that final weariness only Christ can speak words of comfort and cheer. But He can. He can so sustain with His words him that is weary that, amid the swellings of Jordan, he shall be unafraid. Some one spoke to Dr. James Hamilton, as he lay dying, about the "dark valley." "Dark valley?" he said; "there is no dark valley here." Sustained by the words of Christ about the Father's house and the life beyond, he footed that dark and dreary last mile with a singing heart and a shining face. He had got the victory over faintness and fear through Jesus Christ. I preach that Christ who can sustain the weary to you. I would fain be a comforting preacher, a strengthening, heartening, hope-inspiring preacher. But the comfort and the strength and the hope are not in any preacher's gift. They are only in the gift of the Christ whom he preaches. But He knows how to sustain the weary. He has comfort for sorrow, forgiveness for sin, courage in face of fear.

> Art thou weary, art thou languid,
> Art thou sore distressed?
> Come to Me, saith One, and, coming,
> Be at rest!

And if you come, your sorrow and sighing shall flee away; you shall have a garland for ashes, the oil of joy for mourning, the garment of praise for the spirit of heaviness.

Great Sermons by Great Pulpiteers

Spurgeon's Sermons on the
Cross of Christ
ISBN 0-8254-3687-7   160 pp.   (pb)

Spurgeon's Sermons on Family
and Home
ISBN 0-8254-3688-5   160 pp.   (pb)

Spurgeon's Sermons on New
Testament Men, Book One
ISBN 0-8254-3783-0   160 pp.   (pb)

Spurgeon's Sermons on New
Testament Miracles
ISBN 0-8254-3784-9   160 pp.   (pb)

Spurgeon's Sermons on New
Testament Women, Book One
ISBN 0-8254-3782-2   160 pp.   (pb)

Spurgeon's Sermons on Old
Testament Men, Book One
ISBN 0-8254-3772-5   160 pp.   (pb)

Spurgeon's Sermons on Old
Testament Men, Book Two
ISBN 0-8254-3789-x   160 pp.   (pb)

Spurgeon's Sermons on Old
Testament Women, Book One
ISBN 0-8254-3781-4   160 pp.   (pb)

Spurgeon's Sermons on Old
Testament Women, Book Two
ISBN 0-8254-3790-3   160 pp.   (pb)

Spurgeon's Sermons on the
Parables of Christ
ISBN 0-8254-3785-7   160 pp.   (pb)

Spurgeon's Sermons
on Prayer
ISBN 0-8254-3691-5   160 pp.   (pb)

Spurgeon's Sermons on the
Resurrection
ISBN 0-8254-3686-9   160 pp.   (pb)

Spurgeon's Sermons on
Soulwinning
ISBN 0-8254-3787-3   160 pp.   (pb)

Spurgeon's Sermons on Special
Days and Occasions
ISBN 0-8254-3786-5   160 pp.   (pb)

Available from Christian bookstores, or

kregel
PUBLICATIONS

P. O. Box 2607 • Grand Rapids, MI 49501-2607

Journey Group Bookmark

Accountability Questions

Instructions:

- Plan on meeting for at least 1/2 hour.
- Same-gender pairs only.
- One person reads the questions; both share their answers.
- Question 9 is to help hold you accountable for an issue God is calling you to deal with.
- There is no place here for judgment. Offer each other only support.

---

1. Have you been a verbal witness to someone this week about the good news of Jesus Christ?
2. Have you exposed yourself, either accidentally or intentionally, to sexually alluring material or have you entertained inappropriate sexual thoughts this week?
3. Have you lacked any financial integrity this week?
4. Have you been honoring, under-standing, and generous in your important relationships this week?
5. Have you lied or shaded the truth to look better to others this week?
6. Have you given in to an addictive behavior this week? If so, explain.
7. Are you harboring anger, resentment, or bitterness toward someone?
8. Have you secretly wished for someone's misfortune?
9. (Your Personalized Accountability Question)_____

   _____

   _____

10. Were you faithful in your reading and praying, and did you hear from God? What will you do about it?
11. During this conversation today, have you lied, left out parts of the truth, or left a mis-impression with me that needs to be cleared up?

My Most Wanted List

"My prayer is not for them alone. I pray also for those who will believe in me through their message, that all of them may be one, Father, just as you are in me and I am in you. May they also be in us so that the world may believe that you have sent me. I have given them the glory that you gave me, that they may be one as we are one."

Jn. 17:20-22

"The Son of Man has come to seek and save what was lost."

Lk. 19:10

Each day, pray specifically for these who are Wanderers...

_____

_____

_____

_____

_____

_____

_____

Lord, prepare the heart of _____ to hear the gospel. Mt. 13:23

Lord, raise up a worker to bring the gospel to _____. Lk. 10:2b

Lord, send me to be a witness to _____. Isa. 6:8

Pray daily as Jesus instructed in Luke 10:2b:

"Ask the Lord of the harvest, therefore, to send out workers into his harvest field."